BORDER THEORY

BORDER THEORY

The Limits of Cultural Politics

Scott Michaelsen
and David E. Johnson, editors

University of Minnesota Press
Minneapolis
London

Published by the University of Minnesota Press
111 Third Avenue South, Suite 290
Minneapolis, MN 55401-2520

http://www.upress.umn.edu

Printed in the United States of America on acid-free paper

Library of Congress Cataloging-in-Publication Data

Border theory : the limits of cultural politics / Scott Michaelsen and
    David E. Johnson, editors.
        p.   cm.
    Includes bibliographical references and index.
    ISBN 0-8166-2962-5 (hardcover : alk. paper). — ISBN 0-8166-2963-3
(pbk. : alk. paper)
    1. Boundaries.   2. Boundaries in literature.   3. Geopolitics.
4. Political anthropology.   5. Ethnicity.   6. Multiculturalism.
7. United States — Boundaries — Mexico.   8. Mexico — Boundaries — United
States.   I. Michaelsen, Scott.   II. Johnson, David E., 1959–
JC323.B65   1997
306.2 — DC21   97-3356
                                                                      CIP

Contents

Acknowledgments

My work on this book could not have been accomplished without help from two sources: first and most important, a year-long Fellowship for 1995–96 from the American Council of Learned Societies and, second, a faculty development grant (spring 1995) from the University of Texas at El Paso.

Scott Michaelsen

Border Secrets: An Introduction

David E. Johnson and Scott Michaelsen

A "border" is always and only secured by a border patrol. Where Scott Michaelsen works, in El Paso, Texas, on the U.S.-Mexico border, one sees the most clearly virulent form of border production literally in the backyard of the university. Along the Rio Grande are miles upon miles of cement trenches, chain-link fences, light-green paddy wagons, uniforms, binoculars, and soon, perhaps, steel walls, as well as multiple paranoid discourses of national and racial contagion. This book is concerned with borders like this, but more often the focus is on the sorts of "soft" borders produced within broadly liberal discourse: benevolent nationalisms, cultural essentialisms, multiculturalisms, and the like — in short, the state of "border studies." As border theorist Renato Rosaldo noted in his keynote address at the 1995 American Ethnological Society meeting, a trickle of U.S.-Mexico border studies has turned into a flood in the wake of, among other influential works, Gloria Anzaldúa's *Borderlands/La Frontera: The New Mestiza* (1987), Rosaldo's own *Culture and Truth: The Remaking of Social Analysis* (1989), D. Emily Hicks's *Border Writing: The Multidimensional Text* (1991), and Ruth Behar's *Translated Woman: Crossing the Border with Esperanza's Story* (1993), as well as essay collections such as Héctor Calderón and José David Saldívar's *Criticism in the Borderlands* (1991). These books focus primarily on the U.S.-Mexico border — the birthplace, really, of border studies, and its methods of analysis.

The idea of the "border" or "borderlands" has also been expanded to include nearly every psychic or geographic space about which one can

1

thematize problems of boundary or limit. In collections such as Gustavo Pérez Firmat's *Do the Americas Have a Common Literature?* (1990) and Alfred Arteaga's *An Other Tongue: Nation and Ethnicity in the Linguistic Borderlands* (1994), the focus expands to include Latin American, Caribbean, and internal U.S. borders. A further expansion of the border concept is evident in the essays collected in this volume. The readings presented here refer, among other things, to a wide range of anthropological, sociological, feminist, Marxist, European postmodernist and poststructuralist, postcolonial, ethnohistorical, and race/ethnicity theory, all now presumed to bear significant genealogical and logical relation to border studies in the Americas—the focus of which is expanded once more to include, among other things, the U.S.-Canadian border, U.S. sectionalism, and American immigrants' diasporic experience.

We imagine one possible meaning for our book's title to be simply this: the "limit" for border theory's growth is the reinscription of the various disciplines as instances of border studies. As an explicit example of this tendency, Alejandro Lugo's essay in this collection ends with a call for "antidisciplinarity," which is, in effect, a "transdisciplinarity" in that it imagines a borderlands anthropology supplemented by history (primarily a history of modernity, including histories of the state and the academy), sociology (Marxist, as well as the history of bourgeois sociology), feminism, and the like in order, in a Gramscian "war of position," to offer "effective resistance against" "the state, theory, and power." For Lugo, all of the disciplines and their histories must be brought to bear on the problem of the borderlands if the theorizing of it is not to be blind to the role of nationalist and capitalist "structure" and "order" in dominating and disciplining the border. Lugo imagines the disciplines re-fusing under the heading of "border studies" in order to refuse and challenge border dominations.

In short, like "race" and "gender," and then "nation" and "sexuality," the intellectual entry point of the "border" is one of the grand themes of recent, politically liberal-to-left work across the humanities and social sciences. National interdisciplinary conferences are organized around this theme, and hundreds of papers and books produced in all of the liberal arts disciplines.

In the majority of this work, interestingly, the entry point of "the border" or "the borderlands" goes unquestioned, and, in addition, often is assumed to be a place of politically exciting hybridity, intellectual creativity, and moral possibility. The borderlands, in other words, are *the* privileged locus of hope for a better world. Anzaldúa's and Rosaldo's texts suggest this: although neither would minimize the violence, of every sort, within the U.S.-Mexico borderlands, both authors' arguments about the significance of this geographic area hinge upon such promise. Rosaldo cites and glosses Anzaldúa approvingly in the conclusion to his chapter titled "Border Crossings":

> Gloria Anzaldua has further developed and transformed the figure at the crossroads in a manner that celebrates the potential of borders in opening new forms of human understanding. . . . In making herself into a complex persona, Anzaldua incorporates Mexican, Indian, and Anglo elements at the same time that she discards the homophobia and patriarchy of Chicano culture. In rejecting the classic "authenticity" of cultural purity, she seeks out the many-stranded possibilities of the borderlands. By sorting through and weaving together its overlapping strands, Anzaldua's identity becomes even stronger, not diffused. She argues that because Chicanos have so long practiced the art of cultural blending, "we" now stand in a position to become leaders in developing new forms of polyglot cultural creativity. In her view, the rear guard will become the vanguard. (1993, 216)

The following collection of essays not only theorizes the idea of "border," but also explores the philosophico-political limits of border theory work. Here, for once, the "border" will not be taken for granted, either as an object of study and analytic tool or as a privileged site for progressive political work. Hence a second meaning for our title, *Border Theory: The Limits of Cultural Politics.*

We begin with an understanding that for all of border studies' attempts to produce a cultural politics of diversity and inclusion, this work literally can be produced only by means of—can be founded only upon—exclusions. Several of the contributions to this volume, each in its own way, are intent on mapping these exclusions—whether geographic, ethnic, theoretical, or other—and filling in the gaps in border work. Other pieces suggest an alternative to border studies (the "other" of yet "another" border studies) that involves thinking from an entirely different sort of "ground" — indeed, without the possibility of a ground for determining and securing relation. To think along these lines is to suggest a nonprescriptive "model" for multiculturalism and community.

The model used by liberal-to-left scholars, by border theorists, is the one in which differences count, make a difference, in which particular constellations of practices are understood to be essentially related or organized by some principle of identity. Homi Bhabha suggests that this model amounts to the celebration — even when practiced as what David Palumbo-Liu calls "critical multiculturalism" (15) — of "cultural diversity," the celebration of culture as an "epistemological object" (Bhabha 34); such celebration, Bhabha writes, "gives rise to liberal notions of multiculturalism, cultural exchange or the culture of humanity" (34); it is, finally, the "representation of a radical rhetoric of the separation of totalized cultures" (34). The other "model," which is not one, which presupposes and circumscribes nothing, is one in which differences mean nothing, add up without sum; a "model," then, in which practices can never be totalized to account for identity — indeed, in which there would be no (question of) identity.

The first model imagines a day of nearly infinite judgments about otherness (at least, judgments concerning the other's very existence) — but judgments, finally, that are not judgmental. One version would be acknowledging and respecting the other's identity in its alterity without presuming much of anything about the other; or, in a slightly more interactive mode, learning about the other's identity without producing a system of inflections, hierarchies. Benign and friendly judgments, these, without content and/or value.

We know this to be theoretically impossible. Such judgment, inevitably, is exclusion, and is necessarily made from a position entirely incommensurate with the other. It is always already a kind of prejudice, and the very possibility of more familiar forms of such — the determining of categories of and candidates for the inferior, the unnatural, the debased. As a model for multiculturalism, it is ineluctably exclusive: constructive of borders around identities, the fault lines today being precisely those differences that seem to matter and "make a difference"—gender, race, color, ethnicity, class, religion, sexuality, to name the most obvious.

The second model is one of radical inclusivity, and not because "we" are, as Tzvetan Todorov claims in *On Human Diversity,* all fundamentally alike at the level of our humanity. This community, if it is one, has no ground, but is nevertheless "founded," according to Jean-Luc Nancy, on our being-in-common:

> Being *in* common means that singular beings are, present themselves, and appear only to the extent that they compear (*comparaissent*), to the extent that they are exposed, presented, or offered to one another. This compearance (*comparution*) is not something added on to their being; rather, their being comes into being in it. (1991, 58)

The second model does not begin with the principle of identity. It is no longer a question of inclusion or exclusion, no longer a question of taking it personally, no longer a question of affiliation (brotherhood) or identity. Differences make no difference and cannot, as a consequence, secure legislation against anyone. This is not to say that there is no judgment, only, rather, that judgment will be unfounded, without precedent, and fraught with typically unthought ideological implications. We take this to be Bhabha's point when he writes that "culture only emerges as a problem, or a problematic, at the point at which there is a loss of meaning in the contestation and articulation of everyday life, between classes, genders, races, nations" (34). At stake is the "structure of the problem" of cultural limits, something that proponents of cultural diversity, in their "well-intentioned moralist polemics against prejudice and stereotype" (34), cannot describe. In focusing attention on the limit of culture, the border of its possibility, Bhabha distinguishes between cultural diversity on the one hand and "cultural difference," which "is the process of the *enunciation* of culture as 'knowledge*able*,' authoritative, adequate to the construction of systems of identification" (34), on the other. Cultural difference is, then, the "process of signification through which statements *of* culture and *on* culture differentiate, discriminate and authorize the production of fields of force, reference, applicability, and capacity" (34). Cultural difference would thus be the "foundation" for any possible cultural diversity, but it remains a problematic, ambivalent ground, one that threatens the security of the identity, the authority, it supports: "The concept of cultural difference focuses on the problem of the ambivalence of cultural authority: the attempt to dominate in the *name* of a cultural supremacy which is itself produced only in the moment of differentiation" (34). To put it another way, "we" are always at the limit of the enunciation of culture, always awaiting the arrival of culture as the unambivalent ground of and for identity. In the advent of its arrival, Nancy's community is before us. Which is simply to say that "we," this community without ground and without identity, will have to decide about "culture," will have to be responsible both to and for "our" decision concerning "borders" and "difference," if "we" are to bring such effects forward. Or if at all. Every time, for the first time.

To begin to articulate the problem of the border, one can begin literally anywhere — for example, in the back pages of the *New Yorker,* where, in 1993, the American Indian College Fund ran an extremely terse advertisement. The ad tells nothing about the fund's purpose, which involves support of twenty-seven tribal colleges, most of which are located on reservations across the country. The ad contains a single line of copy and a single image. The text — in large, bold letters — reads, "Save A Culture That Could Save Ours." What does this mean? "Culture," that ultimately mysterious word in interdisciplinary conversations at the moment, is at stake. And two particular cultures — "ours" and that of the "American Indian."

On the one hand, the implication is that Amerindian culture is in a kind of danger that can be averted only through a college education. It is at least cause for wonder that an Anglo educational institution must prop up Indian ways of being — that Indians need an Anglo-style education, including an education in who they are — in order to continue to be themselves. But however strange it sounds, this argument is made quite explicit in the information that the American Indian College Fund mails to those who respond to the advertisement. The fund has printed a set of postcards that describe various Indian beliefs, and at the bottom of each card, the fund notes: "This is just one of the many beliefs *that are kept alive by* the 27 tribal colleges. Help save a culture that could save ours" (emphasis added).

Used by permission of the American Indian College Fund.

On the other hand, it is equally curious that Anglo-American culture must save Indian culture in order to save itself. Something ineffable within Indian culture holds the key to "our" survival. One might guess the implication: Indian spirituality, a close relationship to nature, an alternative to a competitive market economy, will save "us" from ourselves. One knows all of these narratives in the late twentieth century. From the standpoint of the implied reader of the advertisement, then, a very complex dialectic and economy are at work. Indians need Anglos (both their money and their methods of education) in order to be *themselves*, which allows Indians to shore "us" up, take care of "our" culture.

So while the ad copy presumes that the reader knows precisely where the border lies between "our" culture and Amerindian culture, the ad says that neither of these two cultures can be, in the future, what they already are, without massive border crossing. An Anglo supplement to Indian culture is needed in order to gather and hold together such culture, and this combined Anglo-Amerindian product is needed, in turn, in order to supplement the Anglo world. The Anglo world secures the Indian world, and Anglo-Amerindian education returns the favor and secures the Anglo world.

The image in the ad is also worth examining. It is a "white" feather nesting within a colored flame. This white/colored image visualizes the ad copy, and imagines a day when that which is white (i.e., Anglo) is encased within that which is colored (i.e., Amerindian). The image also visualizes complex cultural transfer, because the white image is in the shape of a feather, which so typically symbolizes "Indianness" and its relationship to nature, and the colored image is a flame, which symbolizes, most likely, civilization in general, and, in particular, the knowledge provided by a college education. So the image promises a future when that which is "white" will be shaped like an Indian mind, and that which is "colored" will be shaped in the manner of an Anglo mind.

But it is even more complicated, and here is where the text is at its most interesting. The border between the two images is not secured. The bottom of the white feather is not enclosed within the black border; rather, the bottom of the white feather leaks out onto the ad's larger field of whiteness, not only escaping a complete nesting, but demonstrating that the black envelopes the white only as it itself is enveloped by the totality of that which it surrounds. The image is, finally, one in which whiteness reigns, though the white secures its own complex imaging of a preserved whiteness only by the introduction of a seemingly protecting coloredness. That which is colored is then both an external and internal border for the white.

It is perhaps predictable that the ad, through the use of the word *could*, imagines that cultural transfer and interrelationship between Anglos and Amerindians is still to come, as if, in the late twentieth century, two separate cultures exist that can now—if "we" choose—inform and even ground each other. This is a modified multiculturalist affirmation of difference: bare multiple-culturalism combined with a vision of a more complex, mixed future, albeit with the distinction between cultures always preserved. Perhaps it goes without saying that this is a particular narrative of modernity: the world begins in simple difference or alterity (Europe and its others), and, following colonialism, it ends happily in complex reciprocity.

Judged as a politics, what such a narrative, or model of both a present and an ideal future, necessarily leaves behind as a trail of debris is an opening for virulent forms of differentiation — on both sides. Amerindians can, within the bare terms of the ad, use its language to indict whiteness in general as, at least, self-destructive. And Anglos can too easily use the rhetorical resources of the ad to produce simple reversals on the fund's implied message: Amerindians' contributing to the salvation of Anglos looks to some like backwardness, technophobia, antimodern tree hugging, anticapitalist laziness, and the like.

In other words, multicultural or liberal notions of difference are also, at one and the same time, fuel for a rhetoric of dislike or even hate. One can always read a narrative of differentiation either way, depending upon one's largest political sensibilities. And unless one can imagine a world composed of nothing but liberal sensibilities (and this is, indeed, impossible, given that the differential field of political ideas demands that all positions within the field exist), the result is that virulent whiteness and coloredness continue (see Bourdieu 185). Liberal politics, then, inevitably reproduces the conditions of hate.

Recognizing the traps of this discourse, however, does not necessarily plunge one into pessimism, because it is possible to rethink the border — in this case, the border "between" Anglo and Amerindian cultures. It is not necessary to think that the modern world proceeds from separate and distinct, preexisting cultures toward more complex formations. One can, instead, think of the complexity — the profound interrelationship of the very ideas of European and indigenous cultures — as a product of colonialist thought from its inception. The cultural knots — the sorts of borders that strangely elide the difference between inside and outside — are products of beginnings. What is typically described as identity difference is nothing more than an effect of an identity relationality that makes it seem as if cultures are still to be "crossed" rather than, as David Murray has suggested, analyzed for their "constant interplay" (3).[1]

If colonial encounters in general produce the problematic rhetoric of the American Indian College Fund, then one possible project is *de*-thinking — thinking backward — the status of the differences themselves and imagining a future not more but less complex or mixed. This means forgoing the "saving" of cultures, and instead destructuring one's sense of them. It involves making studies of "culture" as maximally difficult as possible in the name of a future sparser and sparer in its understanding of peoples and cultures. This means doing away with modern anthropology, sociology, and ethnohistory's ideas of culture, as well as these disciplines' tropes of complexity, typically assembled under the prefixes *inter, trans, bi,* and *cross.*[2] These "traveling logics" can give way to something else — a recognition that cultural borders are effects produced in the mental operation that pulls two groups of people together (in the case of anthropology, ethnographers and their research objects) — (con)fusing them in order to contrast them. The terms of this other way of thinking culture make it impossible to describe singular cultures and their border/crossing. "Border effects," instead, trace back to abyssal discursive relationalities.

To put it in terms of the American Indian College Fund advertisement, the fund cannot have its cake and eat it, too. The language of multicultural differentiation and mixture is betrayed by the black/white border within the image that does not successfully mark out where the cultural border lies and how it can be crossed. In the ad, the border crossing has always already taken place, with the seemingly privileged figure of coloredness always already colonized.

Two of the best-known elaborations of border theory — Anzaldúa's *Borderlands/La Frontera* and Hicks's *Border Writing* — expose the problems and tensions inherent in theorizing border crossing. And both texts bear some relationship to the *New Yorker* ad. First, both establish the same kind of difference — the same historical divide — between modern and premodern worlds. This is an old story. In these texts, the premodern world consists of separate and distinct cultures or territories and the modern of culture crossings. Hicks calls this later process, borrowing from Deleuze and Guattari, the "deterritorialization" of culture and language (xxiv), whereas Anzaldúa speaks of a multiplicity of "borderlands" — "the psychological borderlands, the sexual borderlands and the spiritual borderlands," which "are not particular to the Southwest" and which, in fact, are disseminated across borders and into every body that inhabits the world, whether these bodies reside near geographic borders or not (pref., n.p.).

Second, both texts, like the ad, are concerned with saving all individual cultures from destruction, and Anzaldúa in particular is concerned with saving subjectivities from the increasing cultural fragmentation that puts such subjectivities at risk. But both Hicks and Anzaldúa believe that cultural isolationism poses grave dangers, even though Anzaldúa *also* sees "borderlands' " subjectivity as "plagued" and "torn" due to cultural "transfer," "collision," "clash," "strife," and "attack" (78). In both cases, salvation involves increasing attention to border crossing: a kind of coming to consciousness of proliferating psychological and/or linguistic crossings. For Anzaldúa, those subjects who speak "Chicano Spanish" in the U.S.-Mexico borderlands are wounded subjects, but sometimes, today, they are becoming conscious of these effects of border crossings. And even Anglos living in Iowa are already border crossers, though without knowing it or feeling it. They are hunkered down in an illusory, self-enclosed white subjectivity. Anzaldúa asks of Anglos or whites "to be *met halfway*" (pref., n.p.). "Whites" are "to be our allies" in the future (85), she argues, and she addresses whites in the following way: "Admit that Mexico is your double, that she exists in the shadow of this country, that we are irrevocably tied to her. Gringo, accept the doppleganger in your psyche" (86). Such a modification of consciousness will produce a world of border subjects that preserves "the heterosexual white man's or the colored man's or the state's or the culture's or the religion's or the parent's" ways of being-in-the-world as part of an amalgam or fusion that is "just ours, mine": "And suddenly I feel everything rushing to a center, a nucleus. All the lost pieces of myself come flying from the deserts, and the mountains and the valleys, magnetized toward that center. *Completa*" (51).

Hicks's metaphor for this same process is that of the hologram: "In the same way that one part of a hologram can produce an entire image, the border metaphor is able to reproduce the whole culture to which it refers" (xxxix). She imagines a complex project of global wellness that preserves all existing cultures and languages by stitching together the border subjectivities that embody them toward an in-principle uncompletable yet still necessary and ideal conception of wholeness (xxix). The difference between Anzaldúa and Hicks on this point is that Anzaldúa forecasts absolute, holistic completeness, whereas Hicks strategizes a "less solid" sort of universality—one that "cannot be dominated so easily" (xxix). In both cases, however, cultures must be forced into increasingly combining relationship with one another in order to save each individual cultural piece or fragment.

Third, both texts, again like the American Indian College Fund ad, premise saving or "healing" the world on recourse to the indigenous. Hicks calls this "nonsynchronous memory" (xxiii). "The word [the world speaks] is sick"; "the global body needs to be healed," she says, and the dangerously fragmented subjectivities of modernity are made well, finally, by a kind of writerly shamanism (xxxi). Hicks says:

> Border writing is the trace of the coyote/shaman ... [in which] the writer ... [is] a shaman who writes in order to cure the reader. ... If the border is a machine, then one of its elements is the *bicultural* smuggler, and to read is to cross over into another side where capital has not yet reduced the object to a commodity, to a place where *psychic healing* can occur. (xxxi)

Anzaldúa, for her part, writes at great length about getting in touch with a pre-Aztec, Nahuatl element inside her: "Plumb the rich ancestral roots" (23); "native cultural roots ... origins" (21). "Let's all stop importing Greek myths and the Western Cartesian split point of view and root ourselves in the mythological soil and soul of this continent" (68). This submerged consciousness, this unconscious, acting as an "officiating priestess" (80), allows one to "deconstruct" the split border subject and "reconstruct" a transborder, pancultural subjectivity that no longer hurts (82–83).

Some serious problems within these theoretical narratives are quite obvious, three of which are worth noting. First, the tensions between tendencies toward universalism and localism are not sufficiently marked. In both cases, Spanish American writing is both unique *and* serves as a kind of final destination for *all* world writing. This is the same double gesture, from reverse perspective, of the cultural history of the West, as Jacques Derrida notes in *The Other Heading*. Europe, according to Derrida, has been figured for hundreds of years as both special *and* universal — and this tension or contradiction is one of the crucial markers of colonialist thought. Both Anzaldúa and Hicks, it might be said, engage in a new but no less tired form of colonialism.

Second, the recourse of both Anzaldúa and Hicks to the seemingly indigenous partakes of some of the most obvious of stereotypes about premodern peoples (that their cultures are dominated by magic, shape-shifting, healing) as well as a decidedly late-Western, "New Age," and, finally, bland universal humanism and/or multiculturalism (we need to "see not just from one side of the border, but from the other as well," says Hicks [xxiii], and we are "on our way to a new consciousness" beyond black and white dichotomies, says Anzaldúa [78]). In these twin and again conflicting tendencies, the indigenous is, on the one hand, "othered" as profoundly antirational and, on the other hand, understood as humanist through and through. Putting to one side the question of just how phantasmagoric these notions of indigenousness are — and they are all profoundly romantic-mythic — the splitting or bifurcating of the historically and perhaps necessarily linked ideas of rationalism and humanism is a highly problematic gesture.

Finally, there is a third unresolved tension in Hicks's and Anzaldúa's texts between the claims to future inclusiveness of all sides of the world's borders and the harsh criticism of facets of Anglo or white culture: capitalism and technologism in Hicks; sexism and heterosexism, among other things, in Anzaldúa. For all their claims to inclusiveness, saving notions of indigenousness in Anzaldúa and Hicks resist and strive to overcome domination by capital, technology, machismo, and heterosexuality. In other words, for every bare multiculturalist gesture in these texts, there is another gesture toward the demonization and repression of a presumed white or Anglo culture.

But the largest problem in these texts involves coming to terms with their conceptualization of completeness and totality. If the world begins in completely separate, unlike, anterior cultures, what guarantees or secures the very possibility of wholeness or wellness — completeness and totality? In Hicks's case, what does a "hologram" look like that is pieced together from unrelated fragments? She uses words like "order" and the "whole," and she uses the Benjaminian metaphor of the "vessel" "piece[d] together" (xxx) — but what guarantees that a totality will emerge from the fragmentary state(s) of culture? And in Anzaldúa's case, what guarantees that "certain 'faculties' — not just in me but in every border resident — and dormant areas of consciousness are being activated, awakened" (pref., n.p.), and that these faculties will produce a kind of writing or communication that translates all "alien" cultures into a pancultural, panlinguistic tongue?

One answer might be that the special notion of "indigenousness" in these texts operates as a kind of universal translator. Hicks certainly implies that there is something so similar about all indigenous cultures, and something so complete unto itself and so well or healthy about the very condition of indigenousness, that, in its essence, it speaks across all modern borders and heals their differences. In Hicks's narrative, all of the different modern cultures emerged out of indigenousness, and that same indigenousness therefore undergirds or underpins modernity — provides a set of hidden connections among cultures that can be called back into being. For Hicks, then, the wholeness of the hologram is guaranteed only when the fragments of modernity are lacquered over with a heavy coat of indigenousness, drawn from its deep well.

Anzaldúa's text works much the same way, even though it is only hemispheric in outlook. Indigenousness is different from modernity because it is preduality, prebinary — it is a heady mixture of anything and everything before elements and concepts were separated out from one another and organized hierarchically. Modernity (read: duality, or difference) emerges directly out of this rich, inchoate, and protean stew, and can be, therefore, redissolved back into its constituting indigenousness.

But something else altogether can be argued concerning these images of totality and completeness. Or, at least, it is possible to suggest another pathway for thinking that was open to Anzaldúa and Hicks. A theory of borderlands need not return to the homelands.

Both Anzaldúa's mysterious, untapped "faculties" and Hicks's "nonsynchronous memory" are nothing more or less than the embodiment of the complex of "border effects" — a transcultural or global "outer edge or border [that] can also be considered an inner fold" (Derrida

1984, 14). They both involve the sensing of relationality *interpreted* as an exterior completeness and totality that, at one and the same time, *feels* interiorized — and this can be understood as the largest possible but still phantom effect of the project of bordering. It is a version of the "border effect" that produces a sense of individual cultural completeness, logically extended to its maximum — to the culture that is the combination of all independent cultures. Anzaldúa's and Hicks's resorting to "indigenousness" in order to account for such feelings is both a grasping at mythic-nostalgic straws and, on another level, little more than liberal-humanist politics.

But a border is not something that can be crossed by one or the other self-enclosed cultural subject. Nor can all of these borders be assembled and gathered together into a still larger enclosure — whether one calls it "*completa*" or a negative/ideal totality. Instead, a border is always already crossed and double-crossed, without the possibility of the "trans"cultural — whether petit or grand. It is "to be related, without translation, to all the 'trans-'s that are at work here" (Derrida 1984, 172).

To bring Anzaldúa and Hicks to this point means abandoning, finally, any project of "keeping intact one's . . . identity," as Anzaldúa phrases it (pref., n.p.), and then comprehending the cultural or linguistic self as necessarily incomplete, coming to be, held open to "outside" cultures, while, at the same time, as having always already enfolded the other within itself, with the border between the inside and outside, in principle, unclosable. Such an other way of thinking produces defamiliarizing border readouts without the possibility of laying it on the line — or at least a straight or straightforward one. Borders everywhere, but a world where no geographer's or cartographer's science is up to the task of mapping. And once this is grasped, who can say what the "one," the "many," the "othered," or the "whole" sum total might be capable of rethinking — or actively forgetting to think?

The "border" in border studies remains the problem, set before Anzaldúa's "one" and the "other" as the site for "keeping intact one's . . . identity." It is the place, in short, of a certain property, and of a certain properness. You might say that one belongs there, that we will find ourselves there, facing one another across that divide. Such is the upshot of Calderón and Saldívar's introduction to *Criticism in the Borderlands,* in which they describe that volume's project as an attempt to place the borderlands—the literature and criticism, the culture, then, of the U.S. Southwest—before a national audience, explaining that while the "widening of the literary canon" has benefited many, "much work still lies ahead, however, especially in the field of Chicano literature; although many men and women have entered the academy, our literature and scholarship have yet to receive full institutional support or national attention" (1). This work "lies ahead" of "us" like a problem, a limit or border, to which "we" come and that "we" will have to cross. But not all of "us": there are exclusions operating in this borderlands anthology, exclusions that, as part of the introduction, serve to authorize the collection's coherence and publication. "Chicano culture, as viewed by Chicana and Chicano critics as well as by European and Latin American scholars, is an expression of a social group that has given *the* distinctive cultural feature to the American West and Southwest" (2). In sum, the borderlands belong to Chicano culture, to Chicano cultural and self-expression. It is a right of property.

As such, moreover, it must be constituted within a narrative of possession, a genealogy of occupation. At stake is a relation to the origin, the right to determine it:

> Although Colonial Novohispano and Mexican cultures in this region date back to the mid-sixteenth century and beyond, taking into account Native American *mestizo* roots, the literature produced by these groups should be ideologically and institutionally situated within the national literatures of Spain and Mexico. A Spanish chronicler of the area which was later to form the northern regions of the viceroyalty of New Spain, Cabeza de Vaca or Coronado writing in the sixteenth century, regardless of whatever sympathy he may have had for Native Americans, is not a Chicano but a Spaniard. (2)

On the one hand, as in Anzaldúa and Hicks, there is the suggestion of a relation to an indigenous *mestizaje,* of an origin without history; on the other hand, there is the desire to determine the origin of Chicano cultural expression as a *principio* without the taint of Spanish colonialism. Cabeza de Vaca is no Chicano despite passing several years in and through what would become the South Texas valley—the scene of

Rolando Hinojosa's fictions—and despite moving among that originary *mestizaje.*[3] In excluding conqueror-writers like Cabeza de Vaca and Coronado, *Criticism in the Borderlands* effectively argues that contact with others, being among others, makes no difference. There is contact, perhaps no end of contact, but it makes no difference. This exclusivity implies that the rule of Chicano identity is not to be among others, but to be among Chicanos: it is constitutive of an enclave. The cultures in contact, then, in the sixteenth century, like *Criticism in the Borderlands*'s understanding of Chicano culture today, apparently maintain their respective purities, their identities, without and before the other—a kind of aboriginal Native American *mestizaje* that in its aboriginality becomes pure, on the one hand, and on the other a Spanish cultural "purity" influenced for centuries by the presence in Spain of Jews and Moors. The two, constituted of mixing without rule, exist in the borderlands, unmixed—without any intercourse. And this despite what Calderón and Saldívar call "the four hundred years of a Mexican *mestizo* presence in our borderlands" (7). This would be the rule, the *arché* of Chicano culture.

Calderón and Saldívar no doubt are aware of the exclusion; they remark it as an effect of another definition of Chicano identity: "If we limit Chicano or Mexican-American artistic forms to political boundaries, they have existed in oral or written form since the Texas-Mexican War (1836) with greater awareness of cultural differences from Mexico after the U.S.-Mexican War (1846–48)" (2). The possibility of Chicano or Mexican American cultural identity results from an Anglo-American intervention in already colonized territory.[4] Given this definition of Chicano identity, the exclusion of Cabeza de Vaca is not one: he belongs to an earlier historical-political narrative. Yet the new model for Chicano identity remains exclusive despite its apparent geopolitical inclusivity, for it includes as Chicanos only those who are both inscribed genealogically within the geopolitical borders of the U.S. expansion into formerly Mexican territory *and* resistant to Anglo-American domination:

> Although we are not dismissing the various ideological discourses on the borderlands prior to the mid-twentieth century, we are arguing in this volume for a Mexican-American or Chicano intellectual perspective.... From our vantage point in the twentieth century, we can posit that such

a perspective must have emerged in the borderlands in mid-nineteenth century when Mexican-Americans, Chicanos, or *mestizos* began to project for themselves a positive, yet also critical, rendering of their bilingual and bicultural experience as a resistive measure against Anglo-American economic domination and ideological hegemony. (4)

The importance of resistance in the formation of Chicano identity no doubt explains the place of Américo Paredes in Calderón and Saldívar's Chicano studies: "The presence of Paredes is especially evident throughout our volume, for his book, *'With His Pistol in His Hand'*, was a highly conscious, imaginative act of resistance that redefined the border" (Calderón and Saldívar 5).[5] It is, perhaps, at the site of "resistance" that the discourses of Chicano, border, cultural, and ethnic studies articulate themselves with postcolonial studies.[6] They will all, more or less, participate in Lugo's Gramscian "war of position." To the extent that these various "studies" take sides, occupy one side of the border against another—engage in resistance against assimilation or collaboration—they all share in the same problems, indeed, in precisely those problems announced here in the context of Chicano studies and border theory more generally.

Calderón/Saldívar Chicano studies essentializes Chicano identity around the figure of resistance: in short, there will be no Chicano assimilationists. No doubt this enables Calderón and Saldívar to discount the political Right's embrace of Richard Rodriguez as a Mexican American spokesman.[7] He isn't one of "us." The exclusion of Rodriguez exposes a hegemonic desire, what Juan Bruce-Novoa calls the "monological unity" (1994, 242 n. 1), of the Calderón/Saldívar version of Chicano studies and its definition of Chicano identity.

The problem is that although resistance may not, finally, be necessary to Chicano identity, it most certainly is to Calderón/Saldívar-constituted Chicano studies, for "resistance" locates the border, cites it between "us" and "them" in such a way that a field or discipline is constituted. And although the field of Chicano studies could have been founded without the notion of resistance—for the geopolitical-historical definition offered to exclude Cabeza de Vaca would alone have sufficed—it serves another purpose: namely, that of the dream of purity.

Calderón/Saldívar Chicano studies effectively tells all those who would be Chicanos that it is not enough to have been born in a certain place at a certain time of a certain biological-cultural genealogy. It tells them they will have to choose and, further, that they will have to *know* what they choose; they will have to resist and they will have to do so consciously. They will have to take sides. And they will have to know what side they've taken. This would be the crisis of identity without the risk, for all Chicanos will decide for "us"; they will all be like "us." Our resistance against their assimilation. No Chicanos on the other side, *el otro lado.* Chicano identity is inscribed, as is every other identity, within the horizon of the politics of opposition. Yet Todorov, in *The Conquest of America,* cautions that "we shall never be sure that by *not* behaving like them we are not in fact on the way to imitating them" (254). Or, even were we to grant the possibility of knowing that we resist, and of knowing what amounts to resistance, as Derrida points out in the preamble to "The Ends of Man," such opposition "does not upset the given order":

> It would be illusory to believe that political innocence has been restored, and evil complicities undone, when opposition to them can be expressed in the country itself, not only through the voices of its own citizens but also those of foreign citizens, and that henceforth diversities, i.e. oppositions, may freely and discursively relate to one another. That a declaration of opposition to some official policy is authorized, and authorized by the authorities, also means, precisely to that extent, that the declaration does not upset the given order, is not *bothersome.* (114)

It is always possible, in other words, that we will never know where we stand and, knowing where we stand, knowing what side we've taken or come to occupy, we won't nevertheless find ourselves elsewhere. What passes, then, for resistance, for opposition, and, thus, for identity? Or perhaps there is only passing resistance and the passing away of identity. Identity: it comes to pass.

Perhaps, then, there are very few Chicanos; perhaps there are none. A strategy for inclusion grounded upon an exclusion, a principle of inclusivity (resistance, opposition) that, when pushed hard enough, effectively denies access to all—and this to *preserve* Chicano identity, to save it from others, and not, as Benjamin Alire Sáenz suggests in his contribution to this volume, to rethink Chicano as "an identity that waits for the day that it is no longer necessary."

Sáenz's essay makes clear what so much of Chicano studies — and ethnic studies in general — fails to note: identities don't travel well. They don't work well abroad, among others; and home, too, is always foreign, always on the other side of the border. Sáenz notes: " 'Chicano' in those years meant nothing. There was no context, no social or political necessity for that identity. But it was my time in Europe and my summer in Africa that taught me that I did not belong in those places. I was a foreigner there — and would always be a foreigner. I came to the conclusion that I had a people — that I belonged to a people, a community." But the place he thinks he belongs is not his either: he has just recounted the story of a young woman who told him to "criticize Mexico... — criticize your own country." In Europe, the Chicano is European, American, white; in the United States, the Chicano is Mexican. Always out of place, improperly sited, at home and abroad: this will be the "ground" of the Chicano, of Chicano identity, if there is one, and, perhaps, of a certain "people" and "community." Or, to address the problem in terms of Louis Kaplan's reading of *The Pilgrim*, Chaplin's film set in the "no-man's-land" of the Tex-Mex borderlands, the boarder — the one who dwells, who is at home — is always on the other side of the border. Indeed, we will never be able to tell, to hear, the difference between the border and the boarder.

This is a very different terrain from the one marked out by Calderón and Saldívar, by Anzaldúa, and by Hicks. It is, perhaps ironically, the space traversed by Cabeza de Vaca in *Naufragios*. But this is not to argue in favor of Bruce-Novoa's assertion of Cabeza de Vaca's Chicanicity, an inclusion grounded on the identity of personal experience (see note 3); on the contrary, it is to site Cabeza de Vaca at the edge of the decision about his place, at the limit of inclusivity and exclusivity. At the border of meaning, which is, according to Jean-Luc Nancy, the place of *mestizaje* (1994). It is also where Rolena Adorno finds him in "The Negotiation of Fear in Cabeza de Vaca's *Naufragios*." For Adorno, Cabeza de Vaca's movement between Amerindian groups allowed those groups to come into contact. Thus Cabeza de Vaca mediated Amerindians as a kind of shaman, without, however, occupying an essential place between them: "This magical power did not mean that the Spaniards were the principal parties in the negotiations between the marauding groups and their victims, but rather the catalysts to the exchange: they helped produce the desired pillaging and could be counted upon not to covet its rewards" (67). His place within these exchanges, then, is extrinsic; nothing accrues to his place. It is productive of nothing but the possibility of relation among and between others. He is a cipher at the edge of an economy of cultural production. He gains nothing in relation to these others—neither a new, Amerindian identity nor the preservation of a Spanish one. His place is entirely emptied out. He will come to occupy the site of an unidentified "we" (Todorov 1984, 199): entirely empty, neither inclusive nor exclusive; a community, a plurality, that produces no culture to which "we" belong, no identity "we" can call our own. This "we" takes no sides in the "war of position," has no place there.

On the one hand, to the extent contemporary Chicano studies of the Calderón/Saldívar sort defines itself, defines *Chicano* in terms of resistance and opposition to hegemonic discourses of the nation, Cabeza de Vaca has no place there: he is no Chicano. On the other hand, Bruce-Novoa's inclusion of Cabeza de Vaca within the genealogical narratives of Chicano literature and Chicano history is no less problematic in that it depends on the guarantee of shared experiences. This sort of inclusion is an exclusion waiting to happen; it is effectively the same as Calderón and Saldívar's insistence on "Chicano" as a relation to Anglo-American discourses of national identity, as long as the relation is the one "we" all share: one of opposition, of resistance.

At stake in these gestures of inclusion and exclusion is a policing of the border of culture and of the borderlands in general as the location of Chicano culture, a certain legislation that governs access to culture and cultural identification. Again, this is not a problem unique to Chicano studies. In an article published in *American Quarterly,* the flagship journal of the American Studies Association, Betsy Erkkila suggests that "current paradigms of American literary studies ... encourage a separatist and atomized model of literary and cultural studies in which whites do whites, men do men, women do women, blacks do blacks, latinos do latinos, and there is very little dialogue among or cultural encounter beyond these relatively fixed ethnic and gender bounds" (564). Border studies and/or multiculturalism reach their limit in monadology: a world of "created simple substances or monads" that "have no windows, by which anything could come in or go out" (Leibnitz 181, 179).

Yet, while it is true that other critical discourses both implicitly and explicitly have recourse to borders — geopolitical *and* metaphorical — it is equally true that Chicano studies, more than any other, has refocused critical attention on the concept of the border. Chicano studies — more than ethnic studies or postcolonial studies or U.S.-Mexico border studies — has made the idea of the border available, indeed necessary, to the larger discourses of American literary studies, U.S. history, and cultural studies in general. And precisely because Chicano studies has come to occupy the border — the political-geographic one between the United States and Mexico and the concept of the border person, the *fronterizo* — and to claim it, as Hicks and Anzaldúa do, as a kind of birthright, and as Renato Rosaldo does, as the site "of creative cultural production," *Border Theory* must mark out an other relation to it. *Border Theory* inscribes itself neither simply within Chicano studies nor simply without it: neither inclusive nor exclusive, it traces the limit (of the border) of disciplinary and discursive identity.

The border is policed, access denied or permitted, always on the ground of reading, interpretation. Roberto González Echevarría points out that "the law (*legislar,* from 'to read') is above all a system of reading and writing, a prescribed way of interpreting" (67). Rosaldo's *Culture and Truth,* which is perhaps the most important text in the growing canon of multicultural anthropology and which occupies the center of the most recent Chicano studies, is organized around certain problems of reading, problems that have, finally, the force of law. No fewer than three times, Rosaldo provokes a crisis of interpretation by marking scenes of reading and the decisions they demand. But his point is not that it is rigorously impossible to decide for or against a certain reading, and that, this shadow of undecidability notwithstanding, "we" must decide without precedent, without rule. Nor does he, faced with such a legislative problem, conclude that the question of reading effectively opens the subject to the aporetic structure of the border of subjectivity. No: Rosaldo's crises of reading are, rather, sites of exclusion and affiliation.

Culture and Truth's remaking of social analysis, its repositioning of "the cultural force of emotions" (2) depends on how "we" read A. R. Radcliffe-Brown's reading of Andaman Islanders' "weeping" rite (52–53), deciding "whether or not the weepers actually feel anything" (52); on how "we" read Karl Marx's "anti-Semitic stereotypes," whether "we" read them straight or not, in context or out (190–93); and, finally, though it comes first in *Culture and Truth,* on how "we" read Rosaldo's "use of personal experience" (11). According to Rosaldo, "we" will decide that Andaman Islanders do feel something when they weep their welcome; that Marx, when read *in context,* was not an anti-Semite; and that, most important, "we" sympathize with Rosaldo's use of personal experience, namely, his description of Michelle Rosaldo's death and his reaction to it.[8]

The crisis, however, is not one; there is no other choice, for to decide otherwise would be, quite simply, inhuman: as Rosaldo points out, "unsympathetic readers could reduce [his text] to an act of mourning" (11), in the same way, for example, that Radcliffe-Brown, Rosaldo notes, "regards [Andaman Islanders'] tears as mere playacting" (53). Unsympathetic readers, of course, are those who do not share emotions with others or, in the case of *Culture and Truth,* with "us." But within the context of *Culture and Truth*'s argument — basically that humans share an emotional structure that makes multiculturalism possible — unsympathetic readers, because they lack such fellow feeling, the possibility of sympathetic identification with the other, which makes us human, are dead, and thus no longer human. *Culture and Truth*'s "we" in other words will be inclusive of all humans, of the *living.* If you are human, you will be one of "us"; to prove you are alive, however, to prove your humanity, you must agree with "us," you must sympathize. There is in this totalizing gesture masked as inclusive multiculturalism something of what Rosaldo calls "the Green Card phase" of institutional diversification. "Institutions of higher learning appeared to tell those previously excluded," Rosaldo explains, " 'Come in, sit down, shut up. You're welcome here as long as you conform to our norms' " (x). This would be called, if it weren't already called multiculturalism, a theory of assimilation grounded upon a fundamental exclusion, an exclusion so thoroughly buried it goes virtually unnoticed, almost unread.

No doubt *Culture and Truth* constructs an inclusive community, a "we" that "you" and "I," among others, can join, be part of; such community comes at a certain cost, however, and though that cost won't be "our" humanity—for that will be given "us" upon "our" inclusion—it will be any possibility of an ethical relation to others. Indeed, this community costs "us" others. And it does so precisely by reducing the risk of reading, by reducing the problem it puts before "us"—whoever "we" are, living or dead.

On the one hand, we have multicultural inclusivity grounded in legible universal human emotions—tears, for example—that do not, however, require interpretation because "we" (all humans) agree on their import; on the other hand, we have an inclusive, expansionist multicultural American literary history grounded on principles of inclusion that produce a certain hegemonic Chicano identity. How, for example, does *Criticism in the Borderlands* justify Cabeza de Vaca's exclusion from a widened American literature, a multicultural one, except to say that he is a Spaniard? Effectively, *Criticism in the Borderlands* would exclude him on the grounds that he is not one of us, not a product of U.S. Anglo-American cultural and economic domination, *and* that he was one of them—a Spaniard, a conqueror—his sympathy for us mestizos notwithstanding. In the first half of the sixteenth century, what exactly is a Spaniard, whether here, in the Americas, or there, in Europe?

Of tears and Spaniards, then, two transparent scenes that make clear the grounds for legislating against a certain anthropological narrative of the other and Cabeza de Vaca. In a way, the question for multiculturalism would be, For whom do Spaniards cry? For themselves or for others? How do they know? And, for that matter, how do "we" tell the difference between a Spanish tear and a Chicano one? Or are they/we all merely playacting, feigning authentic tears, authentically shedding crocodile tears for the other?

What of Cabeza de Vaca's tears? In *Naufragios*—the *relación* of a nine-year stay/journey among, between, with those fundamentally mestizo Native Americans, written by a "Spaniard," according to Calderón and Saldívar, who will be recognized neither as Spanish nor as Amerindian by "Spaniards" or by "others" in 1536, and both recognized and not recognized as Chicano in 1991—Cabeza de Vaca and other "Spaniards" cry among themselves and among others. Shipwrecked, cast naked upon the shore, Cabeza de Vaca writes:

> Así, estuvimos pidiendo a Nuestro Señor misericordia y perdón de nuestros pecados, derramando muchas lágrimas, habiendo cado uno lástima no sólo de sí, mas de todos los otros, que en el mismo estado veían.... Los indios, de ver el desastre que nos había venido y el desastre en que estábamos, con tanta desventura y miseria, se sentaron entre nosotros, y con el gran dolor y lástima que hubieron de vernos en tanta fortuna, comenzaron todos a llorar recio y tan de verdad, que lejos de allí se podían oír, y esto les duró más de media hora. Cierto ver que estos hombres tan sin razón y tan crudos, a manera de brutos, se dolían tanto de nosotros, hizo que en mí y en otros de la compañía creciese más la pasión y la consideración de nuestra desdicha. (1989, 120–21)

> [And thus we were imploring our lord for mercy and pardon for our sins, shedding many tears, each one bewailing not only his own plight but that of all the others whom he saw in the same state.... When the Indians saw the disaster that had come upon us and the disaster we were in, with so much ill luck and misery, they sat down among us and, with great grief and pity they felt on seeing us in such a desparate plight, all of them began to weep loudly, and so sincerely that they could be heard a long way off, and this lasted more than half an hour; and certainly, to see that those uncivilized and savage men, like brutes, were so sorry for us, caused me and others in our company to feel still more grief and the full realization of our misfortune.] (1993, 42)

"We" cry for ourselves and the other cries for "us," also, but "our" tears need interpretation, need explanation, for tears can never be certain; despite their transparence, they are rather murky emotional indicators, if they mark emotions at all.[9] Cabeza de Vaca's "y tan de verdad" signals the ambiguity of tears — authentic or feigned, tears of joy or sorrow, tears of pity or self-pity; they must be contained, situated within a narrative of survival in the face of the longest odds. So long, in fact, that despite the "truth" of these Amerindian tears, that they are on behalf of "our" pain, a pain with which the Amerindians sympathize, and despite the effect these tears have on "us," namely, that "we" feel ourselves and our pain even more truly in the wake of these tears, nevertheless, these others threaten "us." After feeding and warming "us," Cabeza de Vaca explains that the Amerindians carry "us" to a house they had made for "us" and desde a una hora que habíamos llegado, comenzaron a bailar y hacer grande fiesta, que duró toda la noche, aunque para nosotros no había placer, fiesta ni sueño, esperando cuándo nos habían de sacrificar. (1989, 122)

[by an hour after the time we arrived they began to dance and make great revelry (which lasted all night), though for us there was neither pleasure nor revelry nor sleep, waiting to know when they were going to sacrifice us.] (1993, 43)

How do "we" read the other, the other's tears, the other's revelry? How do "we" read "our" own tears? The problem for Cabeza de Vaca, simply, is to negotiate the signs of the other, to read the watermark of tears. Salvation *or* sacrifice, salvation *and* sacrifice. A certain consummation of the self, then, its completion in the tears of the other.

If there is a rule for reading the other, it remains a secret; and if "our" understanding of ourself hinges on "our" reading of others, then "we," too, the rule or law of "our" identity, remains a secret — a secret among others, perhaps; a secret that cannot (not) be told among others, a secret that cannot (not) take a toll on "us."

Anthropology comes after the secret understood as the private knowledge of culture, that which the other holds in reserve, that which in its reservation preserves the other and sustains the other's culture. And it is, perhaps, since Lévi-Strauss's theft of the proper name in *Tristes Tropiques* that anthropology has suffered a crisis before the secret: to take it or leave it (272–80). This crisis remains legible in recent feminist ethnography, like that of Ruth Behar and Barbara Tedlock, but also in Elizabeth Burgos's *Me llamo Rigoberta Menchú y así me nació la conciencia*. In the prologue to the first edition, Burgos explains that although she had intended to speak to Menchú about death on the last day of their eight-day stay in Paris, she developed a certain reticence, thinking that direct discussion of Mayan rituals of death would prove "premonitoria" (17). Her reluctance takes the shape of a reservation, the putting-on-reserve of certain aspects of Mayan culture. Burgos understands these rituals to be so intimately Mayan that discussion of them with a non-Mayan could prove destructive. This is the anthropological fantasy of the secret of the other, that knowledge that must be kept inside or within a certain culture. It marks the limit of culture. And although Menchú takes the liberty of recording, on her own, a discussion

of those rituals, it is nonetheless not clear that she doesn't share Burgos's understanding of one's relation to culture, for *Me llamo Rigoberta
Menchú* concludes, after nearly three hundred pages of revelation, with
Menchú claiming that although she has given "una imagen de [mi
pueblo]. . . sin embargo, todavía sigo ocultando mi identidad como in-
dígena. Sigo ocultando lo que yo considero que nadie sabe, ni siquiera
un antropólogo, ni un intelectual, por más que tenga muchos libros, no
saben distinguir todos nuestros secretos" (1983, 271).[10] The self occults
the secret in order to reserve to herself her identity, in order not to give
it away. If the secret is a content, a *datum,* to be guarded, shared only at
the risk of death,[11] then *Me llamo Rigoberta Menchú* blows smoke in the
anthropologist's face, telling her secrets in order not to give herself
away.

It is access to some such secret that *Criticism in the Borderlands* denies Cabeza de Vaca, and it is access to this secret, the secret self that
you can't see, that *Culture and Truth* never challenges in its reading of
Sandra Cisneros's *The House on Mango Street* as resistant to a certain
patriarchal discourse of Chicano culture and identity. In "Changing Chicano Narratives" (chapter 7 of *Culture and Truth*), Rosaldo writes that
"young Chicano authors have written against earlier versions of cultural authenticity that idealized patriarchal regimes that appeared autonomous, homogeneous, and unchanging" (161), but in the case of Cisneros anyway, this challenge to patriarchal versions of authenticity, for
Rosaldo, does not result in a disavowal of authenticity in general. His
point, in other words, is not that there is no authentic Chicano culture,
but only that Chicano culture isn't simply what Américo Paredes claimed
it was.

A good portion of Rosaldo's analysis of Cisneros concerns "My Name,"
the brief text that explains Esperanza's relation to her name and her
desire to rename, "baptize" herself anew, with "a name more like the
real me, the one nobody sees" (163; Cisneros 11). The name she would
choose, though she admits that she is "always Esperanza," would be "Zeze
the X. Yes. Something like Zeze the X will do" (163; Cisneros 11). Rosaldo can't read the name, and although his analysis works the line between Esperanza's patrimony and her matrimony, exposing the sexual
politics of a certain Chicano community, it is unable to see that there is

no "invisible, real self" (163), certainly not one that isn't exposed from the beginning. Rosaldo leaves Esperanza's secret alone, leaves it to her, despite being told, in Esperanza's choice of a name, that no one is at home. Esperanza hides nothing: X is the sign of the unknown, the undetermined variable, and it is not simply unknown to Rosaldo, but to Esperanza, too, so much so that, finally, not even Zeze the X will do. Not even that name names her self. Only a name *like it* will do. *The House on Mango Street* tells all the secrets of Esperanza, tells all the secrets she knows, tells them to others in order to keep them. In order, perhaps, to keep herself. The name, then, is a problem, "that which one poses or throws in front of oneself, either as the projection of a project, of a task to accomplish, or as the protection created by a substitute, a prosthesis that we put forth in order to represent, replace, shelter, or dissimulate ourselves, or so as to hide something unavowable — like a shield . . . behind which one guards oneself *in secret* or *in shelter* in case of danger" (Derrida 1993, 11–12). And yet, what the name would secret and secrete, would protect by projecting itself as a prosthesis, "itself" has the structure of an aporia: that for which there is precisely "*no longer any problem*" (12), or no longer any chance "of sheltering ourselves behind what could still protect the interiority of a secret" (12).

The secret, in short, is the border of identity, the limit between inside and outside, between self and other. But secrets, like tears, *secrete* without reason. At the very least, cultural secrets, which are always on display, in public, exposed to and shared among others, among ourselves as others, preserve and occult nothing; they are meaningless. Rosaldo won't look in that direction; his course has another heading: he writes that "it would be difficult to exaggerate the major role played by the narrative analysis of Paredes, Galarza, and Cisneros in my charting a path for renewing the anthropologist's *search for meaning*" (166). No doubt anthropologists — understood as broadly as possible, Barbara Tedlock claims that "in today's rapidly changing multicultural world, we are all becoming ethnographers" (xii) — will find something, a secret or two; and, no doubt, filling their notebooks, they'll come up empty.[12]

Border Theory rethinks the place of the border in border studies. More specifically, it challenges the current dream of prevailing border discourses that the so-called borderlands are the site of a new cultural production, a new *mestizaje*, as it were, fundamentally more tolerant than other cultural paradigms. *Border Theory*, then, jeopardizes not just the border, whether of political-geographic or metaphoric realities, but the limits of any attempt to theorize the border. At stake is the *value* of the border, both as a cultural indicator and as a conceptual tool. Of what use, finally, are concepts like "culture" and "identity" if their invocation, even in so-called multicultural contexts, is also exclusive, colonial, intolerant?

To the extent that the cultural borderlands of the U.S. Southwest have been privileged as the site of the production of border discourses, the essays collected in this volume solicit the frontiers of the borderlands, shake them up, on the one hand, in Part I, by reading the borderlands and the discourses they produce and that produce them and, on the other hand, in Part II, by remarking the border elsewhere and otherwise. The volume represents a double strategy, then, of concentration and dissemination, of focusing on the borderlands in order to displace them and of looking away from them in order to locate them elsewhere.

Border Theory: The Limits of Cultural Politics thus collects the work of younger scholars and writers who are not as yet identified with border studies and who are not working in fields or within theoretical frames traditionally associated with border studies, but whose work nevertheless has implications, on the one hand, for the rearticulation of border discourses and, on the other hand, for the reinscription of the disciplines in which the contributors are boarders — American literature, anthropology, ethnic studies — as instances of border studies.

For each of the contributors to this volume, border studies as currently constituted inadequately theorizes the border and its political import. For Alejandro Lugo, it neglects the totalizing power of capitalism and the state; border studies' "theory of multiple subjectivities" forgets the way in which such subjectivities prop up "the politics of difference under state citizenry" and a "late capitalism characterized not only by the fragmentation of the production process, but also by the fragmentation of the labor force."

For both Benjamin Alire Sáenz and Elaine K. Chang, border theory is too nostalgic for home, homelands, a final — and imaginary — destination for hope, healing, and security. "It is too late for me to forge a return to my great-grandmother's culture," writes Sáenz, and he cautions that Gloria Anzaldúa's strategy is "not so different from Englishmen appropriating the 'classical' culture of the ancient Greeks as their own." Chang's piece is designed to move border studies away from "villain/victim" narratives. Responding to feminists' dissatisfaction with the collapse of the distinction between "life and text" in postmodern discourse, Chang suggests that attempts to uphold such a "strictly or merely binary" method of thinking play into the hands of essentializing, totalizing, and dominating accounts of race, gender, age, and the like, and make "victims" of people of color, women, and the young by determining their ground, their sites of origin and destination, in strictly "material" terms.

Similarly, Russ Castronovo takes issue with the "nice stories" offered by border studies (Paredes, Anzaldúa) — tales that he links to African American slave narratives of the nineteenth century, told on both sides of the Mason-Dixon line. These all are "classic hero" tales in which "a text overcomes the impediments of being marginal to two or more cultures, and indeed ironically benefits from these historical limitations and prejudices, to undermine . . . oppressive structures," and the academy's often naive reading of such stories fails to take account of recontainment procedures enacted through conditions of publication, distribution, and framing of such texts, and by particular audiences and their reading practices.

For Louis Kaplan, the problem is a "border analysis" mortgaged to an unthematized notion of "history (or biography)," with its attendant themes of racial/ethnic/cultural origins, traditions, and straight-line trajectories. In short, the discourse of history produces closed-system, "soundproof," internally coherent subjects, at the level of the individual and/or group, and fails to attend to the problematic of the "signature (or bioautography)," which better reflects identity's "permanently threatened" status — its eternal and built-in deliberation over "what it might or might not take to be its own."

One could synthesize these critiques of border studies and suggest that they search, as a group, for ways to rethink and reroute border studies' tendency to imagine the problem of proliferating border identities as its own solution once true or historically accurate stories about marginalization and hybridity have been told; once ancient pasts are remembered; once peoples are properly differentiated and situated and, at the same time (which amounts to a later historical time), properly amalgamated or coalesced. The contributors to this book, then, find the identity politics of border studies' most prominent instantiations naive and wanting in quite similar ways. The two sections of this volume, "The Borderlands" and "Other Geographies" — cohere in their attempt to trouble the proper place of the border, its propriety and properness in the formation, at the very least, of discourses of identity. Indeed, in its fretting of the borders of identity — so many names, prostheses, protecting/projecting one's identity, exposing and sheltering it at the same time — Sáenz's essay in particular resonates, though not unequivocally, in all the others.

But, in a certain way, *Border Theory* comes apart at the seam, its unity exacerbated by the plurality of critical perspectives presented in it, ranging from Foucauldian and Gramscian influenced Marxism (Lugo, Castronovo) to various deconstructions (Kaplan, Johnson, Michaelsen) to postmodern feminisms (Chang) — theoretical positions that are not necessarily compatible. These theoretical biases are themselves modulated by the writers' particular disciplinary affiliations: anthropology (Lugo), American literatures (Johnson, Chang, Castronovo, Michaelsen), comparative literature (Kaplan). And this diversity is further complicated by the presence of an afterword written by a trained historian, Patricia Seed, and by the presence of a haunting and hauntingly double-voiced "personal" essay by "Chicano writer" Benjamin Alire Sáenz.

Although the volume is "itself" interdisciplinary, gathering the work of scholars/writers from various disciplines, it nevertheless registers the tension such work should elicit, but all too rarely does, for any ethical interdisciplinarity necessarily disrupts the ground of at least two disciplines: the one the practitioner leaves and the one he or she enters. Such border crossing — or, in Kaplan's terms, bo(a)rder crossing — should be problematic. It is not — far from it: the emphasis on interdisciplinarity as the hallmark of "good" academic/scholarly work and as the savior of the disciplines, interdisciplinarity as the sign of disciplinary rejuvenation, the sign of renaissance, should already point toward the bankruptcy of disciplinary work and of the concept of the border as currently constituted in border studies.

More than one of the essays that follow challenge, in varying degrees of explicitness, the necessity and efficacy of the border discourses that separate and constitute disciplines, cultures, identities. It would be a mistake, however, to assume that any or all of the authors agree on strategies for dismantling bordered positions or even on a vocabulary, a language, translated or not, for convening the negotiations necessary to rearticulating them. It would be an even larger mistake to think that all or any of the contributors to this volume would appear at such a negotiation and that if they did, certain of them would not, perhaps, argue for the value of disciplines and, more generally, for the further production and description of cultural differences.

Indeed, several of the essays included here continue to address the border as the site of the encounter between a dominant culture and a resistant one, both of which require a certain identification. This, of course, remains the model of the "borderlands" border studies group, and it worries Castronovo's fine description of the tensions along the Mason-Dixon line, as well as, perhaps, Lugo's rendering of the discourses of nationalism in anthropological theories of the state and Chang's discussion of runaway subjectivity. The interest of these essays testifies to the potency of the prevailing border narrative.

A related point might be made with regard to the sorts of methodological reimaginings and utopian longings evidenced in this collection. The texts of Castronovo and Chang work toward a greater particularity or specificity in border narratives — producing readings of local geographies and conditions and/or power relations as border identities shift over time. Different borders and borderlands are different, and the differences proliferate as border subjects engage one another, relate. Freedom for Castronovo, home for Chang and Sáenz — these are extremely elusive goals or dreams that nevertheless are approximated or at least approached by means of at once more powerful *and* specific analytics and articulations of culture. Castronovo's new historicist model of subversion/containment, for example, is a totalizing method for border analysis that results in a description of endless microstruggles—endless cultural identity reformulations, each of which must be taken into account. Lugo's antiuniversalist politics—his endorsement of a Gramscian or Foucauldian "war of position"—and Chang's sense of "guerrilla" movement in "breaks left open" within the postmodern, late-capitalist city are analogous strategies for the representation of shape-shifting, multiplying, increasingly fragmented subject positions and for the charting of their potentially subversive implications. The hope in these texts rests upon an ability to map *more* possibilities within an ever-expanding field of identity positions (Chang notes, for instance, that "to celebrate [identity] illegibility" is akin to celebrating "dead" subjects). And, in this way, we might note these contributors' partial kinship with crucial presuppositions within major border studies work: intellectual positivism, humanism, agency, and an at least implicit commitment to the promise of identity hybridization and multiplication.

But Chang's attempt to turn the corner on a streetwalker, so to speak—to remark her inscription of identity as, precisely, inscription itself—and Kaplan's related effort to textualize identity point in another direction, as does Sáenz's triple willingness to rethink an identity politics of "fragments," as his title implies, perhaps to the limit of what he calls the "posthuman" (although he openly acknowledges that such subjects of the future would not be "living" ones), to question the notion of the "active subject" with "radical" potential, and to break with a politics or even an epistemology of shared, coherent "culture."

Our own individual contributions to the volume seek to extend, but perhaps reconfigure, these tendencies in Chang's, Kaplan's, and Sáenz's critiques by questioning whether any revision of border studies' objects of study, protocols, or procedures would "better" represent the border. It is the border—not the limit *of* the border and the subjects who inhabit borderlands, but the limit that *is* the bo(a)rder—that needs scrutiny if we are to begin to imagine the limit of exclusions, whether racisms, ethnocentrisms, and cultural chauvinisms or, relatedly, academic disciplinary ones. All of which are implicit in even the most well-intentioned formulations of the discipline(s), of the disciplinary activities, of border studies.

Notes

1. We have done some violence to Murray's line in order to avoid his reference to the *"cross*-cultural." To repeat: we understand "crossing" as merely an effect of what is actually a network of strangely related identities. This is in line with Fredric Jameson's recent comments on the concept of "culture," which he says "is not a 'substance' or a phenomenon in its own right" but rather "an objective mirage that arises out of the relationship between two groups. This is to say that no group 'has' culture all by itself: culture is the nimbus perceived by one group when it comes into contact with and observes another one" (33). "Culture must thus always be seen as a vehicle or a medium whereby the relationship between groups is transacted" (34). It is "the space of the symbolic moves of groups in agonistic relation to each other" (38–39).

2. To take only the example of ethnohistory and its literary studies equivalent, ethnocriticism, the logic of the "cross-" dominates famous work by figures such as James Axtell (for example, *The Invasion Within*) and Arnold Krupat. In Krupat's work, the idea of the "bicultural" or "composite" text is implicitly connected to an argument on behalf of cultural diversity or multiculturalism (see the second chapter of *For Those Who Come After* and the conclusion to *Ethnocriticism*). But not all ethnohistory works this way. Richard White's notion of the "middle ground," for example, is a near relation to the kind of thinking we are recommending. White hints at another way of locating the problem of culture by suggesting that cultures were created literally at the moment of colonial contact. Mary Louise Pratt's notion of the "contact zone" — described in the opening pages of *Imperial Eyes*— is a potentially analogous idea.

3. Not everyone, not even every Chicano, sees it this way. Juan Bruce-Novoa writes that Cabeza de Vaca was the first Chicano, and that "los iniciados en la cultura chicana reconocerán ya la similitud con [Cabeza de Vaca]. Tan múltiples resultan las asociaciones que deslumbran: el salir del país natal en busca de riqueza en un territorio desconocido salvo a través de las leyendas hiperbólicas; el desengaño de la realidad difícil y aun humillante al llegar; la pérdida del contexto cultural original a cambio del nuevo, hostil, enajenante, capaz de reducir al emigrante a la esclavitud; el aprendizaje lento en que, a través de duras penas y la mímésis, el emigrante comienza a mejorar su posición entre los nativos hasta dejar de ser un mero criado para pasar a rendir servicios que le permiten más movilidad" (1993, 305). Calderón and Saldívar's rejection of Cabeza de Vaca's Chicanicity seems to responder to Bruce-Novoa's claim, which first appeared in Mexico in 1990, for his inclusion within a certain genealogy of Chicano literature—a border dispute, then, within the "borderlands" concerning the definition of *Chicano*. The irony, of course, is that whereas Calderón and Saldívar argue in the introduction to *Criticism in the Borderlands* for the expansion of the American literary canon, their dismissal of Cabeza de Vaca from the Chicano family tree would have the effect of reducing the canon by (at least) one: in 1990 Cabeza de Vaca was included in *The Heath Anthology of American Literature*.

4. The "or" in Calderón and Saldívar's "Chicano or Mexican-American" functions as a coordinating conjunction, marking synonymity. This is a political strat-

egy, for Chicanos and Mexican Americans have often marked a difference among and between themselves. Some still do; see Sáenz's contribution to this volume as well as Bruce-Novoa (1994, 226–27). The focus on U.S. Anglo-American intervention in the mestizo Southwest deflects attention from the region's Hispanic colonization: the four hundred years of mestizo history to which Calderón and Saldívar refer produced the same sort of cultural and economic displacement as the one that began again and from the North in the mid-nineteenth century. The production of Mexicans resulted from a no less violent encounter between Spaniards and Amerindians than that between Mexicans and Anglos.

5. For a more detailed account of Paredes's place within a resistant Chicano studies, see R. Saldívar (1995). For counternarratives of Paredes's work, see Rosaldo (1991, 1993), and Bruce-Novoa (1994).

6. See, for example, the introduction to David Palumbo-Liu's *The Ethnic Canon*, in which Palumbo-Liu argues that the upshot of these discourses should be a "critical multiculturalism" that "may be able to draw forth the potential for resistance and change within the academy and society at large" (3). Bhabha, too, participates in the rhetoric of resistance, but he does not invoke resistance or opposition as the position of a particular culture—of Chicano culture, for example; it is, rather, an effect of "cultural difference" or of the enunciation of culture. "Hegemony," Bhabha writes, "depends on the production of alternative or antagonistic images that are always produced side by side and in competition with each other. It is this side-by-side nature, this partial presence, or metonymy of antagonism, and its effective significations, that give meaning (quite literally) to a politics of struggle *as the struggle of identifications* and the war of positions" (29). "The war of positions" to which Bhabha refers comes to him in the context of reading Stuart Hall; it is, then, the same war to which Lugo refers through Gramsci in his contribution to this volume. Bhabha's interest, in *The Location of Culture* and elsewhere, is to remark the limit of the in-between of hegemony: "The language of critique is effective not because it keeps forever separate the terms of the master and the slave, the mercantilist and the Marxist, but to the extent to which it overcomes the given grounds of opposition and opens up a space of translation: a place of hybridity, figuratively speaking, where the construction of a political object that is new, *neither the one nor the other*, properly alienates our political expectations, and changes, as it must, the very forms of our recognition of the moment of politics" (25). Finally, Bhabha concludes that "we should remember that it is the 'inter'—the cutting edge of translation and negotiation, the *in-between* space—that carries the burden of the meaning of culture. It makes it possible to begin envisaging national, anti-nationalist histories of the 'people.' And by exploring this Third Space, we may elude the politics of polarity and emerge as the others of our selves" (38–39). The "Third Space," to the extent it avoids polarity and, thus, polarization and positionality, remains unfounded, always to be thought, always to come.

7. For almost hysterical readings of Rodriguez designed to delimit his canonical authority and to discount his Chicanicity on the basis of his assimilation, see Alarcón, J. Saldívar, R. Saldívar (1990), Sánchez. It is perhaps instructive to read the essays by Alarcón and Sánchez alongside R. Saldívar's contribution to *The Ethnic*

Canon (1995); the essays appear to mark the limits of Calderón and Saldívar's version of Chicano studies: on the one hand, elegiac inclusion of Paredes; on the other, hysterical dismissal of Rodriguez. There would appear to be no "middle ground," no place to avoid the rhetoric of oppositional identity.

8. For a full-length reading of Rosaldo's text on this matter, and one that sets his argument in the context of reformist sentimentalism, see Michaelsen.

9. On tears, Derrida writes: "Why does terror make us tremble, since one can also tremble with cold, and such analogous physiological manifestations translate experiences and sentiments that appear, at least, not to have anything in common? This symptomatology is as enigmatic as tears" (1995a, 55). See also Georges Bataille *(1993),* which begins with a discussion of tears.

10. "Nevertheless, I'm still keeping my Indian identity a secret. I'm still keeping secret what I think no-one should know. Not even anthropologists or intellectuals, no matter how many books they have, can find out all our secrets" (Burgos 1984, 247).

11. According to Barbara Tedlock, beheading is the penalty for revealing certain Zuni secrets (52).

12. On the secret and culture in the context of a critique of anthropological discourse, see Mario Vargas Llosa's novel *El hablador;* on the secret and the archive, its necessary publicness, see González Echevarría; and on the aporetic structure of the secret in general, see Mark C. Taylor, "Secretions," in *Tears,* and Jacques Derrida, among other texts, *On the Name,* in which Derrida writes: "There is in literature, in the *exemplary* secret of literature, a chance of saying everything without touching upon the secret. When all the hypotheses are permitted, groundless and ad infinitum, about the meaning of a text, or the final intentions of an author, whose person is no more represented than nonrepresented by a character or by a narrator, by a poetic or fictional sentence, which detaches itself from its presumed source and thus remains *locked away [au secret],* when there is no longer even any sense in making decisions about some secret behind the surface of a textual manifestation (and it is this situation which I would call text or trace), when it is the call of this secret, however, which points back to the other or to something else, when it is this itself which keeps our passion aroused, and holds us to the other, then the secret impassions us. Even if there is none, even if it does not exist, hidden behind anything whatever. Even if the secret is no secret, even if there has never been a secret, a single secret. Not one" (29–30).

Works Cited

Adorno, Rolena. 1993. "The Negotiation of Fear in Cabeza de Vaca's *Naufragios.*" *New World Encounters.* Ed. Stephen Greenblatt. Berkeley: University of California Press.

Agamben, Giorgio. 1993. *Infancy and History: Essays on the Destruction of Experience.* Trans. Liz Heron. London: Verso.

Alarcón, Norma. 1995. "Tropology of Hunger: The 'Miseducation' of Richard Rodriguez." *The Ethnic Canon: Histories, Institutions, and Interventions.* Ed. David Palumbo-Liu. Minneapolis: University of Minnesota Press.

Anzaldúa, Gloria. 1987. *Borderlands/La Frontera: The New Mestiza*. San Francisco: Aunt Lute.

Arteaga, Alfred, ed. 1994. *An Other Tongue: Nation and Ethnicity in the Linguistic Borderlands*. Durham, N.C.: Duke University Press.

Axtell, James. 1985. *The Invasion Within: The Contest of Cultures in Colonial North America*. New York: Oxford University Press.

Bataille, Georges. 1993. *The Accursed Share*, vols. 2–3. Trans. Robert Hurley. New York: Zone.

Behar, Ruth. 1993. *Translated Woman: Crossing the Border with Esperanza's Story*. Boston: Beacon.

Bhabha, Homi K. 1994. *The Location of Culture*. New York: Routledge.

Bourdieu, Pierre. 1991. *Language and Symbolic Power*. Ed. John B. Thompson. Trans. Gino Raymond and Matthew Adamson. Cambridge: Harvard University Press.

Bruce-Novoa, Juan. 1993. "Naufragios en los mares de la significación: De *La relación de Cabeza de Vaca* a la literatura Chicana." *Notas y comentarios sobre Alvar Núñez Cabeza de Vaca*. Ed. Margot Glantz. Mexico City: Grijalbo.

———. 1994. "Dialogical Strategies, Monological Goals: Chicano Literature." *An Other Tongue: Nation and Ethnicity in the Linguistic Borderlands*. Ed. Alfred Arteaga. Durham, N.C.: Duke University Press.

Burgos, Elizabeth. 1983. *Me llamo Rigoberta Menchú y así me nació la conciencia*. Barcelona: Seix Barral.

———. 1984. *I, Rigoberta Menchú: An Indian Woman in Guatemala*. Trans. Ann Wright. London: Verso.

Cabeza de Vaca, Alvar Núñez. 1989. *Naufragios*. Ed. Juan Francisco Maura. Madrid: Cátedra.

———. 1993. *Castaways*. Ed. Enrique Pupo-Walker. Trans. Frances M. López-Morillas. Berkeley: University of California Press.

Calderón, Héctor, and José David Saldívar, eds. 1991. *Criticism in the Borderlands: Studies in Chicano Literature, Culture, and Ideology*. Durham, N.C.: Duke University Press.

Cisneros, Sandra. 1991. *The House on Mango Street*. New York: Vintage.

Derrida, Jacques. 1982. "The Ends of Man." *Margins of Philosophy*. Trans. Alan Bass. Chicago: University of Chicago Press.

———. 1984. "LIVING ON * Border Lines." *Deconstruction and Criticism*. Ed. Geoffrey Hartman. New York: Continuum.

———. 1992. *The Other Heading: Reflections on Today's Europe*. Trans. Pascale-Anne Brault and Michael B. Naas. Bloomington: Indiana University Press.

———. 1993. *Aporias*. Trans. Thomas Dutoit. Palo Alto, Calif.: Stanford University Press.

———. 1995a. *The Gift of Death*. Trans. David Willis. Chicago: University of Chicago Press.

———. 1995b. *On the Name*. Trans. David Wood. Palo Alto, Calif.: Stanford University Press.

Erkkila, Betsy. 1995. "Ethnicity, Literary Theory, and the Grounds of Resistance." *American Quarterly* 47.4: 563–94.

González Echevarría, Roberto. 1990. *Myth and Archive: A Theory of Latin American Narrative.* Cambridge: Cambridge University Press.

Hicks, D. Emily. 1991. *Border Writing: The Multidimensional Text.* Minneapolis: University of Minnesota Press.

Jameson, Fredric. 1993. "On 'Cultural Studies.'" *Social Text* 34: 17–52.

Krupat, Arnold. 1985. *For Those Who Come After: A Study of Native American Autobiography.* Berkeley: University of California Press.

———. 1992. *Ethnocriticism: Ethnography, History, Literature.* Berkeley: University of California Press.

Leibnitz, Gottfried Wilhelm. 1973. *Philosophical Writings.* Ed. G. H. R. Parkinson. Trans. Mary Morris and G. H. R. Parkinson. London: Dent-Everyman.

Lévi-Strauss, Claude. 1992. *Tristes Tropiques.* Trans. John Weightman and Doreen Weightman. New York: Penguin.

Michaelsen, Scott. 1995. "Problems for Emotional Politics: The Rise of Sentimentalist Cultural Studies." *Over Here: Reviews in American Studies* 15.1–2: 79–90.

Murray, David. 1991. *Forked Tongues: Speech, Writing and Representation in North American Indian Texts.* Bloomington: Indiana University Press.

Nancy, Jean-Luc. 1991. *The Inoperative Community.* Ed. and trans. Peter Connor et al. Minneapolis: University of Minnesota Press.

———. 1994. "Cut Throat Sun." *An Other Tongue: Nation and Ethnicity in the Linguistic Borderlands.* Ed. Alfred Arteaga. Durham, N.C.: Duke University Press.

Palumbo-Liu, David. 1995. *The Ethnic Canon: Histories, Institutions, and Interventions.* Minneapolis: University of Minnesota Press.

Pérez Firmat, Gustavo, ed. 1990. *Do the Americas Have a Common Literature?* Durham, N.C.: Duke University Press.

Pratt, Mary Louise. 1992. *Imperial Eyes: Travel Writing and Transculturation.* New York: Routledge.

Rosaldo, Renato. 1991. "Fables of the Fallen Guy." *Criticism in the Borderlands: Studies in Chicano Literature, Culture, and Ideology.* Ed. Héctor Calderón and José David Saldívar. Durham, N.C.: Duke University Press.

———. 1993. *Culture and Truth: The Remaking of Social Analysis,* 2d ed. Boston: Beacon.

Saldívar, José David. 1991. *The Dialectics of Our America: Genealogy, Cultural Critique, and Literary History.* Durham, N.C.: Duke University Press.

Saldívar, Ramón. 1990. *Chicano Narrative: The Dialectics of Difference.* Madison: University of Wisconsin Press.

———. 1995. "The Borders of Modernity: Américo Paredes's *Between Two Worlds* and the Chicano National Subject." *The Ethnic Canon: Histories, Institutions, and Interventions.* Ed. David Palumbo-Liu. Minneapolis: University of Minnesota Press.

Sánchez, Rosaura. 1995. "Calculated Musings: Richard Rodríguez's Metaphysics of Difference." *The Ethnic Canon: Histories, Institutions, and Interventions.* Ed. David Palumbo-Liu. Minneapolis: University of Minnesota Press.

Taylor, Mark C. 1990. *Tears.* Albany: State University of New York Press.

Tedlock, Barbara. 1992. *The Beautiful and the Dangerous: Dialogues with the Zuni Indians.* New York: Viking Penguin.

Todorov, Tzvetan. 1984. *The Conquest of America: The Question of the Other.* Trans. Richard Howard. New York: Harper & Row.

———. 1993. *On Human Diversity: Nationalism, Racism, and Exoticism in French Thought.* Trans. Catherine Porter. Cambridge: Harvard University Press.

Vargas Llosa, Mario. 1987. *El hablador.* Barcelona: Seix Barral.

White, Richard. 1991. *The Middle Ground: Indians, Empires, and Republics in the Great Lakes Region, 1650–1815.* Cambridge: Cambridge University Press.

Part I

The Borderlands

ONE

Reflections on Border Theory, Culture, and the Nation

Alejandro Lugo

border *n* 1: an outer part or edge 2: BOUNDARY, FRONTIER...
4: an ornamental design at the edge of a fabric or rug
syn BORDER, MARGIN, VERGE, EDGE, RIM, BRIM, BRINK
borderland *n* 1a: territory at or near a border: FRONTIER b: an
outlying region
borderline *n:* a line of demarcation
bordure *n:* a border surrounding a heraldic shield
Webster's New Collegiate Dictionary

frontera (de frontero.) f. *Confín de un Estado* [Limit of a state]
2. *Fachada* [ornamental design] ... 5. *Límite*
frontería (de frontero) f.ant. *Frontera; hacer frente* [To confront]
frontero, ra *Puesto y colocado enfrente* [Situated in front]
Diccionario de la Lengua Española

Heterotopia: disorder in which fragments of a large number of
possible orders glitter separately in the dimension, without law or
geometry, of the heteroclite.... in such a state, things are laid,
placed, arranged in sites so very different from one another that it is
impossible to find a place of residence for them.
MICHEL FOUCAULT, *The Order of Things*

We live in a time and space in which borders, both literal and
figurative, exist everywhere.... A border maps limits; it keeps people
in and out of an area; it marks the ending of a safe zone and the
beginning of an unsafe zone. To confront a border and, more so, to
cross a border presumes great risk. In general people fear and are
afraid to cross borders.... People cling to the dream of utopia and
fail to recognize that they create and live in heterotopia.
ALEJANDRO MORALES, "Dynamic Identities in Heterotopia"

The Borders of Border Theory

If we wanted to carry out an archaeology of border theory, how would we identify its sources and its targets? Where would we locate its multiple sites of production and consumption, formation and transformation? What are the multiple discourses producing images of borders almost everywhere, at least in the minds of academics? In trying to answer these questions, more with an exploratory spirit than with a definitive one, let us say that the sites, the sources, the targets, and the discourses can be variably characterized by the following: previously marginalized intellectuals within the academy (i.e., women and other minorities), the outer limits of the nation-state (i.e., the U.S.-Mexico border region), the frontiers of culture theory (i.e., cultural borderlands vis-à-vis cultural patterns), the multiple fronts of struggle in cultural studies (i.e, the war of position), the cutting edge (at the forefront) of theories of difference (i.e., race, class, gender, and sexual orientation), and finally (at) the crossroads of history, literature, anthropology, and sociology (i.e., cultural studies).

In this essay I argue that in order to understand its political and practical importance, we must reimagine border theory in the realm of the inescapable, mountainous terrains of Power (Foucault, 1978) as it has operated in the past two hundred years in the West (Foucault, 1978; Derrida, 1966), and as it has been imbricated in the academy, in culture theory, in the global contexts of late capitalism, and in the last analysis, and perhaps most important, in the realms of the changing "nation" (Anderson, 1991) and "state" (Hall, 1986).[1]

This privileging of the "nation/state," on my part, relates to a current theoretical and political concern that has practical implications for the opening of more inclusive spaces under globalization, especially for the coming twenty-first century: *the deterritorialization* of the nation, politics, culture and border theory, and, finally, human agency (Ong, 1995; Morales, 1996; Martín-Rodríguez, 1996). For Alejandro Morales, "Michel Foucault's concept of heterotopia explains border culture," and "life in the chaos of heterotopia is a perpetual act of self-definition gradually deterritorializing the individual" (1996, 23, 24). Regarding feminist practice in the global setting, Aihwa Ong argues that "diasporic feminists (and we should all be somewhat mobile to be vigilant) should develop a denationalized and deterritorialized set of cultural practices. These would have to deal with the tough questions of gender oppression not only in that 'other place'. . . but also in one's own family, community, culture, religion, race, and nation" (1995, 367). Finally, just as Manuel Martín-Rodríguez, following Deleuze and Guattari, argues that a "minor language" can erode a "major language from within," I argue that the border region and border theory can erode the hegemony of the privileged center by denationalizing and deterritorializing the nation/ state and culture theory: "In other words, minor languages erode, as it were, a major language from within, deterritorializing it, breaking up its system's supposed homogeneity" (Martín-Rodríguez, 1996, 86).[2]

Much more specifically, my analytic framework is the following: I will try to draw the contours of two theoretical parallelisms, both of which are constituted by seemingly disconnected conceptual preoccupations. On the one hand is the critical articulation between Gramsci's notion of *the state and its dispersal* and Foucault's notion of *power and its deployment*;[3] on the other is Anderson's critique of the nation and Rosaldo's critique of culture in anthropology. I am particularly interested in Gramsci's uses of the terms "state," "force relations," and "war of position" and how they might relate to Foucault's "relations of force" and his faith in "the strategical model rather than the model based on law" as well as his strategic belief that "politics is *war* pursued by other means" (Foucault, 1978, 93; emphasis added). I argue here that these connections of resistance against folk notions of the "head of the king [and] the spell of monarchy" (Foucault, 1978, 88–89) — that is, "the state/ the law"[4] — are quite telling in themselves about the ways in which we have come to think about social life and culture inside and outside anthropology, which is my interest here. These critiques call for multiple discourses, wars of position, situated knowledges, positioned subjects, and different arenas of contestation in everyday life. Thus, the analysis presented here should help explain the recent production of theories of borders in our Westernized imagination. I will examine this articulation between border theory and the West, within anthropology, by juxtaposing Anderson's critique of the nation as an imagined community with Rosaldo's critique of culture as shared patterns of behavior.[5]

By reflecting on these parallelisms—that between Gramsci's notion of the state and Foucault's notion of power (both being *dispersed* entities) and that between Anderson's notion of the imagined community and Rosaldo's cultural patterns (both being *homogeneous* entities)—I hope to show how border theory in the late twentieth century in anthropology (i.e., Rosaldo's "cultural borderlands") cannot be properly understood unless it is situated, willy-nilly, vis-à-vis changing discourses about the state, the nation, and culture in the nineteenth and twentieth centuries, at least as these imagined categories and periodizations are examined in the works of Rosaldo himself (*Culture and Truth*, 1993), Anderson (*Imagined Communities*, 1991), Foucault (*History of Sexuality*, 1978), and Stuart Hall ("Gramsci's Relevance for the Study of Race and Ethnicity," 1986).

By locating border theory at the crossroads of culture theory in anthropology, and at the crossroads of ideologies of the state and the nation, which in turn produced "anthropologies" that represented national hegemonic traditions (American, British, and French), I hope to show the political and epistemological limits under which we teach, write, do research, and theorize. My main argument here is that border theory itself can contribute effectively to the exploration of these limits, as long as it is recognized to be (as theories of social life tend to be) a product of the codification of a "multiplicity of force relations . . . which by virtue of their inequalities, constantly engender states of power" (Foucault, 1978, 93).

The Current State of Culture: Cultural Borderlands vis-à-vis Cultural Patterns

Cultural borderlands should be understood, first of all, in relation to the previous dominant discourse about culture: cultural patterns. Renato Rosaldo has been very precise about the limitations of what he calls the "classic vision of unique cultural patterns":

> It emphasizes shared patterns at the expense of processes of change and internal inconsistencies, conflicts, and contradictions. By defining culture as a set of shared meanings, classic norms of analysis make it difficult to study zones of difference within and between cultures. From the classic perspective, cultural borderlands appear to be annoying exceptions rather than central areas of inquiry. (1993, 27–28)

Although I agree with Rosaldo's critical assessment of the social and political implications of the ideology of "cultural patterns," my vision of the way those cultural patterns have been constituted in the theoretical imagination of classic anthropologists is a bit different. In fact, the historical process through which we have come to theorize and think about culture, society, cultural patterns, and borderlands should not be taken for granted, or as a given, if we want, as Foucault puts it, "to cut off the head of the king" (1978, 88).

I propose here that the attempt to decipher the complex relation between "structure and practice" was and has been a dominant thinking channel or tool through which the concept of culture has been imagined, though more implicitly than explicitly. Let us see how the latter contention is manifested in the writings of some of anthropology's major and recent practioners. By considering the sociopolitical and historical context in which anthropologists wrote, I hope to shed some light on why, after all, a discourse on culture and society emerged. The following discussion will eventually bring us back to an analysis of the roles of the state, the law, and the nation in shaping our formulations of the concept of culture and of social life in general.

Marshall Sahlins has explicitly associated the concept of culture with a double existence: "In the dialectic of culture-as-constituted and culture-as-lived we...discover some possibility of reconciling the most profound antinomy of social science theory, that between structure and practice: reconciling them, that is, in the only way presently justifiable—as a symbolic process" (1982, 48). Regarding "society," however, Sherry Ortner has also identified a dialectical polarity in what she calls "practice theory," which constitutes the attempt to understand "how society and culture themselves are produced and reproduced through *human intention and action*" (1984, 158; emphasis added). Ortner argues that "the modern versions of practice theory...appear unique in...that society is a system, that the system is powerfully constraining, and yet that the system can be made and unmade through human action and interaction" (159). Ortner's similar treatment of both "society" and "culture" is less conspicuous, for our purpose here, than the way she imagines these theoretical constructs through pervasive critical dualisms: system and action, human intention and action. Sahlins's imaginings about culture, as lived and as constituted, also reproduce the pattern I am exposing here: the double existence of culture.[6]

Sahlins subjects this dialectic in culture to his "structure and history" approach (1981, 1982, 1985; see also Rosaldo, 1980), whereas Ortner associates the dialectic in society with a general theory of "practice" (1984). Ortner in fact argues that this focus on "practice" emerged in the early 1970s as a result of such historical conjunctures as the New Left movement; she also suggests that "practice theory" became articulated in American anthropology when Bourdieu's *Outline of a Theory of Practice* was translated into English in 1978.[7]

In what follows, I suggest that the anthropological notion of culture constituted by the articulation of beliefs and action, structure and practice, culture as constituted and culture as lived, system and action, was the historical product of a specific "academic" response to the political relation between the state/the nation and its citizens — a relationship that can be traced to the nineteenth century. In fact, these larger sociohistorical forces became crystallized in Western academia through Durkheim's (1933[1893], 1965[1912]) invention of society and through Mathew Arnold's (1963[1867–68]) production of culture.

Culture and the State

Previous to the late 1960s, certain socioeconomic and political events of the Victorian era contributed to the continued suppression of the explicit treatment of the structure/practice relation embedded in the concepts of "culture" and "society": to talk about human practice or praxis was to talk about history, conflict, change, and social transformation — theoretical concepts that could easily expose the colonial and capitalist encounters/enterprises of the nineteenth century and the first half of the twentieth century. Thus, until the early 1970s, the discourse on culture and society in the social sciences, and especially in anthropology, was dominated by the systematic analysis of the coordination of such dualisms as the individual and society, the individual and culture — ignoring the political implications of "practice" (for examples of this pattern, see Durkheim, 1933[1893], 1965[1912]; Malinowski, 1944; Benedict, 1934; Radcliffe-Brown, 1952; Barth, 1966).

Consequently, due to the political suppression of conceptual binaries, which included "practice," the notions of "society" and "culture" were to be discussed in terms of "order," "harmony," "rules" (Durkheim, 1933[1893], 1965[1912]), "shared patterns of beliefs" (Boas, 1963[1911]; Benedict, 1934), and an antichaotic condition (Weber, 1977[1905]). Political scientist Perry Anderson has appropriately noted that the work of Durkheim, like that of Weber and Pareto, was haunted by "a profound fear of the masses and premonition of social disintegration" (1968). He claims quite explicitly that sociology at the turn of the twentieth century "emerged as a bourgeois counter-reaction to Marxism," which, of course, was arguing at the time that class conflict was inevitable. It must be noted, however, that Durkheim was as much against the greedy capitalist on the loose at the time as against the "immorality" of the masses. Both of these threats confirmed for him, as an employee of the French state, the need of rules to monitor and control both the working classes and the utilitarian entrepreneur.

The intensification of class conflict had emerged as a product of industrial capitalism within the "West"; additionally, broader sociopolitical tensions were generated as a result of the retraction of some European colonialisms due to the nineteenth-century nationalist movements in Spanish America and Central Europe. The expansion of U.S. colonialism at the turn of the twentieth century also contributed to a generalized problem of the body politic within and outside the West (see Anderson, 1991; Foucault, 1978; Hall, 1986). Foucault and Stuart Hall treat 1870 as a key historical moment regarding, respectively, the production of new sexualities and the expansion of the new imperialist colonialisms.[8] According to Gramsci and Hall, this period in the later part of the nineteenth century constitutes a historical transition in the nature of the "State" from a monarchical, dynastic body politic and its *subjects* to a "State" (read: nation/nation-state) in which the *subjects* become *citizens*, and thus become loosely tied to the direct control of a centralized, lawlike apparatus; in this new political regime, individuals are indirectly monitored through the state's *dispersal of power* (Hall, 1986; Foucault, 1978). This process must be properly explained in the historical and geographic contexts of each newly emerging nation around the world.[9]

Stuart Hall describes Gramsci's vision of this critical transformation in Western history:

> Gramsci bases this "transition from one form of politics to another" historically. It takes place in "the West" after 1870, and is identified with "the colonial expansion of Europe," the emergence of modern mass democracy, a complexification in the role and organization of the state and an unprecedented elaboration in the structures and processes of "civil hegemony." What Gramsci is pointing to, here, is partly the diversification of social antagonisms, the "dispersal" of power, which occurs in societies where hegemony is sustained, not exclusively through the enforced instrumentality of the state, but rather, it is grounded in the relations and institutions of civil society [schooling, the family, the factory, churches and religious life, and so on]. (1986, 18)[10]

Weber documented the bureaucratization of modern institutions around the same time, after 1870 and into World War I (1958[1920]). The "war of position" necessary for effective political resistance against the dispersal of power, and characterizing the new state of the "State" is powerfully stated in military terms:

> The "war of position"... has to be conducted in a protracted way, across many different and varying fronts of struggle.... What really counts in a war of position is not the enemy's "forward trenches" (to continue the military metaphor) but "the whole organizational and industrial system of the territory which lies to the rear of the army in the field" — that is, the whole structure of society, including the structures and institutions of civil society. (Hall, 1986, 17, paraphrasing Gramsci)

Today's realization of the transformation of the nature of *the cultural* (from homogeneity to heterogeneity) as manifested by both "cultural studies" and the postmodern preoccupation with "dispersal," has clearly influenced Renato Rosaldo's redefinition of "culture" in terms of "borderlands," fragmentation, and contestation (as opposed to the exclusivity of shareability, coherence, and uniformity). It is necessary to quote Rosaldo at length from his book *Culture and Truth* (1993):

> The fiction of the uniformly shared culture increasingly seems more tenuous than useful. Although most metropolitan typifications continue to suppress border zones, human cultures are neither necessarily coherent nor always homogeneous. More often than we usually care to think, our

everyday lives are crisscrossed by border zones, pockets and eruptions of all kinds. Social borders frequently become salient around such lines as sexual orientation, gender, class, race, ethnicity, nationality, age, politics, dress, food, or taste. Along with "our" supposedly transparent cultural selves, such borderlands should be regarded not as analytically empty transitional zones but as sites of creative cultural production that require investigation. (207–8)

In the past, however, from the moment Marxism became a threat to late-nineteenth-century European order, Marx and his followers were not only negatively sanctioned (suppressed) in major sociological and anthropological circles, but "metropolitan typifications" of culture and society (i.e., Durkheimian and Weberian traditions) quite willingly continued "to suppress" any alternative means of studying and analyzing social life in its entirety, that is, in a manner that such phenomena as disorder, chaos, fragmentation, contestation, resistance, and "the border zones" could be rigorously scrutinized. The notion of "cultural border-lands" seems to be closely associated with social identities or subjectivities—that is, age, gender, class, ethnicity—however, for purposes of explaining what Sherry Ortner calls "human intention and action" or what Sahlins denotes as "structure and practice," Renato Rosaldo still depends on the dual aspect of social life that, I have argued, has characterized our imaginings about both culture and society.

For example, while analyzing the work of literary theorist Kenneth Burke, Rosaldo wrote:

Recent social thinkers [Giddens, 1979; Ortner, 1984] have updated Burke's style of analysis by identifying the interplay of "structure" and "agency" as a central issue in social theory. Most central for them, in other words, is the question of *how received structures shape human conduct, and how, in turn, human conduct alters received structures.* (1993, 104; emphasis added)

Thus, if the initial understanding of the "state" was complicitly associated with rules, laws, and order, which must be followed or obeyed by its citizens or subjects, Victorian anthropologists (British, American, and French) quite willingly, with the same juridical attitude and "morality," traveled to other "non-Western" societies uncritically searching for the rules, traditions, orders, and coherent social systems to which human subjects (or informants, in the anthropologists' case) must accommodate and adhere. By "uncritical," I mean that these early-twentieth-century scholars did not necessarily articulate in their writings the impact of the state on the production of social science itself. It is also true, however, that the dominant discourse on "law and society" had a key humanitarian angle that was used against an earlier vision of "natives" as lacking law and therefore having no rights to life and property.

Nonetheless, the Victorian focus on morality, order, and the law, with its many angles, dominated the anthropology practiced until the early 1970s, when the civil rights, New Left, and feminist movements and the decolonization of previously colonized "nations" disinterred both critical thought and critical theory from the academic cemetery deliberately constructed by "metropolitan scholars" (see Rosaldo, 1993, chap. 1). Now that we recognize that "modern societies" constitute "arenas" of different social contestations, are we looking for similar contestations, fragmentations, dispersals, disorders, and chaos within and in "other" societies,[11] just as our ancestors looked for order, shared patterns, and coherent systems here and elsewhere?

Perhaps what is of major importance here is that our metaphors of social life have also been transformed along with our notions of culture, society, and the state. There has been a very persuasive replacement, not only displacement, of a metaphoric trope: the biological organism, which was supposed to maintain itself in equilibrium through systemic (political) order and (social) harmony, has been decidedly supplanted by the "war" metaphor, which sheds light on how "society" and "culture" constitute hegemonic battlefields where contestation itself (instead of reciprocity) is inescapably pervasive. As Foucault suggestively questions, "Should . . . we say politics is *war* pursued by other means?" (1978, 93; emphasis added).[12]

Thus, although Gramsci's work on the state and culture seems to have been "discovered" as late as the 1950s and 1960s as a result of the sociopolitical movements of Birmingham, England (see Raymond Williams's *Politics and Letters,* 1979), through Gramscian "cultural studies," the state has come to be imagined vis-à-vis its dispersal of power within "civil society" by being deployed on a battlefield of multiple social relations. Since the mid-1980s, through the critiques of such scholars as Renato Rosaldo, Donna Haraway (1986), and James Clifford (1986), American anthropologists have begun rigorous (re)search on the deployment, dispersal, and, ergo, fragmentation of society and culture, where identities and experiences are constantly being contested in specific sites or localized centers of power, such as the factory, the cafeteria, the bus, and even the restroom.[13]

Nonetheless, despite the influence of cultural Marxism, the notion of culture used in cultural studies has its strong connection to the culture concept constituted by "structure and practice" and that has characterized most academic conceptions or imaginations about the social and the cultural. Paul Willis, author of the classic *Learning to Labor,* says the following with regard to his use of the "cultural": "I view *the cultural,* not simply as a set of transferred internal *structures* (as in the notion of socialisation) nor as the passive result of the action of dominant ideology downwards (as in certain kinds of marxism) but at least in part as the product of collective human *praxis*" (1977, 3; emphasis added; note the inevitable duality—structure/praxis). Based on Gramsci, Hall presents the following definition of culture:

> One might note the centrality which Gramsci's analysis always gives to the cultural factor in social development. *By culture, here, I mean the actual, grounded terrain of practices, representations, languages and customs of any specific historical society.... I would also include that whole distinctive range of questions which Gramsci lumped together under the title, the "national popular."...* They are a key stake as objects of political and *ideological* struggle and *practice.* (1986, 26)

The dual aspect (ideology/practices, structure/praxis) associated with a general definition of culture, although not central, is self-evident. Along with this implicit double existence, in the past decade or so, as I have noted, we have simultaneously treated, much more explicitly, culture as an arena of different social contestations. James Clifford notes, "Culture, and our views of it, are produced historically, and are actively contested" (1986, 18). He adds, "Culture is contested, temporal and emergent" (19). Its temporality, its instability, its contingency, and thus its fragmentation all give form and content to the theory of borderlands that Rosaldo (1993) and Anzaldúa (1987) call for in and outside social analysis.

Yet to limit the concept of culture to "contestations" while not recognizing its double life (as we tend to do regarding new theories of borders, culture, and social life) is to confuse culture with Gramsci's notion of the "State" in "modern societies." As Stuart Hall correctly argues about Gramsci:

> Gramsci elaborates his new conception of the state. . . . it becomes, not a thing to be seized, overthrown or "*smashed*" with a single blow, but a complex formation in modern societies *which must become the focus of a number of different strategies and struggles because it is an arena of different social contestations.* (1986, 19; emphasis added)

In fact, I must emphasize that Gramsci associated culture not only with practices and representations, but also with the "national popular." Why is culture and the idea of nation or nationalism so closely interrelated by Gramsci?

Culture and the Nation: Imagined Communities

In the late twentieth century, both culture and the state are perceived to be dispersed as well as consolidated or centralized. Yet we have privileged, in the past ten years, the dispersed and the fragmented. How were nationalism, the state, the nation, and culture perceived in the nineteenth century? In a pre-Rosaldo phase, culture was imagined, almost exclusively, to be shared, patterned, and homogeneous. So, in a similar way, throughout the nineteenth century and the first half of the twentieth century, the nation, according to Benedict Anderson, came to be imagined in homogeneous time, and as an imagined community: "The nation is always conceived as a deep, horizontal comradeship. Ultimately it is this fraternity that makes it possible, over the past two centuries, for so many millions of people, not so much to kill, as willingly to die for such limited imaginings" (1991, 7).

These imaginings—whether from the first decade of the 1800s (Creole nationalism, i.e., Mexico) or from the 1820s or the 1850s of Central Europe (so-called vernacular/linguistic nationalisms, which were opposed to the hegemony of Latin) or from the "official nationalism" prior to the end of World War I (a nation/dynasty combination)—all culminated in the now threatened "nation-state" that became the international norm after 1922 and at least until the 1970s. By the 1970s the nation-state was politically and economically transcended, or at least challenged, by the strategic fragmentation of the manufacturing production process around the globe in late capitalism. In the specific case that has concerned my larger writing project (Lugo, 1995), the Mexican state has been challenged by the deployment of *maquiladoras* not only throughout Mexico, but throughout the border metropolis of Ciudad Juarez; they are located in more than ten industrial parks strategically established in different sections of the city.

Thus, the imagined community Anderson identifies in the idea of the nation is the imagined (shared) community Rosaldo identifies in the classic anthropological concept of culture, which was conceptualized in the period of "official nationalism" (around and after 1850; Arnold published *Culture and Anarchy* in 1868) and discursively deployed throughout the consolidation of the "nation-state" (between 1922 and 1970).[14]

Two major historical forces (or, in Gramsci's terms, *force relations*) that led to the nation as an imagined community were the emergence of print capitalism (the novel and the newspaper) and the gradual collapse of the hegemony of Latin (a collapse that gave rise to vernacular nationalisms within Europe). Before these major historical and complicated political processes led to the initial versions of the nation (before the nineteenth century—more specifically, before 1776), the political imagination regarding such taken-for-granted conceptualizations as "society" or "social groups" was characterized by fragmentation, intermarriage, and cultural and social heterogeneity—all predating a homogeneous imagined community.

For instance, Benedict Anderson has written in relation to this prenation, premodern stage, "The fundamental conceptions about 'social groups' were centripetal and hierarchical, rather than boundary-oriented and horizontal" (1991, 15). With regard to the dynastic, monarchic realm, Anderson notes that,

> in the older imagining, where [kingship] states were defined by centres, borders were porous and indistinct, and sovereignties faded imperceptibly into one another. [Are not these border crossings?] Hence, paradoxically enough, the ease with which pre-modern empires and kingdoms were able to sustain their rule over immensely heterogeneous, and often not even contiguous, populations for long periods of time. (19)

Regarding sexual politics, Anderson makes it very clear that, "in fact, royal lineages often derived their prestige, aside from any aura of divinity, from, shall we say, miscegenation? For such mixtures were signs of superordinate status [thus] . . . what 'nationality' are we to assign to the Bourbons?" (20–21). Consequently, assigning an essentialized "national" or "cultural" identity to any subject (as opposed to *citizen*) or to any, let us say, intersubjective collectivity, before the nation, was not only difficult, but probably impossible.[15]

It is evident that heterogeneity preceded the "imagined community" — the nation, the nation-state, nationalism, all of which, I argue, influenced our notions of culture and society during the nineteenth and most of the twentieth century. Thus, the heterogeneity discovered in the late twentieth century in theories of borderlands and fragmentation should not be limited exclusively to the collapse of classic norms — from the mid-1960s to the mid-1980s — rather, our theories of culture, society, and identity should be analyzed in the contexts of much longer historical processes, such as (1) the first attempts "to cut off the head of the king" in the early nineteenth century and (2) the political transformation and/or reproduction of the nation-state, throughout and in the late twentieth century. Even more productively, we must conduct additional comparative research on the heterogeneity of the late twentieth century and the heterogeneity associated with prenation contexts and politics — not that heterogeneity cannot coexist with homogeneity, but this strategy might serve as a point of departure from a possible prison house of border thought.[16] At the same time, however, we must recognize that such identities as class, gender, sexuality, and ethnicity, as they are articulated in the late twentieth century, are products of the 1900s; in particular, they are products of a long history of resistance — the working-class, feminist, gay and lesbian, and civil rights movements of the 1960s, as well as of the decolonization of Africa and Asia since the late 1950s (Rosaldo, 1993).

We can now claim, then, that in the 1990s the "State" has been strategically dispersed, both by current Gramscian thinking and by late capitalist multinational corporations in this historic moment characterized by the dispersal of manufacturing production processes throughout the world. Unfortunately, Benedict Anderson not only ignores the role of late capitalism in the redefinition of the nation-state after 1965, but also does not perceive that the fascism of Mussolini had been produced through and by the ideology of the nation, which Anderson himself limits to an amorous feeling of patriotism. Anderson also ignores the major threat to the formation of the nation-state in the first decades of the twentieth century: the attempt to internationalize (read: denationalize; deterritorialize) the working classes.

It is perhaps at this analytic juncture that we must systematically articulate Rosaldo's theory of multiple subjectivities (so much needed for our understanding of the politics of difference under state citizenry) with pervasive late capitalism — which can be characterized not only by the fragmentation of the production process, but also by the fragmentation of the labor force. Is it possible to reconcile the following seemingly irreconcilable statements about the politics (and economics) of difference? First, Rosaldo argues:

> Social borders frequently become salient around such lines as sexual orientation, gender, class, race, ethnicity, nationality, age, politics, dress, food, or taste. . . . such borderlands should be regarded not as analytically empty transitional zones but as sites of creative cultural production that require investigation. (1993, 207–8)

And second, June Nash notes, regarding the current global accumulation of capital: "Sectors of the labor force based on gender, ethnicity, age, and education within both industrial core and peripheral nations are differentially rewarded and these differences, along with wage differences, between nations, determine the long-run movement of capital" (1983, 3).

Adding the wage differential to the "borderlands" equation or theory does not allow us to separate "border zones" as "sites of creative cultural production" from "border zones" as "sites of lucrative manufacturing production" in the globalization of capital. Thus, is the theory of borderlands a critique or handmaid of capitalist discipline in this historical moment? Historically and theoretically, it can be both. Just as we must extend cultural borderlands into a critique of late capitalist production, so we must transform the political economy of June Nash into a critical, global theory of multiple cultural subjectivities, which in fact Rosaldo offers. After all, one alternative lies in situating our theoretical concepts about social life not only in the larger contexts of history, nationalism, and power, but also in micro contexts of cultural specificity as well as in the Foucauldian recognition that academic research

is a question of orienting ourselves to a conception of power which re-
places...the privilege of sovereignty with the analysis of a *multiple and
mobile field of force relations,* wherein far-reaching, but never completely
stable, effects of domination are produced....And this, not out of a spec-
ulative choice or theoretical preference, but because in fact *it is one of the
essential traits for Western societies that the force relationships which for a
long time had found expression in war, in every form of warfare, gradually
became invested in the order of political power.* (1978, 102; emphasis added)

From the Nature of the State to the State of Nature

The foregoing emphasis on war, contestation, and power relations in
society and culture, more than a faithful commitment to communist
utopias, constitutes a heterotopic strategy of resistance and opposition
to the extreme conservatism permeating Durkheimian thinking. The
latter influential paradigm, however, is tied more to Hobbes, who wrote
for an earlier British monarchy, than to Durkheim himself, who was
reacting against late-nineteenth-century labor unrest (Anderson, 1968).
In assigning the generalized transformations of societies to specific historical periods — for example, to 1870s historical events (both Durkheim
and Gramsci) or, for that matter, to 1970s political occurrences and
outcomes — one runs the danger of reducing the complexity of human
relations to socially situated experiences (practice), which are in turn transformed into generalized visions of the world (structure). The problematic trick presents itself when the latter (structure) are confused with
the former (practice), not in the recognition that one can lead to or
challenge the other. The unfixity of either "structure" or "practice" allows
for the analysis of the *unintended* consequences of culture and its politics, past or present.

"Situated knowledges" (Haraway, 1986) in themselves are not necessarily, and have not always been, part of the "war of position" that Gramsci promoted. Durkheim's position about the state, morality, and society was consciously situated as well, but vis-à-vis the state's need, of the
times, to restore so-called social order — both from capitalist rapacity
(the greedy capitalist) and from worker unrest. Under late capitalism,
Durkheim's vision of the state is in fact being dismantled by multinational corporations, particularly in Mexico, more specifically at the
U.S.-Mexico border, and by a much-needed border theory that is pro-

duced by border subjects who claim citizenships that transcend boundaries (see Anzaldúa, 1987; Rosaldo, 1993; Morales, 1996; Lugo, 1996).

Throughout most of the history of social science thinking, and, in fact, as early as 1642, Hobbes argued in *Leviathan* (1978[1642]), and in Latin (that is, before "the nation"), that the state of nature is inherently about chaos, disorder, and war, and that the only remedy is to impose a sovereign—the king—so that order and harmony will exist. Thus, we must realize that actual social life does not tend to obey "official mandates" or the most recent "theoretical paradigms." Human relations did not necessarily transform themselves from "chaos" to "order" under Hobbes, nor from "order" to "chaos" under Marx, nor from "chaos" to "order" (back again) under Durkheim, nor will they change from pure "order" to pure "disorder" under Gramscian, postmodernist, and/or borderland thinking.[17] Thus, just as culture changes, so does the state; needless to say, our concepts about them are also transformed, according to distinct historical specificities.

Social life changes and reproduces itself both through cultural-historical contingencies and through the arbitrary, though still symbolically constituted, imposition of a politically legitimated force. It is our business to study the former and a matter of human integrity not only to scrutinize the latter, but, more important, to prevent it. It is necessary that we continue our analytic flow from "Culture" to "culture," from the "State" to the "state," from "Order" to "order," from "Patterns" to "patterns," and, lastly, from "Chaos" to "chaos." As Geertz persuasively noted in 1973, the anthropologist still "confronts the same grand realities that others . . . confront in more fateful settings: Power, Change, Faith, Oppression . . . but he confronts them in obscure enough [I'd say clear enough]—places . . . to take the capital letters off them" (21). It seems, after all, that one of postmodernism's major contributions to sociocultural analysis is, as Benítez-Rojo argues in *The Repeating Island: The Caribbean and the Postmodern Perspective,* its "lens," which "has the virtue of being the only one to direct itself toward the play of paradoxes and eccentricities, of fluxes and displacements" (1992, 271)—that is, toward the simultaneous play of order and disorder, coherence and incoherence, chaos and antichaos, contestation and shareability, practice and structure, culture and history, culture and capitalism, and, finally, patterns and borderlands (Rosaldo, 1993). We should not privilege a priori one or the other; instead, we must continuously suspend each category in order to analyze their eccentricities. It seems to me that only by following these suggestions was I able to juxtapose the analysis of assembled goods in *maquiladoras* with the analysis of the fragmented lives of the *maquila* workers who assembled them, both in the larger contexts of history and the present, the global economy and the local strategies of survival, and, finally, in the more intricate, micro contexts of culture and power.

Conclusion

By examining Gramsci's notion of the state and its dispersal, Foucault's notion of power and its deployment, Anderson's critique of the nation, and Rosaldo's critique of culture, I have tried to spell out my critique of cultural analysis, cultural studies, and culture and border theory, as these are imbricated, willy-nilly, in nationalist, capitalist, late-capitalist, and related projects of politically legitimated force. My specific argument throughout the essay, however, has been fourfold. First, I have argued that dominant (and dominating) anthropological conceptions of culture and society have been historically constituted by such dialectic dualities as beliefs and practices (Boas, 1940[1920]), "symbolic structures and collective behavior" (Geertz, 1973b, 251), structure and agency (Rosaldo, 1980, 1993; Bourdieu 1978), human action and intention (Ortner, 1984), and culture as constituted and culture as lived (Sahlins, 1981, 1982, 1985).[18] Second, I have asserted that received academic conceptions of culture and the border, and of social life for that matter, have been heavily (but, for the most part, unconsciously) influenced by our capacity and incapacity to acknowledge the distinct transformations that the nature of the Westernized "state" has gone through in the past two hundred years (the recent academic recognition of everyday experiences along the U.S.-Mexico border region is a recent manifestation of this transformation, especially with the creation of Free Trade [Border] Zones around the world). Third, I have contended that these academic conceptions of culture and border have been the historical products of either political suppressions or political persuasions and of other types of resistance (i.e., the emergence of minority scholars who have experienced life at the borderlands) to the center's domination. Finally, I have argued in this essay that culture, constituted by both beliefs and practices, is not necessarily shared or contested, and that the crossroads and the limits or frontiers of these beliefs and practices (border theory) constitute, in turn, the erosion of the monopoly of culture theory as "cultural patterns," *from within* (to follow Martín-Rodríguez, 1996, 86).

What is the role of anthropologists in the production of a cultural theory of borderlands in the interdisciplinary arena? Anthropologists today can certainly redefine themselves vis-à-vis the emergent and newly formed academic communities that now confront them. In the late twentieth century, as Renato Rosaldo (1994) consistently argues, anthropologists must strategically (re)locate/(re)position and "remake" themselves in the current scholarly battlefield of power relations.

In order to be effective in this conceptual/political relocation, however, both anthropologists and nonanthropologists who think seriously about the cultural must ask themselves the following question (which Roland Barthes would pose to anybody regarding the nature of interdisciplinarity): Is the concept of culture an object of study that belongs to no particular discipline? Only an *anti*disciplinary mood would provide an answer in the affirmative. A cultural theory of borderlands challenges and invites academics to recognize the crossroads of *inter*disciplinarity, where "ambassadors" are no longer needed. Once the challenge and the invitation are accepted, border theory itself can simultaneously transcend and effectively situate culture, capitalism, and the academy at the crossroads, but only if it is imagined historically and in the larger and dispersed contexts of the nation and of Power (Foucault, 1978).

Otherwise, the *deterritorialization* of the state, theory, and power — and, thus, effective resistance against them — is impossible. Yet those of us who theorize about the border (especially previously marginalized theorists) must recognize that our border has been simultaneously a *bordure*: a border surrounding *a shield*. Unfortunately, shields against capitalism and other agents of oppression are not common among less privileged border subjects, such as factory workers and other working-class men and women inhabiting the U.S.-Mexico border region (Lugo, 1995; Limón, 1994). Until we democratically distribute these shields, those who perhaps need them the most will remain marginalized. After all, as Alejandro Morales argues in "Dynamic Identities in Heterotopia," "In general people fear and are afraid to cross borders.... People cling to the dream of utopia and fail to recognize that they create and live in heterotopia" (1996, 23).

Although much remains to be done, there is no doubt that border theory has proven to be an effective alternative for some of us who used to fear not only to cross borders but to challenge them.

Notes

This essay is part of a larger project titled "Fragmented Lives, Assembled Parts: A Study in Maquilas, Culture, and History at the Mexican Borderlands." I am very grateful to Nancy Abelmann, Jane Collier, George Collier, Bill Kelleher, Bill Maurer, Renato Rosaldo, and Marta Zambrano for commenting on earlier versions of this essay. I am, of course, solely responsible for any errors. With much respect, admiration, *cariño*, and gratitude, I dedicate this essay to Professor Renato Rosaldo.

1. In this essay, *the nation* and *the state,* though usually imbricated with each other, are used to refer, respectively, to a changing imagined community (Anderson, 1991) and to a changing governance apparatus (Hall, 1986). These specific uses, and their implications for culture and border theories, are examined throughout the essay. The examination of these categories and their implications, however, is intended to be illustrative of the social and political problems that must be, and have not yet been, addressed in the literature that concerns us here; thus, though this essay reflects on the state of culture and the nation during the past two hundred years, it does not constitute in itself an exhaustive historical project. I wish mainly to point out some limitations and some new readings of these topics.

2. "Deterritorializing" from "within" is a multilinear process and a complicated political project. It is multilinear because there are several fronts of struggle: the nation-state, contested communities, theory itself, and the individual subject, among many others. It is a complicated political project because agents inhabit multiple locations. For instance, I write this essay from diverse, but interconnected, positions: as a cultural anthropologist who did fieldwork among *maquila* (factory) workers and who was trained in American institutions; as a Mexican who was born in Ciudad Juárez, Mexico, but who became Chicano while continuing my elementary, secondary, and university schooling in Las Cruces, New Mexico. While living in Las Cruces, I visited Ciudad Juárez every weekend until I was twenty-two years of age; thus, I am also a borderer (*fronterizo*) whose everyday experiences could be unpredictably located at the Mexico (Ciudad Juárez)/Texas (El Paso)/New Mexico (Las Cruces) borders. Whatever my multiple locations and possibilities, however, in this essay I would particularly like to reflect on why, as academics, we have come to think seriously about "culture" and "borders" to begin with.

3. In *The History of Sexuality,* Foucault writes, "The purpose of the present study is in fact to show how deployments of power are directly connected to the

body" (1978, 151). These "deployments of power" are imbricated with the deployments of sexuality in the modern West. In part 4 of the same work, titled "Deployment of Sexuality," Foucault examines in detail the objectives, methods, domains, and periodizations through which power operated and dispersed itself from the late eighteenth century to the late nineteenth century in Europe (see 75–131). He also argues that power is omnipresent: "The omnipresence of power: not because it has the privilege of consolidating everything under its invisible unity, but because it is produced from one moment to the next, at every point, or rather in every relation from one point to another" (93).

4. Foucault writes: "Law was not simply a weapon skillfully wielded by monarchs; it was the monarchic system's mode of manifestation and the form of its acceptability. In Western societies since the Middle Ages, the exercise of power has always been formulated in terms of law" (1978, 87). He adds: "One is attached to a certain image of power-law, of power-sovereignty, which was traced out by the theoreticians of right and the monarchic institution. It is this image that we must break free of, that is, of the theoretical privilege of the law and sovereignty, if we wish to analyze power within the concrete and historical framework of its operation. We must construct an analytics of power that no longer takes law as a model and code" (90).

5. Interestingly, in his analysis of the nation, Anderson uses the same periodization that Foucault uses to examine the deployment of sexuality—the late eighteenth and nineteenth centuries. For the most part, Rosaldo limits himself to the twentieth century.

6. In fact, Sherry Ortner organizes her highly influential essay on "practice theory" (1984) along such dialectics as system/action and structure/practice.

7. In "Cultural Reproduction and the Politics of Laziness," I try to show how this double life of culture (in the work of Sahlins, Ortner, and Bourdieu) is manifested inside an electronic *maquila* through an analysis of how specific notions of laziness at the workplace reproduce ideologies of masculinity and machismo (Lugo, 1995; also see Lugo, 1990).

8. Foucault associates this periodization—"1870"—with the production of the homosexual as "a personage, a past, a case history, and a childhood, in addition to being a type of life" (1978, 43). He adds: "We must not forget that the psychological, psychiatric, medical category of homosexuality was constituted from the moment it was characterized—Westphal's famous article of 1870 [*Archiv für Neurologie*] on 'contrary sexual relations' can stand as its date of birth.... The sodomite had been a temporary aberration; the homosexual was now a species" (43).

9. In the case of Mexico, the question of *mestizaje* and *lo mexicano*, as national projects, emerged at the same time the nation-state was trying to consolidate itself immediately after the Mexican Revolution of 1910–20.

10. In addition to these institutions of civil society, Foucault adds "a multiplicity of discourses produced by a whole series of mechanisms operating in different institutions... demography, biology, medicine, psychiatry, psychology, ethics, pedagogy, and political criticism" (1978, 33). Regarding their *dispersal*, Foucault explicitly and forcefully notes, "So it is not simply in terms of a continual extension that

we must speak of this discursive growth; it should be seen rather as a dispersion of centers from which discourses emanated, a diversification of their forms, and the complex deployment of the network connecting them (34).

11. Of course, the "self/other" distinction has been both contested and problematized in recent writings of culture.

12. In his experimental ethnography *Dancing with the Devil*, José Limón applies the metaphor of war in ways I am suggesting here, but following Gramsci's "war of maneuver" and "war of position." In the following quotation, Limón uses the metaphor of war quite appropriately to depict the racial struggle between Mexicans and Anglos in South Texas: "For it is a basic premise and organizing metaphor for this essay that since the 1830's, the Mexicans of south Texas have been in a state of social war with the `Anglo' dominant Other and their class allies. This has been at times a war of overt, massive proportions; at others, covert and sporadic; at still other moments, repressed and internalized as a war within the psyche, but always conditioned by an ongoing social struggle fought out of different *battlefields*" (1994, 15–16).

13. See chapter 6 of my manuscript "Fragmented Lives, Assembled Parts" (1995). Also, feminist anthropologists have been at the forefront of this "new" and exciting anthropology (see especially the provocative and theoretically sophisticated volumes *Uncertain Terms*, 1990, edited by Faye Ginsburg and Anna Tsing, and *Women Writing Culture*, 1995, edited by Ruth Behar and Deborah Gordon).

14. Of course, this notion of culture, as shared patterns of behavior, still reigns in some quarters.

15. See my analysis of prenation, dynastic, monarchic, and heterogeneous New Spain and New Mexico in my chapter titled "Hegemony and History in the Invention of Borderlands Geography" (Lugo, 1995).

16. See Lugo (1995, chap. 2) for the encounters of conquest both Hernán Cortés and Juan de Oñate had with uncertain, unidentified, and perhaps yet unnamed groups of people in the coast of "México" and in what came to be New Mexico.

17. One of the most important contributions of Renato Rosaldo's thinking is precisely Rosaldo's sensitivity to analysis of power as it is found in *both* patterns and borderlands, chaos and order, subjectivity and objectivity, and culture and politics. None of these entities holds a monopoly on truth. This is Rosaldo's most important message regarding culture, identity, and power/knowledge.

18. I have also argued that within anthropology, if "practice and structure," "beliefs and action," do not explicitly appear in early anthropological debates about culture and the individual, the individual and society, the individual and social structure, or culture and the environment, it is because "practice," as category of analysis, was suppressed due to its implication for political mobilization on the part of colonized subjects, the working poor, and other subaltern subjects — the usual targets of anthropologists throughout most of the twentieth century. Also, anthropologists have historically privileged such analytic domains as cognition, symbols, the environment, decision making, the superorganic, and personality, among many others, in trying to get to the cultural or the social in human beings. Yet all these categories acquire meaning for academics only to the extent that they can explain

or interpret people's "beliefs and actions." Thus, we return to the structure/practice duality that, I argue, has constituted our dominant discourse on culture — so far.

Works Cited

Anderson, Benedict. 1991. *Imagined Communities: Reflections on the Origin and Spread of Nationalism.* London: Verso.

Anderson, Perry. 1968. "Components of the National Culture." *New Left Review* 50.

Anzaldúa, Gloria. 1987. *Borderlands/La Frontera: The New Mestiza.* San Francisco: Aunt Lute.

Arnold, Mathew. 1963[1867–68]. *Culture and Anarchy,* ed. J. Dover Wilson. Cambridge: Cambridge University Press.

Barth, Frederik. 1966. *Models of Social Organization* (Occasional Paper No. 23). London: Royal Anthropological Institute.

Behar, Ruth, and Deborah A. Gordon, eds. 1995. *Women Writing Culture.* Berkeley: University of California Press.

Benedict, Ruth. 1934. *Patterns of Culture.* Boston: Houghton Mifflin.

Benítez-Rojo, Antonio. 1992. *The Repeating Island: The Carribean and the Postmodern Perspective,* trans. James E. Maranis. Durham, N.C.: Duke University Press.

Boas, Franz. 1940[1920]. *Race, Language, and Culture.* New York: Free Press.

———. 1963[1911]. *The Mind of Primitive Man.* New York: Collier.

Bourdieu, Pierre. 1978. *Outline of a Theory of Practice.* New York: Cambridge University Press.

Clifford, James. 1986. "Introduction: Partial Truths." In *Writing Culture: The Poetics and Politics of Ethnography,* ed. James Clifford and George E. Marcus, 1–26. Berkeley: University of California Press.

Derrida, Jacques. 1978[1966]. *Writing and Difference,* trans. Alan Bass. Chicago: University of Chicago Press.

Diccionario de la Lengua Española. 1992. Madrid: Real Academia Española.

During, Simon, ed. 1994. *The Cultural Studies Reader.* London: Routledge.

Durkheim, Emile. 1965[1912]. *The Elementary Forms of the Religious Life,* trans. J. W. Swain. New York: Random House.

———. 1933[1893]. *The Division of Labor,* trans. George Simpsom. New York: Free Press.

Foucault, Michel. 1978. *The History of Sexuality,* vol. 1. *An Introduction,* trans. Alan Sheridan-Smith. New York Random House.

Geertz, Clifford. 1973a. "Thick Description: Toward an Interpretive Theory of Culture." In *The Interpretation of Cultures,* 3–30. New York: Basic Books.

———. 1973b. "Religion as a Cultural System." In *The Interpretation of Cultures,* 87–125. New York: Basic Books.

Giddens, Anthony. 1979. *Central Problems in Social Theory: Action, Structure, and Contradiction in Social Analysis.* Berkeley: University of California Press.

Ginsburg, Faye, and Anna Tsing, eds. 1990. *Uncertain Terms: Negotiating Gender in American Culture.* Boston: Beacon.

Hall, Stuart. 1986. "Gramsci's Relevance for the Study of Race and Ethnicity." *Journal of Communication Inquiry* 10(2): 5–27.

Haraway, Donna. 1986. "Situated Knowledges: The Science Question in Feminism and the Privilege of Partial Perspective." *Feminist Studies* 14(3): 575–99.

Hobbes, T. 1978[1642]. *Leviathan.* New York: Liberal Arts.

Limón, José E. 1994. *Dancing with the Devil: Society and Cultural Poetics in Mexican-American South Texas.* Madison: University of Wisconsin Press.

Lugo, Alejandro. 1990. "Cultural Production and Reproduction in Ciudad Juarez, Mexico: Tropes at Play among Maquiladora Workers." *Cultural Anthropology* 5(2): 173–96.

———. 1995. "Fragmented Lives, Assembled Goods: A Study in Maquilas, Culture, and History at the Mexican Borderlands." Ph.D. diss., Stanford University.

———. 1996. "Border Inspections." Paper presented at the annual meeting of the American Anthropological Association, San Francisco, November.

Malinowski, Bronislaw. 1944. *A Scientific Theory of Culture and Other Essays.* Chapel Hill: University of North Carolina Press.

Martín-Rodríguez, Manuel M. 1996. "The Global Border: Transnationalism and Cultural Hybridism in Alejandro Morales's *The Rag Doll Plagues.*" In *Alejandro Morales: Fiction Past, Present, Future Perfect,* ed. José Antonio Gurpegui, 86–98. Tempe, Ariz.: Bilingual Review.

Morales, Alejandro. 1996. "Dynamic Identities in Heterotopia." In *Alejandro Morales: Fiction Past, Present, Future Perfect,* ed. José Antonio Gurpegui, 14–27. Tempe, Ariz.: Bilingual Review.

Nash, June. 1983. "The Impact of the Changing International Division of Labor on Different Sectors of the Labor Force." In *Women, Men, and the International Division of Labor,* ed. June Nash and María Patricia Fernández-Kelly, 3–38. Albany: State University of New York Press.

Ong, Aihwa. 1995. "Women Out of China: Traveling Tales and Traveling Theories in Postcolonial Feminism." In *Women Writing Culture,* ed. Ruth Behar and Deborah A. Gordon, 350–72. Berkeley: University of California Press.

Ortner, Sherry. 1984. "Theory in Anthropology since the Sixties." *Comparative Studies in Society and History* 26(1): 126–66.

Radcliffe-Brown, A. R. 1952. *Structure and Function in Primitive Society.* New York: Free Press.

Rosaldo, Renato. 1980. *Ilongot Headhunting, 1883–1974: A Study in Society and History.* Stanford, Calif.: Stanford University Press.

———. 1993. *Culture and Truth: The Remaking of Social Analysis.* Boston: Beacon.

———. 1994. "After Objectivism." In *The Cultural Studies Reader,* ed. Simon During, 104–17. London: Routledge.

Sahlins, Marshall. 1981. *Historical Metaphors and Mythical Realities: Structure in the Early History of the Sandwich Islands Kingdom.* Ann Arbor: University of Michigan Press.

———. 1982. "Individual Experience and Cultural Order." In *The Social Sciences: Their Nature and Uses,* ed. William H. Krustel, 35–48. Chicago: University of Chicago Press.

————. 1985. *Islands of History.* Chicago: University of Chicago Press.

Weber, Max. 1958[1920]. *The Protestant Ethic and the Spirit of Capitalism.* New York: Charles Scribner's Sons.

————. 1977[1905]. "'Objectivity' in *Social Science and Social Policy.*" In *Understanding and Social Inquiry,* ed. B. Dallmayr and T. McCarthy, 24–37. Notre Dame, Ind.: University of Notre Dame Press.

Webster's New Collegiate Dictionary, 8th ed. 1974. Springfield, Mass.: G. & C. Merriam.

Williams, Raymond. 1979. *Politics and Letters: Interviews with New Left Review.* London: Schocken.

Willis, Paul. 1977. *Learning to Labor: How Working Class Kids Get Working Class Jobs.* New York: Columbia University Press.

TWO

In the Borderlands of Chicano Identity, There Are Only Fragments

Benjamin Alire Sáenz

A bill is coming in that I fear America is not prepared to pay.
JAMES BALDWIN

The time for undiscriminating racial unity has passed.
TONI MORRISON

My wife and I go to an opening reception at the newly opened Barnes & Noble bookstore. We are disappointed because it looks like a mall. What did we expect? The store is full of people who gather around food tables and gawk through the aisles. People visit and chat with one another. My wife and I look at each other and finally whisper: "*There's no one here but white people.*" El Paso is 70 percent "Hispanic" (I hate that word). The West Side, where the bookstore was built, is the whitest part of El Paso. The clientele assembled here tonight *is* decidedly white. My wife and I become uncomfortable. We drink a cup of coffee. We leave. We drive to a book reception — Texas Western Press is celebrating the publication of its latest book. I feel obliged to attend because I am on the editorial board. My wife and I again notice that everyone there is white. "What is this?" I ask myself. "White Night?" I remembered living in Lafayette, Louisiana. There was a blues joint where Black people hung out, but on Tuesdays the "Blacks" would clear out and the place would fill up with "white" people. The locals referred to Tuesdays at that place as "White Night." I never knew if the term was used ironically or not. Tonight, I remember that place. We make small talk (there is no "big" talk at such events). My wife, Patricia, is an associate judge. I am used to attending events with her where many (if not most) of the people are "Hispanics." At the reception, my wife and I keep looking around, then nod at each other knowingly. We leave. Why do Patricia and I notice that we are the only Chicanos at these events when nobody else around us seems to notice — or care? Why do *we* notice? And them — why don't *they* notice?

> *The term* Chicano *is supposedly derived from* Mexicano, *which comes from* Mexica *(pronounced "meshica"), who are generally known as Aztecs. Unfortunately, the term began to be utilized in a pejorative sense. It was likened to the disparaging term* greaser *or* wetback *by some Anglos. In the 1960s it became popular as Chicanos began to seek political and social reforms. It is at this point where the term becomes problematic and a source of indifference to me.*
>
> *First of all, I am a first-generation American citizen, whose parents both immigrated to the United States from Mexico in the 1960s. As a child I was compelled to appreciate the newly found freedoms and opportunities my parents were experiencing. I was provided with an education that up until recently I believed was more than adequate. Through history, literature, and government courses in high school, I was indoctrinated with patriotic American values that were basically devoid of any prominent Chicano influences. The term* Chicano *was used as a pejorative and referred to radical and reactionary individuals who were the antithesis of what I was taught that this country represented. Consequently, I became content on questioning the classification in which I was categorized. When asked about my ethnicity I simply replied that I was Mexican or Mexican American. I avoided the term* Hispanic *because it seemed extremely generic.*
>
> *Although the civil rights movements of the 1960s are often looked upon as a favorable period for many minorities, it seems that in the area in which I grew up (Fabens, the Lower Valley), Mexican Americans who chanted "Brown Power" and "Viva La Raza" were a mere triviality.*
>
> *It is nice knowing that Chicano was the name Mexican Americans chose for themselves. However, this term seems more applicable to people who grew up in the 1960s. As a child of the 1980s, I am comfortable with being classified as a Mexican American. "Mexican" does not negate my Native American ancestry and "American" reemphasizes the place of my birth.*[1]

In response to one of my assignments, one of my undergraduate students casually announced, with no discernible rage in his voice, "I don't read gringo poets." His absolute separatist stance appalled me. I confess, I experienced a moment of complete outrage, and I reacted more out of spontaneous reflex than reflective intelligence. My anger was evident, and I made no attempt to hide it. "I'm not about to put up with racist discourse in this class, got that? You *will* read Anglo poets or you will drop my course." He looked at me quietly. Later, I tell myself that I overreacted. I know what lies behind his words: *I have been erased. Ergo, I will erase. I have been hated. I will hate.* There is a compelling logic here.

Later, he wrote me a poem in which my person was represented. I was not exactly the hero. I asked him to visit my office. We talked. But we came to no real solutions. The student (a very dark, Indian-looking Chicano) was disappointed by my response. He was completely disillusioned with me. *What kind of a role model was I, anyway?* Not that he said that, not outright, but his eyes accused. I told him I was not the enemy. But there he was — in my office, and he was staring at me and his eyes kept saying: very definitely not the real thing — not a *real Chicano.* I hate playing the game of "who is more Chicano than whom." (It's a variation on a game currently played in Washington between Newt Gingrich and Bill Clinton: Who is more middle-class than whom?) I detest pissing contests.

I think about this student. It is tempting to dismiss him. But his rage is very real and it is a dangerous thing to dismiss rage. Rage never just disappears — it boomerangs back, and if it doesn't hit me, it will hit someone else. I cannot allow myself to forget that I have felt what he feels. I am not free of hate. I am not free of rage with regard to the subject of identity, and I do not really believe anybody else in that classroom is free of rage either. Most of us merely carry our race-based mistrust in a more acceptable manner (especially those of us who are holding very serious dialogues with a "dominant culture" and have a great deal invested in those dialogues). Some of us deny the relevance of race- or ethnicity-based identities simply by invoking a democracy-based identity that is supposed to supersede all other arguments and discourses: "We are all Americans. We are all equal." This particular strategy is facile, lazy, and anti-intellectual, and has more to do with denial and erasure than with examining our material culture and how that material culture is decidedly built upon inequalities.

I think about this "radical" student later in the day. His argument is decidedly unsubtle, unnuanced, superficial, reactionary. But the possibility exists that his attitude really offended me because I am embarrassed by the way he handles his rage (which has everything to do with his identity). Why do I find his position unacceptable? *Bad politics. Very bad politics. And the premises behind his politics? Well, those are bad, too.* I chew on this. I am not so unlike him. I too have been formed by racist discourse — and yet I have just demanded that he not engage in that discourse in my class because I find the way he talks about this disagreeable. Knowing, as I do, the very real reasons behind his rage and knowing, as I do, the way most of my colleagues ignore the material circumstances of our student population, why should he play the role of the accommodationist? Should I shoot the messenger because he has articulated an attitude we all know is just beneath the surface? He did not produce himself. He is a product. And the word *product* here should not be confused with *victim*. Though we may all occupy different positions in the material world, *we are all* the products of the cumulative discourses around us. None of us is as much an "active subject" as we'd like to imagine. We are all contained by these discourses — especially the discourse of capitalism — and few of us are able to break through to a "radical" talk that is outside of these discourses. All of us make feeble attempts. And isn't this student trying?

Some would say that this young man's rage was produced by an inflammatory separatist Chicano rhetoric that does nothing but produce a climate of hatred and mistrust — and this is partially true. *Partially true.* But this is too easy an answer — too easy because it masks more complex issues and protects a plethora of guilty parties. When faced with the "in your face" talk of some African Americans, Chicanos, "radical" feminists, or members of Queer Nation, we would do well to remember that one of the reasons this kind of talk bothers us has a great deal to do with the "talk" we have adopted. We are trained to use a certain discourse, have grown accustomed to using a different kind of grammar. Most of us who teach in universities have been reproduced by tamer, more genteel rhetorics, but it is disingenuous to pretend we are free of violence simply because we appear to have more control over our actions. The pretense of civility in our places of employment (especially in universities) is just that—a pretense.

I cannot forget this one important thing: this man has something very real invested in his "identity politics." This is serious business. He is fighting back. *Maybe I am the enemy.*

> *I have a curious relationship with the word* Chicano. *I don't mind being called a "Chicana," but I have problems using the label to describe myself. It's not that I don't feel like a Chicana, or I'm embarrassed by my culture or even by the word itself. I usually end up calling myself a Mexican American. The word Chicana inevitably stumbles out of my mouth clumsily like I'm pronouncing a foreign word. I don't know why. I'm not offended by it, I just can't seem to get used to using that word.*

The evening's conversation is easygoing, not too provocative, light, something you would expect from a dinner party held in honor of a visiting lecturer. Near the end of the evening, the woman seated next to me asks: "Why do you insist on calling yourself a Chicano writer? Why not simply call yourself a writer?" She does not ask the question belligerently, but there is a firm tone behind her question that demands an answer, a challenge perhaps. And yet I know that no answer I give will satisfy the questioner. I take a sip of wine. A series of answers run thorough my mind: "If I called myself a Jewish writer, would you ask me the same question? Would you ask why I insisted on my Jewishness? If I called myself an 'American' writer, would you ask why I insisted on my Americanness?" Too aggressive. Another possible answer—one more mysterious, subtle, more suggestive, more worthy of the writer she imagines me to be: "I don't want to call myself anything." I see myself smiling at her. What would she do with *that* answer? But the answer doesn't suit me—I don't like being in the wisdom business. Far too many poets have bored me with their humanistic wisdom that under serious scrutiny turns out to be as thoughtful as *The Bridges of Madison County.* Another answer races through my mind. "Exactly what about the term *Chicano* bothers you? Clearly the label of *writer* (an identity label if there ever was one) doesn't bother you a bit. Why not? Isn't *writer* a problematic identity for you? Why not?" But I don't want to get into an argument, and *that* answer sounds too much like an ambush. "Well," I say, "I'm comfortable with that identity. I choose it." I say this partially because it's true and partially because people are comfortable when anything that is being discussed is framed in terms of "choice" — part of a democratic rhetoric we are all steeped in.

She doesn't skip a beat. "But doesn't calling yourself that limit you? Why would you want to be so limited?"

"Why does it limit me?" I ask. *Of course it limits me. It limits me because when many whites see that word, they won't pick up the book. Serious readers want to read "universal literature," "world literature."* "All writers have their limitations." I say. I'm angry now, and I know it. And I know why I am angry, but I also know that I will not go into any diatribes. I do speak passionately, though I am very bad at hiding my emotions. I suggest to her — and by now the entire table — that I have no wish to distance myself from the history of a people I consider to be my community. I tell her that I am unapologetically political. I tell her that this country has no right to demand historical amnesia from its citizens. I praise the memory of my parents, who were seasonal cotton pickers. I am romanticizing the image of the farmworker shamelessly. She nods her head. But I see she is not completely satisfied by my answer. I have, however, managed to silence her. Does this mean I have won the argument? She is suspicious of my "choice" — finds my "identity" false, though she does not say it. She feels *Chicano* is divisive, an unnecessary and inappropriate political intrusion. *Yes, yes, we all come from immigrant stock. Just be a writer and cut the crap.* Writer, now there's an identity. The conversation is lively, but she is not convinced of anything I have said. I assume that *Chicano* threatens her because it asserts — and insists upon — difference. Difference for difference's sake? Is that what she imagines? And I am equally suspicious of her assumptions. *She* does not have to discuss *her* identity. She does not have to hold it up for public debate, for "intellectual" scrutiny. Doesn't she have an identity? *Tell me, what is it like to be white?* What are the politics of her "chosen" identity? I imagine her answer would sound something like this: "Come, come, we are educated and civil. We are all the same. We all love, we all hate, we all dream, we all will die. We feel. We all feel." I imagine that she tells me this, and I imagine my response: "Yes. And some die sooner than others, and some live better than others, and some work harder than others, and some have a great deal more than others. *Work makes freedom.* Clearly work makes some freer than others."

As I drive home with my wife, I tell her that "gringos" just don't get it.

> While I would consider myself a "Mexican American," I will always call myself a "gentleman." My parents instilled codes of honor and respect in me. I was taught the history of my culture and my family. My familial background and attitude centers on education, ambition, and demeanor. Some would call this elitism or even snobbery. I would say that I differentiate by class—not according to money or status, but by ambition and determination.... When I think of the term Chicano, I associate it with the Chicano movement. Chicano is a reference point to a time of advocating and protesting for civil rights and acknowledgment from the ruling classes. All right, where did I get this definition? I got it from my family. Each member seems to have their identity grounded in the experiences of their formative years.
>
> My relation to the term Chicano is based on my literal relation to any Chicanos.... I would call my uncle a Chicano based on his student experiences at Cal-Berkeley and Texas-El Paso during the late 1960s and early 1970s. I know he can refer to himself as a Chicano because he "was there."
>
> Please understand that I am not chastising anyone who calls themselves a Chicano. I am merely associating them with a time period.... The Chicanos I know from outside the 60s/70s time frame are people who identify with the ideas and ideals of that time frame. It is their loyalty and sense of roots to that time that they wear the term Chicano like a badge. While it comes to finding an identity, there is always someone or some cause that gives a label, and eventually a person, identity and respect.
>
> Again, I am not Chicano. Nor am I a Pachuco, Latino, Mexican, Pocho, Hispanic. I won't use the term Chicano because I cannot use the term. If I call myself a Chicano, I am a liar.... Actually, I would be worse than a liar, I would be a hypocrite.
>
> I may not be a Chicano, but I am related to some.

Catholicism. Marxism. Capitalism. Humanism. Chicanismo. I find it impossible to live without organizing principles. I need to organize my identity around certain narratives. I reject certain discourses, certain kinds of talks that do their work on me despite my protestations—which makes me resent those discourses even more ("nationalism" immediately comes to mind). For the good or for the bad, I find it impossible to live without an identity. *No one can live without an identity.* The day of the "posthuman" has not yet arrived, and anyone who thinks it has arrived had better go back and do some serious analysis of the discourses that have (de)formed and shaped our "selves." The debate surrounding identity and identity formations cannot be reduced to obsessions "invented" by academic people of color and sympathetic white progressives who have no real interest in "knowledge" or "standards" or "academic discipline" or "scholarship." The "identity wars" did not begin in 1968, did not begin with Gloria Steinem, did not begin with Malcolm X, did not begin with Langston Hughes, did not begin with Toni Morrison, did not begin with César Chávez, did not begin with Gloria Anzaldúa, did not begin with Rigoberta Menchú, did not begin with Maxine Hong Kingston, did not begin even with Harold Bloom. The West's obsession with identity began with Plato and Aristotle and was extended by (among others) Thomas Aquinas, Augustine, Descartes, Locke, Hume, Heidegger, and Marx.

"Identity" cannot exist without an attendant politics — and everybody engages in identity politics. *Everybody.* We all privilege certain categories or discourses over others and organize ourselves around these discourses: some of us organize our identities around the vague term *human.* Some of us organize our identities around our sexuality. Some of us organize our identities around the countries of our origins. Some of us organize our identities around our genders. I am often enraged when Chicanos (and other "colorful" people) are accused of playing "identity politics." It is like accusing someone of breathing.

It is fair to say that many people (inside academia as well as outside it) resent *the way* people who call themselves Chicanos (and Indians and African Americans and Asian Americans) have played identity politics (at white people's expense, no doubt — at *everybody* else's expense). I recall a passage in Richard Rodriguez's *Hunger of Memory*:

> "Damn!" he said, and his chair rasped the floor as he pushed himself back. Suddenly it was to *me* that he was complaining. "It's just not right, Richard. None of this is fair. You've done some good work, but so have I. I'll bet our records are just about even. But when we go looking for jobs this year, it's a very different story. You're the one who gets all the breaks."
>
> To evade his criticism, I wanted to side with him. I was about to admit the injustice of affirmative action. "Oh, it's all very simple this year. You're a Chicano. And I am a Jew. That's really the only difference between us."
>
> His words stung anger alive. In a voice deceptively calm I replied that he oversimplified the whole issue. Phrases came quickly: the importance

of cultural diversity; new blood; the goal of racial integration. They were all the old arguments I had proposed years before—long since abandoned. After a minute or two, as I heard myself talking, I felt self-disgust. The job offers I was receiving were indeed unjustified. I knew that. All I was saying amounted to a frantic self-defense. It all was a lie. I tried to find an end to my sentence; my voice faltered to a stop.

"Yeah, yeah sure," he said. "I've heard all that stuff before. Nothing you can say, though, really changes the fact that affirmative action is unfair. You can see that, can't you? There isn't any way for me to compete with you. Once there were quotas to keep my parents out of schools like Yale. Now there are quotas to get you in. And the effect on me is the same as it was for them. . . ."

At the edge of hearing, I listened to every word he spoke. But behind my eyes my mind reared—spooked and turning—then broke toward a reckless idea: Leave the university. Leave. Immediately the idea sprang again in my bowels and began to climb. Rent money. I pictured myself having to borrow. Get a job as a waiter somewhere? I had come to depend on the intellectual companionship of students—bright students—to relieve the scholar's loneliness. I remembered the British Museum, a year in silence. I wanted to teach; I wanted to read; I wanted this life. But I had to protest. How? Disqualify myself from the profession as long as affirmative action continued? Romantic exile? But I had to. Yes. I found the horizon again. It was calm.

The graduate student across the room had stopped talking; he was staring out the window. I said nothing. My decision was final. No, I would say to them all. Finally, simply, no.

I wrote a note to all the chairmen of English departments who had offered me jobs. I left a note for the professor in my own department at Berkeley who was in charge of helping graduate students look for teaching positions. (The contradictions of affirmative action have finally caught up with me. Please remove my name from the list of teaching job applicants.)

I telephoned my mother and father. My mother did not seem to hear exactly what I was trying to tell her. She let the subject pass without comment. (Was I still planning on coming for dinner this Sunday?) My father, however, clearly understood. Silent for a moment, he seemed uncertain of what I expected to hear. Finally, troubled, he said hesitantly, "I don't know why you feel this way. We have never had any of the chances before."

We, he said. But he was wrong. It was *he* who had never had any chance before.[2]

As I recall this passage, I open the book to that page and reread it. Ahh, Richard, I sometimes wonder what your friend would have said to *you* if *you* had said: "You're a Jew. And I am a Chicano. That's really the only difference between us." It was only *you* who was playing the affirmative action identity politics game, not him. Not him. He was just a talented individual. And you, you were a member of a group. And he (unlike you) lived in the best of all possible worlds — where there were nothing but "individuals" who always got jobs according to objective criteria and merit. So there was nothing left for you to do but divorce yourself from the "We." "Romantic exile." Isn't that how you self-consciously referred to it? In the face of "contradictions" you simply take yourself out of the game. And yet you insert yourself back into it by writing a book — a "public" book, about what? — *about identity.* And you admit that your writing is political (though you fail to scrutinize the politics of your own writing): "My book is necessarily political, in the conventional sense, for public issues . . . have bisected my life. And, in some broad sense, my writing is political because it concerns my movement away from the company of family and into the city. This was my coming of age: I became a man by becoming a public man" (7). Why, I wonder, is a "public" identity privileged over a "private" one? These terms you use, *public* and *private* — what are they about? If I were to tell you that I became a "man" by becoming a private man, wouldn't you wonder what the hell I was talking about? You seem to imply that the only identity worth having is the identity that privileges a public identity completely immersed in a middle-class discourse. Like you, I too have mastered a middle-class discourse. Unlike you, I find it disingenuous to separate my "life" into the categories of "public" and "private." Is the discourse of family — Chicano or otherwise — a "private discourse"? Since when? You seem not to be at all aware of the fact that the very notion of "family" has been "publicly" produced. And so you have moved away from family. Should I assume that because your family members' lives have not entered into the public domain that their identities are less authentic? And why is it that you assume that a farmworker's life is not "public"? Capitalism — a public discourse if there ever was one — depends on labor. In what sense are the workers' lives that you speak about in "Complexion" private? Is it because they have not mastered English? You say you have become a public man—self-made in a public language—English. But isn't Spanish a public language? All languages are public, Richard. But the talented "individual" wants only to be an "individual"—insists on it. You have become middle-class without so much as analyzing and critiquing that powerful and complex word: "But I write of one life only. My own. If my story is true, I trust it will resonate with significance for other lives. Finally, my history deserves public notice as no more than this: a parable for the life of its reader. Here is the life of a middle class man" (7). The romance of it is too much for me to bear. You have exchanged one identity for another and cloaked yourself in a rhetoric that denies the complex and unequal positions we occupy in this very complicated material world. Escape is not possible. But you are enamored of the image of escape and you embrace the long literary traditions in which you base your aesthetic: "The world is too much with us," the world is only the place where "ignorant armies clash by night" (especially the ignorant armies that battle for bilingual education and affirmative action). There is no community possible for you. There is only exile. There is only that aesthetic gesture that valorizes the alienation of the enlightened individual. This is an old story, Richard. It will not save you. It will not save anyone.

While the words Chicano *and* Chicana *have lost many of the militant connotations they used to hold for me, I still think the terms signify a person who is unhappy and angry with life here and prone to extremism. I know I'm wrong; even my 1974 copy of the* Merriam Webster Dictionary *describes* Chicano *as an American of Mexican descent. That describes me, but my sixties baggage says it doesn't.*

Prejudice and discrimination will always exist: gender, ethnicity, height and weight, level of education, your alma mater, etc. etc. ad nauseam. People like to hate anyone different from them; ethnocentrism insists that "my way" is the only way. At the ripe old age of forty-three, I realize what can and cannot be accomplished in my life or in my country. The best way for me to help my fellow Mexicans to partake of their fair share in this country is to convince them of the power of education. I can encourage them to stay in school, help them fill out forms for financial aid, enroll in college, teach Chicano literature and history, be proud of their heritage and stand up for it, but realize that realistically more can be accomplished with the system than without it. My husband and I have led a good life, in part because we are both well-educated college graduates, and we try to avoid the idiots of all colors who discriminate. I honestly feel that if I share my life experiences and those of my many Mexican friends with my students and let them know that higher education will open the doors that are shut by ethnicity, then I will have succeeded in helping my people, much more than the angry rhetoric of the 60s Chicanos ever did. Actions speak louder than words.

Like Rodriguez, many Chicanos have come to the conclusion that identity politics is the only game in town. (The conservatives who have appropriated Rodriguez's writing must be reminded at every turn that Mr. Rodriguez has built a career around identity politics.) Why is identity politics inescapable? Because we live in a shitty, disgusting world that produces and reproduces appalling inequalities, a society that helps to create suspicions of "others." The politics of identity cannot be separated from these inequalities. Identity politics in the workplace, for all its disturbing problematics, is at least a recognition that we live in a racist society and a demonstration of a willingness to meet and confront that racist society with solutions. I cannot take opponents of affirmative action seriously, not because affirmative action is so delightfully free of "prejudice" and "discrimination," and not because I seriously believe that affirmative action is going to usher in the just world order we have all been awaiting since the day Adam and Eve were exiled from the garden, but because opponents of affirmative action offer no real solutions to those inequalities (which are undeniably, but not exclusively, race and gender based). We ought to have at least learned by now that an objective merit system does not exist. Trying to hire the best person for the job is like judging a literary contest: for every judge, there is a different deserving winner, and each judge will insist that his or her only criterion is "good writing."

Chicano identity is only in part based on the material culture that is formed by the meeting of Mexico and the United States. Chicano identity is ultimately about politics. I do not consider myself a radical (though in the age of Proposition 187 and Newt Gingrich, I certainly qualify as one), but a Chicano identity *is* radical in this one sense: it refuses to be completely contained by that homogeneous, devouring word *American*. People who are overinvested in a nationalistic identity are right to be suspicious of Chicanos.

What about the word Chicano? *I have always had a problem with this word. I think because it used to have a negative connotation that involved the Chicano movement of the 60s and 70s. I have always called myself a Mexican American and clearly deny any association with the word* Chicana. *Until recently I have started to have a problem calling myself a Mexican American. I am at a point in my life where I want to desperately find an identity and call myself accordingly. I have searched within, and asked myself why the word* Chicano *bothers me. I cannot come up with a valid reason to justify my prejudice....I enrolled this semester in a cultural identity class hoping to find my true identity. We have had to read many books written by Chicano authors....I remember the first day of class we were asked to present ourselves to the class. The professor had placed many words on the blackboard that referred to Mexican Americans. He instructed us to use some of those words in our presentations of ourselves. As we neared the end of the presentations, I noted that not everyone used the word* Chicano(a) *to describe themselves. This perplexed me even further.*

...As the weeks go by and I continue to read the struggles that my people, the Mexican people that live in the United States, have struggled, I myself have stirred my heart and my soul. Slowly I find myself admitting to myself that calling myself a Chicana would not be so bad. On the contrary, I am starting to feel great pride in my Chicano Culture.

When I call myself a Chicano, I do not do so unproblematically. Do I privilege the culture to which I was born? Yes. Do I do so out of nostalgia? No. Do I overprivilege my culture? Sometimes. Do I resent gringos? Sometimes. Do I *hate* gringos? No. Do I realize that white or light skin is overprivileged in the country in which I live? Yes. Am I enraged by people who refuse to acknowledge that fact? Absolutely. Am I an essentialist? No.

I live on a border between Mexico and the United States. I sometimes sneer (perhaps unfairly) at Latinos who think the border is only a metaphor. What is so radical about using a very material culture as a literary device to describe an individual's psychological state? I know border culture intimately, the anxieties and mistrust that the very fact of living here raises in people. But I refuse to romanticize my culture. I am fond of saying that I don't do hat dances. In my writings, there is no nostalgia—the people represented there are not poor but happy and they do not lean on cacti. I am not ignorant of other cultures, other traditions, other ways of talking. I am neither provincial nor insulated nor blind to the other discourses that have formed me. I am not a separatist. I am not an extremist. If I wear *Chicano* as if it were a badge, I do so because "to live is to take sides" and it does not seem an unreasonable thing to side with the class and the ethnic group that produced me. On the other hand, Chicano identity has nothing to do with particular cultural characteristics that an individual must have (or attain) in order to be that thing called Chicano. *I am not a neo-Platonist, I am not an essentialist, I am not a cultural purist.* I realize the pitfalls of identity labels (though I reject such easy metaphors that imply an identity — any identity — is something that is facile, put on like a shirt and just as easily exchanged depending on the weather, the mood, or the occasion).

I am Mexican American and until recently, Chicano *conjured images of cholos, tattooed, with thick, black mustaches; low riders; brown skin and dark hair. This prejudice is rooted in an ill-fated first encounter with* Chicano *and my subsequent actions.*

My first encounter happened when I was eight and the year was 1974. My father was stationed in Hawaii and we lived in base housing. In hindsight, the military is an integrated society. I blended among the black, yellow, red, and brown children of the military housing. Thus, I didn't need a category to put myself into. However, I was unprepared for the first encounter.

Of all things, the encounter centers around a T-shirt. The T-shirt showed a clenched, brown fist and the words "Chicano Power!" encircling the fist. Where this shirt came from I don't remember. Nonetheless, I had it and wore it ... once.

On that day, oblivious to any implications this shirt might have, me and a group of friends were walking down a street of our neighborhood, heading toward a ditch that was our playground of choice. We approached four men gathered by a car.

"Chicano power!" one of them blared at us, or I thought us, but realized it was at me. All four men were looking at only me. I noticed they were Mexican Americans. I didn't know exactly what Mexican American, *or for that matter* Chicano, *meant at the time. But because they had dark skin and hair like me, and I was told that I was Mexican American, I deduced they were Mexican Americans, too. One of the men pointed at my shirt. "Chicano power," he said. I looked down and saw the upside-down fist and words.*

"Que pasa, amigo?" another one said.

"Are you a little Chicano?" a third asked with a big grin on his face.

I noticed they all had on tan pants and white T-shirts. I figured they were G.I.s because of their close-to-the-scalp haircuts. Their white heads looked odd atop brown faces. The silent one stepped toward me and I saw a large tattoo on the inside of his forearm. I couldn't make out what it was, but it was black. He didn't say anything at first, just stared at me. Then he asked, "¿Como te llamas?" I didn't understand, so I stayed quiet. He shrugged his shoulders and stepped back to his group. The other three men laughed and one of them said something in Spanish. It became apparent that they had forgotten about me and continued their conversation. My friends and I hurriedly walked off.

My friends nicknamed me "Chicano" and I hated it. The rest of the day, and days following, I heard "Chicano this" and "Chicano that." "Hey, Chicano!" greeted me as I walked to school the next morning. In my mind I seethed with anger and it grew into hate. I didn't want anything to do with those men, their tattoos and their strange language. I took that terrible shirt and threw it into the backyard storage closet. It disappeared among the other rags.

But the fist and words of that cursed shirt became unseen tatoos across my chest. While my nickname disappeared in a few days, these invisible blemishes bore into my body. They were part of my psyche. My mind muddled with questions I never asked.

In so many class discussions, many of my students predictably arrive at the hugely overstated humanistic democratic dictum, "We are all human beings." No need for Chicanos in their world.

It's a curious thing that I don't consider myself "white." I'm clearly some kind of Caucasian—to look at me. I don't look like an Indian. Where is my *mestizaje*? Does my *mestizaje* reside on my skin? In my blood? In my heart? In the way that I think? In the way that I speak? I have a brother who is darker. I have another brother who has blue eyes and light-brown hair. I have European blood. Is there such a thing as European blood? And if there is, is it pure? I never asked these questions when I was a boy. In southern New Mexico, the world where I grew up, my ethnic/racial identity was not questioned. We were *Mexicanos*. The gringos were *Americanos*. Ours was a rural, insular, poor community. Food on the table was more important than arguing identities. All we knew was the world did not belong to us. It belonged to someone else.

I became a cholo when I was thirteen years old. Now, while for many people this seems to be too young of an age to become anything but a seventh grader, anyone who has lived in the varrio *will recognize the fact that thirteen seems to be the age that most young* Mexicanos *"come of age." Entering La Cholada meant entering into a lifestyle that for many varrio youths is inevitable. But don't get me wrong. La Cholada, while holding true to many myths, can also become a valuable learning experience for the* raza *youth that grow up within it. One can come to think of it as a sort of summer camp for the young urban* Mexicanos *that can't afford or don't fit into regular summer camps. An urban Boy Scouts of sorts, where patches are replaced with scars and tattoos. And just as in the Boy Scouts, La Cholada teaches its young members to survive in a world that seems wild to them; a world that will eat them up and destroy them if they are not properly trained to handle it. . . . It is this urban lifestyle that has created the beautiful murals that adorn the walls all over the nation and it is this lifestyle that has formed such powerful organizations as the Brown Berets. But most important, it is this lifestyle that has helped to create an identity for its youth. An identity that the* raza *can grab on to and take pride in. La Cholada has helped to advance the identity of the Chicano and thus has created a pride in a people. A pride that encouraged them to struggle for their self-determination and well-being.*

A graduate student (white) asked me one day how my seminar on Chicano literature was going. "Are you making good little Chicanos?" A joke. A bad joke. I said nothing. He noticed I wasn't laughing. He changed the subject. He is an intelligent man, serious, well-read, thoughtful about many things.

My Chicano literature class that semester was full: twelve Mexican Americans, two non-Mexican Americans (both women, one of whom was British and had grown up in Africa and had immigrated to the United States and the other of whom had grown up in Latin America), no white males. The title of the class was "Chicano Literature, Culture and Identity." I was frustrated by the ethnic and racial makeup of the class. Don't "white" people who live quite literally on the border and who live in a city where 70 percent of the population is Mexican American and attend a university whose Mexican American student population is greater than 60 percent read Chicano literature? Don't they need to know anything about Chicano culture? Chicano identity? *I don't read gringo poets. You will read gringo poets or you will drop the course.*

As the years went by, I learned to love my culture, my people, my color. It did not happen overnight. But to accept being a CHICANA *took great pains. My only consolation was found in the stories of those who shared my pain, who had lived my sorrow, who had lived my disillusionment. Somehow, their stories strengthened me, everywhere I went and in everything I did. It reminded me of how much others had suffered and of how I was in a way indebted to them. I knew I could not let it go just at that. If those before could not then I had too. And all the anger that I felt, at one time, served to empower me. I found my strength and I knew my name . . . CHICANA.*

CHICANA is the name of the person who questions, who challenges, who dares, who risks. The name of the person who will not assimilate, who will not conform. This is what my father tried to teach me when I was a little girl. And this is what I learned. It is the name that says I am and will be. The word recognizes the power in the people. It embodies the anger of being discriminated against. It reminds us of how far we have to go, but does not let us forget how far others have brought us. It is the history of our people in one word.

I often thumb through Gloria Anzaldúa's book *Borderlands/La Frontera*.[3] Ever since I first read this book, I have had a running battle with Anzaldúa. I applaud her political agenda. Unlike that of Richard Rodriguez, her writing cannot be easily appropriated by the Right. She comprehends that identity is formed by a multiplicity of discourses that conflict with one another. That conflict takes root in our bodies. Like W. E. B. Du Bois, Anzaldúa intuits a split consciousness, and she scrutinizes that (self) consciousness. She confronts her sexuality, she confronts a male-dominated world, she confronts a racist society. She challenges an academic discourse by insisting on a more personal-poetic discourse. She speaks unapologetically with the voice of a woman, and it is not surprising that so many women (though her audience is not exclusively female) have championed her work. Hers is the voice of a strong feminist who seeks to empower, but her voice is not the voice of a separatist. I have no quarrels with Anzaldúa's politics. We are on the same side — she is an ally. If Richard Rodriguez is completely mortgaged to an ideology that privileges the category of "individual," than Gloria Anzaldúa is on the other end of the pole: she is the champion of communitarian thinking — something I am reticent to criticize. But ultimately, the basis for the formation of that "community" is unsettling. I find her book engaging, unsatisfying, overly optimistic, and mired in contradictions that cannot easily be overlooked.

In foraging for a usable past, she fetishizes Aztec and Indian culture. Finding solutions (and identities) by appropriating indigenous mythologies is disturbing and very problematic — but even if this were not so, Anzaldúa's project offers very little to Chicanos and Chicanas who live in mostly urban settings. At the very least, her "solutions" are inappropriate for a late-twentieth-century audience. Added to that, appropriating Aztec and/or any Indian culture in order to create a new identity is not so different from Englishmen appropriating the "classical" culture of the ancient Greeks as their own. To be sure, Anzaldúa is more closely related to indigenous culture and history than any Englishman ever was to the culture and history of the ancient Greeks. I, like Anzaldúa, have a mixed ancestry. My great-grandmother was a Tahurumaran Indian from Mexico. But for me to claim her material culture as mine rings hollow. I was raised in a far different environment, and I was formed by that environment. It is too late for me to forge a return to my great-grandmother's culture. This does not mean that I am unconcerned about the deforestation that is destroying the Tahurumaran people of northern Mexico, but I cannot mistake myself for them. I occupy a different position from indigenous peoples and I cannot borrow their identities. In wanting to distance herself from dominant European discourses, which she views as dualistic, oppressive, and racist, Anzaldúa gestures toward mythologies and cultures that I cannot believe are truly her own. Acknowledgment of mixed ancestry is not in itself problematic; it is far better to acknowledge the competing cultures we literally inherit than to base our identities on ridiculous (and dangerous) notions of "purity" and "pedigree" such as those that gave rise to Nazi Germany and the current wars of ethnic cleansing in Eastern Europe. I sympathize with Anzaldúa and I understand very well the impulse that lies behind Anzaldúa's strategy. The subtitle of her book is *The New Mestiza*. By calling herself a mestiza, she takes herself out of a European mind-set. She refuses to refer to herself as "Hispanic" — to do so would be to embrace an identity that admits no competing discourses, that admits only a European history and erases any indigenous consciousness. Her impulse is to defy that her "Indianness" has been destroyed. But her "Indianness" has been destroyed — just as mine has.

I do not find it productive to build a politics and an identity centered on "loss."

Anzaldúa, unfortunately, falls into the dualistic thinking she so eloquently critiques. To categorize the world into "European" and "indigenous" and try to bridge those two worlds under *mestizaje* is to fall squarely into "dualistic" thinking that does not do justice to the complex society in which we live.

"Consciousness" is ultimately what Anzaldúa's project is all about. If we but immerse ourselves in a particular mythology (a non-European, nonlinear discourse), then our sick body politic will be healed (*healing* is a totem word for Anzaldúa).

> It begins where it ends.
> I descend into black earth,
> dark primordial slime,
> no longer repellent to me,
> nor confining.
> The four winds
> fire welds splinter with splinter.
> I find my kindred spirits.
>
> The moon eclipses the sun.
> *La diosa* lifts us.
>   We don the feathered mantle
>   and change our fate. (198–99)

This is how Anzaldúa ends her book, her final solution. I can hardly disagree with Anzaldúa that we live in a society desperately in need of healing — though I would not choose to use that language. She firmly believes that *La diosa,* her goddess figure (whose identity remains vague but is based on the Aztec goddess Coatlicue), will "lift us." She suggests that a return to indigenous ways of thinking will "change our fate." But I find it impossible to appreciate this solution even while I understand the gesture. This is no solution. This is an escape, *not a confrontation.* To return to the "traditional" spiritualities that were in place before the arrival of Cortés and company makes very little sense. The material conditions that gave rise to the Aztec's religion no longer exist. Anzaldúa's language, her grammar, her talk are ultimately completely mortgaged to a nostalgia that I find unacceptable. The resurrection of the old gods (be they "white" or "indigenous") is a futile and impossible task. To invoke old gods as a tool against oppression and capitalism is to choose the wrong weapon.

> Yes, the Chicano and the Chicana have always taken care of growing things and the land. Again I see the four of us kids getting off the school bus, changing into our work clothes, walking into the field with Papi and Mami, all six of us bending to the ground. Below our feet, under the earth lie the watermelon seeds. We cover them with paper plates, putting *terremotes* on top of the plates to keep them from being blown away. Next day or the next, we remove the plates, bare the tiny green shoots to the elements. They survive and grow, give fruit hundreds of times the size of the seed. We water them and hoe them. We harvest them. The vines dry, rot, are plowed under. Growth, decay, birth. The soil prepared again and again, impregnated, worked on. A constant changing of forms, *renacimientos de la tierra madre.*
>
> > This land was Mexican once
> > > was Indian always
> > > > and is.
> > > > > And will be again. (91)

This passage, which ends a section in Anzaldúa's book titled "La conciencia de la mestiza/Towards a New Consciousness," is deeply disturbing to me. The pastoral tradition that she reproduces is overstated, reductive, and offensive. Like Anzaldúa, I, too, worked the land while I was growing up. Alongside my family, I picked cotton and onions, and I have no wish to represent that particular part of my life romantically in the way Anzaldúa does. The politics of "picking seasons" in this country is disgusting, and the entire system it is based on is certainly indecent, and almost entirely corrupt. The phrase "the Chicano and Chicana have always taken care of growing things" turns us into rural peasants with a deep consciousness with regard to our relationship to Mother Earth. The statement needn't be deconstructed because it deconstructs itself. More disturbingly, Anzaldúa engages in an imperialist discourse of ownership over the land with her ending "poem." The "land," whatever it was, was never "Indian," was never "Mexican." And in terms of ownership, the land will never be returned to the indigenous peoples who lived on it before the conquest. It will *never* be again. The conquest was cruel, harsh, and irrevocable. Whatever the future looks like, it will not resemble the past.

As a Chicano artist I became concerned with how, in search for my Chicano origin, I would re-create or re-present the image of Mexico. Then after surveying my fiction, I learned that I have treated Mexico's image in my Chicano writings into three categories: (a) the pre-Columbian Indian, (b) the Mestizo, and (c) Paradise lost.

My maternal Abuela, *a* Zapoteca, *told me that* Chicano *must have come from the Aztec's original name,* Meschicano. *These Indians she told me had come from the mythical Aztlan. Abuela hated Spaniards. Her Spanish husband, my grandfather, made her sleep on the floor next to his bed. And on the day he brought home a white woman, Abuela had to sleep on the kitchen floor so that the white woman could occupy Abuelo's bed. To Abuela, the Spaniard, the Frenchman, the Englishman, and later the gringo represent foreign powers that have violated the indigenous peoples. European culture is synonymous with capitalism, imperialism, and blatant oppression. Although she married my grandfather, she has never absolved him for being white.*

To Abuela, *Mexico was the cradle of a new race. Her daughter, my mother, represented the* mestizaje *process. And for me, the Chicano artist,* mi Mama *is a racial symbol. After my Spanish* abuelo *had exiled my* abuela, *Mother was reared by her Spanish grandmother and Spanish aunts. It wasn't until Mom had turned sixteen that she discovered that her grandmother was not her mother. A jealous cousin made it known to her; in fact, Mom was the only one of her sisters and brothers who was brown. Afterward, Mom crossed the river where the Indios lived. She was never allowed to go there. Now she knew why. She went into the village and found her Indian grandmother and grandfather. They embraced her and cried because she looked so much like their daughter. They showed their grandchild a yellow photograph of her mother for the first time. My mother makes my Chicano* mestizaje *undeniable.*

Abuela *didn't plan to remain in the United States. But with each passing year she found herself working in the canneries of Nebraska and Illinois, dreaming of returning to Mexico. In her dreams and nostalgia, Mexico became the longed-for past. She remembered her village where she ran freely. Her memories of Mexico were beautiful, but to me they were imaginary since as a boy I had never been there. I recall the arguments that Mom and* Abuela *had. Mother argued that* Abuela's *village as she remembered it no longer existed. Mom would grow angry with* Abuela *for fostering the traditional values and images of Mexico that had disappeared long ago. In contrast, Mom had known Mexico as a land of oppression, racism, poverty, and*

immorality. To Abuela, Mexico was Paradise calling her back. To her daugh-
ter, Mexico was a Paradise lost.

The idealization of the "Paradise lost" prepared the way for my encounter
with Mexico. Growing up with Abuela, I heard the tales of a Mexico that
falls farther and farther from the border. Nonetheless, it is where my races
are. It is where my Chicanoness originated. It is the land of pre-Columbian
Indians and where the birth of a new race took hold, a place that was once a
paradise, a paradise perhaps lost forever. Mexico calls for my encounter with it.

Like Richard Rodriguez, I have become "middle-class." I do not wear
that identity with honor. I am almost ashamed of it — given my background, it would be surprising if I wore that label without wincing. I
was recently speaking to a reading club about my novel. I mentioned
something about my ambivalence toward money — I am sometimes
ashamed of having some. "Is that a Hispanic thing?" a woman asked.
"No," I said, "it's a class thing." But there is no denying the way I live my
material existence. I do not live a peasant's lifestyle — nor do I wish to.
I do not believe anybody should live *that* lifestyle. But when I admit to
being middle-class, I do not mean that I am middle-class in the same way
as someone who was born into it — or someone who stepped "down"
into it. And I certainly do not privilege that particular identity over
others. *Chicano,* for some, is a class label — and because they associate
that word with an "underclass," they cannot flee fast enough from it.
But I refuse to associate *Chicano* with a particular class (though I must
confess, I know no rich persons who refer to themselves as Chicanos).

What makes the label of Chicano *particularly powerful in contrast to*
other labels is that the movement gained a voice in the wake of the civil
rights movement. Chicanismo gave expression to the oppression and alien-
ation of their lives. On the heels of the civil rights movement the label be-
came to refer to a political conscience which proclaimed identity, pride, self-
esteem, and they now wanted a slice of the American pie, they wanted pan
con su cafesito. *Their struggle was against the establishment; their accep-*
tance was to be achieved either through peaceful or violent means. Chicanos
were striving to assert their rights as individuals and human beings, such as
the case of Cesar Chavez and the Delano strikes, in which they tried to as-
sert humane working conditions, fair wages, and political recognition. . . .

. . . In the 80s people were more open to accepting the values of the system
of capitalism, free enterprise, and political structures. . . . Americans from Mex-

ican descent are now found in engineering, business, medicine, and science; the idea is to stay away from art, philosophy, all those liberal arts degrees. Now we have people labeling themselves Mexican American *and rejecting the label* Chicano. *They want a piece of the pie but by playing within the rules. Now it is bagel with an espresso.*

I think the term Chicano *is now an option employed by educated and cultivated Americans of Mexican descent, who are still willing to give the illusion that they still believe in La Causa. At best we are an ineffective group. Most feel that they are just plain ol' Americans, not Chicanos, not Mexican Americans. This generic label justifies whatever gains they have made and separates them from the roots which still remain underground and oppressed.*

Patricia and I learned to make tamales this year. My mother and my aunt came over to our house, and they passed on their learning, their art. We gathered some friends and made a day of it. We laughed, we talked, we enjoyed the entire production. We made an altar for *el día de los muertos,* lighting candles to our dead relatives, and it was a ritual we were comfortable with. We keep *santos* in our house, we go to Mass. Patricia and I were both raised in the generation when the word *Chicano* was something powerful and sacred — something to be whispered, something to be shouted. My group of friends threw a party when Nixon resigned. We thought we had won a great war. We celebrated too early — he resurrected before he died.

Patricia and I, we were raised in a particular time, in a particular place. In some ways, we are completely different people from who we were in those days. In other ways, we have remained close to the culture that gave us our names. We extend the rituals we were raised in, reproduce them, but reproduce them differently from the way these rituals were handed to us. The material culture we were raised in helps to center us. It is not surprising we wear *Chicano/a* with ease.

We live in the same area where we were raised. I live forty-two miles from my hometown of Las Cruces, New Mexico. Patricia has returned to her hometown of El Paso. But it would be a lie to say we returned home the same as when we left, and it would be an even bigger lie to say we returned to the same place. We cannot wear our cultural identity in the same way as our grandparents, in the same way as our parents — nor do we want to. We live in a vastly different world from that of my parents, and we want to be a part of that world. And we both know that being a Chicano is not just a neutral description of the cultural borderlands created by the meeting of two countries. *Chicano* implies a politics, and neither of us wishes to run from our politics. We want to struggle with our lives, we want to understand them. We don't want to run. We know that nothing is simple—not even the art of making tamales. That art will not save us. It is, nevertheless, a necessary ritual. A material reminder of a material history.

I was listening to the evening news when Tom Brokaw announced the death of César Chávez. Even now, I can hardly express what that man meant to me, what he means for me still. As I sat in front of the television set that day, I was surprised to find that I was weeping. Perhaps I was remembering the journey that has been my life, and the place César Chávez had played in my coming to political consciousness. So much of his life's work was exposing the ugly way we go about doing business in this country. I am sorely tempted to romanticize his life, but such a romanticization would do him, and his cause, a great disservice. It is an easy thing to admire César Chávez. It is not an easy thing to continue to struggle with hard questions. Too often, we soften our own experiences, react to them, and forget to *think* about them. Maybe that day, listening to the news of César Chávez's death, I was weeping not for the loss of that man's life, but because I wondered where the struggles of the civil rights movement have taken us. For me, it has been a painful journey, no less for me than for Anzaldúa, Rodriguez, and the students whose voices I have interwoven into this essay. But examining my own identity, my own relationship to the word *Chicano,* I must refuse to fetishize my own cultural background. Chicano cannot, must not, be simply a marketing label. I detest "radical chic." In fairness to Richard Rodriguez, I too have been accused of benefiting from affirmative action. I criticize him for running away. I have entered the site of struggle. I was born to it. I am one of the combatants. I cannot pretend I am neutral. I cannot pretend that I am above the identity and culture wars of the late twentieth century. I am, at times, a happy warrior—at other times, a reluctant participant. I am sometimes perfectly at ease discussing the harsh topics of race and ethnicity. At other times, I am full of rage. And sometimes, I just want to take a hot shower, have a drink, and think of nothing at all. But I always come back to the questions.

What Was It All For, Anyway, César, César Chávez?

It was as if you were born already
Knowing you belonged to the kingdom
Of the working damned, the lost land
Of bent backs where short hoes and pesticides
Were worshipped, adored as if they were
Images of La Reina de los Cielos.

César, genetic memory
Is fine (if you go for that sort
Of thing. So California). But you never knew
When to quit, just never learned how to give up
The brittle bones of the dead. Like some obsessed
Archaeologist, you were always digging up
Another anonymous worker: González. Herrera.
García. Hernández. They only exist now as names
On hieroglyphics, untranslatable into pedestrian
English. And, César, they were all
The same, all from a tribe with a particular
Genealogy, all from a long line of drones
Bred for service, bodies destined for picking,
Bodies with instincts for bending.
Descartes's dictum did not apply.
Not to them. They were not meant for thinking.
They knew only the language of work. And they were
Lucky to have jobs, no? What did they have
Without the labor this fertile country gave?

They died
Of natural causes. You say they died of work.
But work *is* a natural cause, César. Even writers
Die of work. Work. I can hear you laughing.
Nothing personal, I know. Go ahead and
Laugh. And anyway, who taught you how to spell
The word *injustice*? People hate it when you use
A word like that. Such a big word, César.
Too big for you. You, who loved the fight, who
Shoved back when you were shoved, you, César,

Should have known better, should have used a more
Flattering strategy. You wore that word out *Injustice*.
It made you sound accusing and superior. Not smart,
César, people got nervous. People hated you
Because you spelled it out—one lettuce
At a time. You told them what it meant.
Literate people don't like to be corrected.
People like food, César. They don't want
To know where it comes from. Don't politicize
Picking seasons. Already, They've politicized
Sex and sexual attractions. And now our Food?

* * * *

You. More popular in death than in life (though
Some confuse you with that other Latin fighter
Who fights opponents he can beat. There's a lesson
There, César). You. Large as the California sun.
In death. You. Heroes are better manipulated when
They no longer have a voice to intervene in
The making of their own mythologies. Listen, César,
People are lining up just to say they touched you,
Wiped the sweat off your brow in the days when you
Were battling Goliath with a sling. *I was there. I*
Marched with him. He was my hero—and the rest
Of us listen, nod seriously. Some of us even
Weep. The ritual is all such good theater.

You're an icon, now,
Sabes? And nobody gives one damned minimum-wage
Dollar that you broke your fasts by going
To communion at your local Catholic Church.
The Body of Christ did not save your causes.

I have a picture.
Of you. I ripped it from a glossy, New York
Mag. The man who took it, more famous than you.
You don't look like a saint or a prophet. You
Look like an ordinary mestizo who is fashionably
Unfashionable. A star, César. Now, no one
Knows why you fought.

In the Lone Star State, *Hopwood v. the University of Texas* threatens to
end any "race"-based scholarships in the state of Texas. Reverse discrim-

ination — that's what they call it. If people without jobs resent people who are rich, is that reverse discrimination? If the worker resents the landowner, is that reverse discrimination? If a woman who is raped detests the man who raped her, is that reverse discrimination? Why is it we refuse to acknowledge that the "affirmative action" debate is based on position and entitlements? Who exactly is entitled to what — and who is positioned (regardless of merit) to receive those entitlements? There is a group of people (mostly white and always upper- and middle-class) who firmly believe that they are the true heirs — that they are entitled to the riches of America. When the entitled are threatened, they fight back. They call the rest of us racists because we, too, want a piece of the inheritance.

I did not grow up with that sense of entitlement. I was one of the barbarians at the gate. I have to laugh at the anxiety caused by affirmative action, refuse this hateful accusation that I hold a job only because I am a Chicano: in the fall of 1992, I became the second "Chicano" to be hired in the English Department at the University of Texas at El Paso — this in a university where more than 60 percent of the students are "Hispanic." Call me cynical, but if our M.F.A. program in creative writing had not had a bilingual dimension attached, I doubt very seriously that I would have landed this job. I have nothing to base this on *except our past hiring practices.*

Once, after a reading, a young woman gave me a note in which she pleaded with me to stop "criticizing" the United States. "Criticize Mexico instead — criticize your own country." The young woman must have been confused as to the country of my genesis. Mexico is not my place — the United States is *my* place (and I resent having to make that point). It is perhaps too easy for me to criticize the country in which I was born and in which I live, easy because I detest "nationalisms" (though I will not pretend to be free of all nationalist discourses and influences). But isn't it true that it is a nationalist discourse that is most offended by the name *Chicano*? A nationalist discourse demands complete acquiescence. You are allowed only one name: American. We are all so sure we know what that label means. To some it means erasure.

No one is born with an "essential" identity. Identities are produced, and they make sense, they have meaning, only in the cultural context of their production. I spent the summer of 1985 in Tanzania. Tanzanians referred to me as *Mzungu* (the word in Swahili for European). I was not differentiated from the other *Mzungus*. To them, I was as white as my "white" friends from Oklahoma and Kansas. And, living there for a summer, I felt "white." I felt European. *I was European.* It was a painful and difficult thing to admit to myself. I studied for four years at the University of Louvain in Belgium. I never felt very "American" when I was growing up in southern New Mexico, but in Belgium, I felt American. *I was American.* That, too, was a painful and difficult thing to admit to myself. *Chicano* in those years meant nothing. There was no context, no social or political necessity for that identity. But it was my time in Europe and my summer in Africa that taught me that I did not belong in those places. I was a foreigner there — and would always be a foreigner. I came to the conclusion that I had a people — that I belonged to a people, a community. When I returned to the United States, *Chicano* became important again because in the place to which I had returned, the inequalities of my society were everywhere to be found. My aim as a person, as a citizen, as a writer, as a teacher, as a Chicano, as a critic, has had, at least for the past ten years, a political project: to help create a "radical democracy." Like my students, I would like to live in a world where "we are all equal," a world where fragmentation isn't the operative modus operandi. I know this is utopian thinking (but I was one of those people who loved Karl Marx precisely because he was a utopian thinker — in 1996 are we allowed to invoke his name?). If I were to let go of my "Chicano" identity, then I would be complicit in the lie that we have arrived at the day of equality. Chicano — the word echoes with a particular history, but that word also exists to condemn our social and political failures. Chicano — it is an identity that waits for the day that it is no longer necessary.

Notes

1. This and other italicized portions of this narrative are excerpts taken from students' responses to an assignment in a "Chicano Literature, Culture, and Identity" graduate seminar that I taught in the spring of 1994 at the University of Texas

at El Paso. I asked each of the participants in the class to address in writing the following topic: "My relationship to the word *Chicano*." I informed my students that I was working on an essay exploring Chicano identity and asked their permission to publish some of their responses. Each student was more than willing to participate in such a project.

2. Richard Rodriguez, *Hunger of Memory: The Education of Richard Rodriguez* (New York: Bantam, 1983), 170–72. Page numbers for further quotations from this work appear in parentheses in the text.

3. Gloria Anzaldúa, *Borderlands/La Frontera: The New Mestiza* (San Francisco: Aunt Lute, 1987). Page numbers for further quotations from this work appear in parentheses in the text.

THREE

On the Border with *The Pilgrim*: Zigzags across a Chapl(a)in's Signature

Louis Kaplan

Pilgrim, n. A traveler that is taken seriously.

AMBROSE BIERCE, *The Devil's Dictionary*

Introducing Chapl(a)in

In the annals of silent film comedy, there is neither a more beloved nor a more invested signature than Charlie Chaplin's. It is literally legendary in that the signature carries its legend along with it. The mythos of Charlie Chaplin has established a fixed context of description and association over the past decades in the mere mention of the proper name or its illumination upon the silver screen. It connotes an entire cast of outcast roles—the little tramp, the pantomimic clown, the nomadic vagabond—with each and every inscription.

In reviewing *The Pilgrim* (1923), the critic Robert E. Sherwood discusses how Charlie Chaplin's art of disguise in this film adds other variations to this repertoire of roles to function as a thinly veiled autobiographical reflection: "Thus, when Chaplin impersonated a convict who disguised himself in clerical garb, he approximated autobiography" (1971 [1923], 107). For Sherwood, the double impersonations of convict and cleric serve to cancel each other out and leave Chaplin straddling approximately in the middle with a rather dubious doubter's identity. "He has retained the identity of Charlie Chaplin; he has remained an agnostic, in the most inclusive sense of the word" (107). Although I have no argument with the end result of Sherwood's appraisal, his analysis overlooks the orthographic operator that structures this shift in signification as applied to *The Pilgrim*. Slightly altering Sherwood's terms, this essay is an attempt at Chaplin's "bio-auto-graphy," or one that organizes a reading of *The Pilgrim* through a play of its signatures and focuses on the comic slippage induced on account of its wavering signature border. This essay focuses on the manner in which the surname of the starring signature scripts the narrative structure of *The Pilgrim* and plays upon a series of identity borders (e.g., cultural and geoterritorial) in the process. But to undertake this analysis, the viewer must overhear the last name and introduce a homophonic overtone into it. Like the filmic genre in which Chaplin is animated, this letter will be silent. It will be seen, but never heard. With the addition of the initial letter of the alphabet, the clown's proper name is led into religious service. As luck and as language would have it, his signature is haunted by a holy writ. There is the man of the cloth in the guise of the tramp in rags. There is a black frock and a white collar lurking in the black-and-white prisoner's stripes. In this borderlining manner, Chaplin faces off with chaplain.[1]

This speculation upon a silent letter and its comic effects is not so far-fetched. For one commentator, the setting up of a slight or silent difference that plays along and with a border is at the metaphysical basis of Chaplin's conception of comedy in general. Chaplinesque humor depends upon such disparities in conjunctions. It involves "a slight difference in the action, or between two actions, which brings out an infinite distance between two situations, and which serves only to bring out that distance" (Deleuze, 1986, 169). Starting from this assumption, the French philosopher Gilles Deleuze reviews how the narrative action and the comedy of *The Great Dictator* (1940) are played out between the physical convergence of the Jewish barber and the Tomanian dictator and the infinite distance between victim and executioner. In *The Idle Class* (1920), where the double-dealing Chaplin plays both Charlie (the impoverished tramp) and Mr. Charles (the rich alcoholic), there is again disparity in the conjunction that qualifies both of these characters for membership in the idle class. In *The Pilgrim* (1923), a slight difference in a signature, or between two signatures, brings out an infinite distance between two situations and serves only to bring out that distance. Between Chaplin and chaplain, or — to go out even further on an allegorical limb fraught with Christian underpinnings—between a thief and a savior, this is the wandering path of *The Pilgrim*.

There is a repeated gesture in *The Pilgrim* wherein this initially silent letter writes itself upon the moving body of the agnostic protagonist in prayer cloth. It is a hand signal that carves out the excessive letter that is up for grabs and in contention. This sign ritualistically accompanies the pilgrim on his wanderings. Whether he is walking past the train station, on the way to the chapel, or giving his sermon, his hands always assume this prayerful pose. In light of Renaissance art history, this pose recalls both the signature and the representation of A. Dürer's infinitely reproducible drawing *Die betenden Hände* (*The Praying Hands*). In line with the effects of the signature and its filmic writing, it is necessary to read these hands as a graphic symbol, as carving out a literal letter. In the contemplation of these scenes, this gesture will be read as an inverted *A*. And when it is read as right side up (as in the pose of prayer), the *A* becomes the hieroglyph for the institution of the church itself and its idealist aspirations at ascendance unto the heavens. Indeed, a close inspection of the stage set that frames the minister's pantomimic and parodic sermon shows the pseudochaplain standing at a church pulpit between two windows, each of which carves out this initial graphic inscription.[2]

In addition to the comic slip implicit in Chaplin's signature, the silent *A* enters the film in another way. This involves the play that it weaves at the homonymic border of *border* and *boarder*. In this oscillating movement, it is as if the Chapl(a)in character were attempting to stabilize the wavering of the signature border by assuming the role of boarder, and thereby attempting to incorporate the silent *A* in this fashion. The first time this occurs is quite early in the film, when the befrocked gentleman is prevented from riding hobo-style under the train (and over the tracks) in classic Chaplin tramp fashion. The conductor escorts him to the proper carriage with this directive: "This is where you will be boarding." However, since this role necessarily involves a parasitic relationship, the attempt at stabilization as boarder is doomed to failure. This is clearly the situation at the Brown family residence later on in the film, where the visiting preacher has been invited to lodge before finding a more permanent dwelling in the community. Here the unexpected

Figure 3.1. The Chapl(a)in's sermon in *The Pilgrim* (1923). Image courtesy of the Museum of Modern Art/Film Still Archives.

entrance of the quasi-chaplain's old partner in crime, Howard Hunting-ton, who manages to sleaze his way into the role of lodger as well, forces his fellow boarder to confront once again the uneasy border on which his own double identity is perched (in terms of its deceitful disguise) and from which he cannot escape so easily.

In each of these scenes, *The Pilgrim* offers and withdraws the letter *A* in straddling the border between Chaplin and chaplain. This is the let-ter the protagonist does not know whether to add to his name, as well as whether it will still spell out Chaplin if and when added. Or, posed otherwise, *The Pilgrim* exposes the *A* that has been residing in his proper name from the very beginning. It is in mediating and meditating upon the addition of this silent *A* in Chaplin that the comic plot of *The Pil-grim* turns and sets into motion its intricate play upon bioautographi-cal, geopolitical, and cinecultural borders.

Plotting *The Pilgrim*

The Pilgrim is a comedic case study in the mistaking of identities or the overlaying and overdubbing of these identities in Chapl(a)in. Once upon a time there was a Chaplin, an outcast and an escaped convict who stole the costume of a chaplain while that holy man was bathing in a river. The newly befrocked convict as clergyman boards a train to the "no-man's-land" of Devil's Gulch in the vicinity of the Texas-Mexico bor-der in order to get as far away as he can from the law.[3] But instead of the clerical disguise providing an infinite distance from identity, the Chap-lin figure is brought into the greatest proximity with the law through the simulacrum of his signature. Upon leaving the train, he stumbles right into the hands of a congregation eagerly awaiting the arrival of their new chaplain and who take the disembarking cleric as their man for the job.

Now he must fill the role and play the part of the minister to the fullest under the name of Phillip Pim. Like a latter-day Hester Prynne, he must recoup, incorporate, and recover the silent *A* in his identity and become a chaplain, and in the process he must repress the charac-teristics of the convict as much as possible. But, of course, the repressed returns with a vengeance — crossing over the signature border and cross-ing up the chaplain in the process. The remnants of this cast-off signature in the form of old and bad habits slip back into the narrative to stage comic effects. While overlooking the specific slip of the signature effect, Donald McCaffrey's analysis does allude to how the comedy in *The Pilgrim* depends upon the reversion of roles and the resurfacing of "worldly ways" that contradict the character's new ideal and otherworldly status. "Much of the comedy evolves from the bogus minister's embarrassments when he reverts to his old ways before stuffy, small-town people" (1971, 86–87).[4] To cite just one instance, the reverend, who appears quite nervous about his upcoming sermon, takes out a cigarette to relieve some of the tension until he sees reproach in the eyes of the elders and has to repress his smoking urge. Recalling the priestly calling, he goes on to deliver a rousing silent sermon based on the biblical story of David and Goliath. Straddling the fence once again between hero and villain, the doubly divided Chapl(a)in assumes and enacts both roles in this amusing classic of pantomime.

Although this is the only explicit use Chaplin ever made of an Old Testament narrative,[5] it is obvious that this particular story acquires allegorical significance for his entire body of comic work, because it depicts the victory of the little fellow and underdog against what seem to be overwhelming odds. It is not surprising to learn that Rudolf Arnheim's review of *The Great Dictator* in 1940 takes up this biblical story in evaluating the terms of the struggle between Charles Chaplin and Adolf Hitler. In Arnheim's transposition of political allegory, the comic Chaplin is depicted as using the intellectual weapons of satire and ridicule (replacing David's stones and slingshot) to take aim at the brute force of the overpowering Nazi regime. "Chaplin had seemed the David who could meet this Goliath with weapons of the spirit, with ridicule."[6]

As in the pantomime in *The Pilgrim*, Chaplin also plays both roles in *The Great Dictator* and, of course, these roles parallel the biblical figures — the Jewish barber as the heir of David pitted against the Tomaniac Goliath, Adenoid Hynkel. Likewise, Hannah Arendt, another German-Jewish émigré who found refuge in the United States, could not resist making the same analogy in her own incorporation of the Chaplin character into a Jewish pariah tradition. Fitting quite nicely into the comedy of disguise at the basis of *The Pilgrim*, Arendt's discussion of the tramp, written in 1944 against the backdrop of the Nazi genocide as a work in progress, is headed "Chaplin as Suspect." Arendt projects onto Chaplin the hope that mind could somehow triumph over matter in sparking a Jewish resistance that would demonstrate how "the human ingenuity of a David can sometimes outmatch the animal strength of a Goliath" (1944, 111).

Now, Chaplin himself also makes explicit reference to this biblical story in a rare literary selection that serves as his ode to "Nowhere," but, unlike his German-Jewish interpreters, the pilgrim journeyman is unable to project himself into any singular identification. In this rhapsodic prose piece signed in the name of Charlie Chaplin, the nomadic wanderer and sad clown dreams of a land beyond the borders of strife where the lamb and the lion — in the forms of David and Goliath — will lie down together in peace and harmony. In addition to his overt reference to the sermon staged in *The Pilgrim*, Chaplin also refers to *The Gold Rush* (1925) and *The Immigrant* (1917) through idealized images that allude to a life beyond struggle. All in all, the vagabond subject riding this "ship of dreams" gives vent to a paradoxical logic that attempts to articulate the other of the border (i.e., "Nowhere"):

> "Nowhere." This is my country. In its port, the ship of dreams drops its anchor. There no rope bars the tired wanderer an exit from the verge of hardship [*Bord der Mühsal*]. There the hunt for gold comes to an end. David and Goliath live side by side in brotherhood. (Chaplin, in Burger, 1929, 7)[7]

It is interesting to point out that the country of Mexico assumes this same idealized and utopian character for the briefest of moments in the final scene of *The Pilgrim*. When he realizes that the sheriff has set him free south of the border, new horizons beckon to our hero. The intertitle reads, "Mexico. A New Life. Peace at Last." But this wish at release quickly undergoes comic deflation when the shootout of some bandits sends the pilgrim scampering back to straddle the borderline.

When the scene shifts from the David and Goliath sermon at the chapel to a Sunday-afternoon tea party at the Brown residence, the pilgrim has become more adapted to his sacred role. In fact, the roles are reversed with the arrival of Howard Huntington (alias Nitro Nick, alias Longfinger). Recognizing his old prison mate, Huntington assumes the swindle in the parson and the chance to share in a monetary killing.

However, Chapl(a)in defends the church funds and puts himself between the long-fingered one and the money until Nitro Nick overpowers the little guy and escapes with the loot. Nevertheless, this Christian act is by no means a clear-cut action. The mistaking of identities and the bor-derlining continue even at this juncture. From the side of the law (i.e., the point of view of the sheriff or of Mrs. Brown's lovely daughter), Nitro's theft and Chaplin's flight after him might be interpreted as the biggest con job yet.

The conclusion reestablishes the ambivalence of the shuttling signa-ture. The pilgrim returns the money to the Browns, but only by com-mitting another theft. Although this establishes a narrative context where David triumphs over Goliath, he plays the good Samaritan only by go-ing outside the bounds of the law rather than by turning the other cheek. There is only one thing for the good-hearted sheriff to do to restore some semblance of order. Sheriff Byran takes the Chapl(a)in to the Mexico-U.S. border and advises his charge to go and pick some flowers on the other side of the line. The lawman is in the process of riding off into the sunset when the obedient tramp — too deceptively innocent to take the hint — comes running back in pursuit of the sheriff with flow-ers in hand. The undaunted sheriff now drags him back to the border and gives his prisoner a swift kick into freedom, or, at least, outside the bounds of his official jurisdiction.[8]

The narrative ends with the signature effect that was its condition of possibility restored to its indecisive equilibrium. Although the pardoned convict breathes a sigh of relief in Mexican territory, this is rather short-lived, for he appears to be caught in the cross fire between two bandits. The final image of the film shows Chapl(a)in receding into the distance, straddling the borderline of both the geographic territories and his own symbolic landscape as he negotiates the line between the law and the outlaw.[9]

Straddling the Final Frontier

The last, poetic image of The Pilgrim has been the subject of numerous critical interpretations over the years. Many have seen it as a kind of metacommentary on the existential condition of the pilgrim and have associated that specific journey with Charlie Chaplin in both his life and filmic writing. Thus, the receding figure represents "the eternal pilgrim in search of a place in the world,"[10] "a symbol of the eternal pilgrim on the tragic roads of the world" (Huff, 1952, 156), or his unstable and border-straddling position foregrounds "the eternally precarious situation of the homeless and stateless refugee" (Asplund, 1976, 132). One notices how all of these statements link the pilgrim with eternity — and therefore with the boundless and borderless. However, these readings overlook in technical terms how the illusion of eternity is generated by (and as) a cinematographic trick that coincides with the closure of the film itself, which is its condition of possibility. Appropriately enough, the bulk of criticism dealing with the famous final borderlining image has offered two ways of going — either as an allegory for Jewish diaspora or within the narrative conventions of the genre of the Texas-Mexico border film.

Jewish Nomadism

The final image of the pilgrim as stateless and homeless refugee links up with the myth of the diasporic and nomadic Jew as eternal wanderer.[11] Although *The Pilgrim* stages the wandering figure squarely within the Christian tradition, there has been a temptation to co-opt it into a matrix of interpretation that links Chaplin to a Jewish sensibility or even with Jewish identity. Adolphe Nysenholc makes just these connections in "Charles Chaplin and the Jewish World" (1991). Shortly after informing the reader that the tramp "will thus be quite naturally associated with the wandering Jew," Nysenholc invokes an unstable figure that implicates *The Pilgrim* in a description of Chaplin's scenography ("a Chaplin scenario is a zigzag line"). Then he offers a direct reference to the film. His retrospective interpretation would seem to transpose the problematics of *The Great Dictator* and Jewish statelessness onto *The Pilgrim* and the Texas-Mexico border. Although Nysenholc continues to speak in universal terms of homelessness, there is no denying that the specific (and unspeakable) fate of European Jewry acts as one point of reference for this reminder: "But when, in the closing scene of *The Pilgrim*, Charlie flees, straddling the borderline between the U.S. and Mexico, chased by the sheriff on one side, and driven back by guerilla fighters on the other, unable to find refuge anywhere, one can not but be reminded of the fate of the homeless and stateless, expelled from wherever they seek to settle" (19). The plight of the pilgrim as homeless refugee might be set off against the globe dance in *The Great Dictator*, where the dictator's mad desire for total territorial domination and Jewish diasporic decimation would put the whole world into his hands.[12]

But the question of Jewish identity not only raises the figure of the expelled wanderer who straddles the border, it also constitutes a topic for heated debate in regard to Chaplin's own identity for which there are no easy answers. To put it quite bluntly, some critics argue that the figure of the wanderer enters into Chaplin's artistic expression as leitmotiv precisely because it is an expression of his own concealed diasporic Jewish identity.[13] In his own lifetime, both anti-Semites like T. W. H. Crosland[14] and philo-Semites like Ludwig Davidsohn in the encyclopedic *Jüdisches Lexikon*[15] claimed a Jewish genealogy for Charles Spencer Chaplin. Even leading Mexican film critic Emilio García Riera (1990, 132) gets into the act by classifying Chaplin as a Jew in his epic six-volume work on the image of Mexico in foreign cinema. Indeed, one might be inclined to say that the wide-ranging speculations about Chaplin's Jewish identity constitute another wavering borderline around which the Chaplin myth has been constructed as it weaves fact and fabulation to the point where, amid a vast body of literature on the subject, the complete resolution of the genealogical mystery has been rendered a near impossibility.[16]

The German-Jewish literary critic Walter Benjamin also takes up the question of the border as it pertains to *The Pilgrim* in a short review titled "Rückblick auf Chaplin" (Looking back at Chaplin) published in 1929. Rather than focusing on the issue of Jewish nomadism and borderlining per se, Benjamin's analysis of the film's European reception focuses on the crossing up of film genres or how the spinning of *The Pilgrim*'s hinges transforms comic tears of laughter into tragic tears of sorrow. Benjamin reports on a peculiar sobbing screening of *The Pilgrim* in postrevolutionary Russia wherein the Communist internationalist audience breaks down and cries, and, paradoxically, shows its own true national colors by means of this tear-jerking incident:

> Chaplin confirms with his art the old recognition that only a world of expression that is determined socially, nationally, and territorially in the

strictest manner finds a largely irreducible and, indeed, highly differentiated resonance from folk to folk. In Russia, the people cried when they
saw *The Pilgrim*, in Germany they are interested in the theoretical side of
his comedies, and in England they love his humor. (1972[1929], 119)

It is not just that Benjamin's Soviet screening poses a reversed reading
of *The Pilgrim* as a film that belongs to something other than the comic
genre. In this scenario, the Marxist-messianist Benjamin finds resonance
with a Communist-inclined Chaplin and his *Pilgrim* exactly at the point
where the film crosses over the territorial border into Russia and, thus,
into the nation that represents the internationalist longings of that age.
But, paradoxically, this gesture is made only to underscore national and
cultural differences. In the heart of the Soviet other, *The Pilgrim* flips,
or crosses borders, from comedy to tragedy.

Benjamin's swift allusion returns to *The Pilgrim*'s own theoretical concern with borders and reinforces the connection between the German
interest in Chaplin and the problematics of *The Pilgrim*. Countering
the simplicity of a reading that would valorize the universal appeal of
the little tramp, Benjamin argues for the folk group as the national, social, and territorial unit by which artistic understanding must be expressed and differentiated. But Benjamin's enlistment of national differences in the reception of Chaplin's art (in its Russian, German, and
English guises) remains decidedly Eurocentric in that it excludes the
very borderline at stake in the plot of *The Pilgrim*. It ignores the cultural and historical specificity of the Texas-Mexico borderline circa 1923
and the memorable scene of its traversal that plays out this same tension between national borders and borderless ideals.

Tex-Mex Borderlining

In staging the final scene on the Texas-Mexico border, *The Pilgrim* taps
into and puts into play the narrative conventions of Hollywood that
make this site the primary locus of cinematic action. Following the investigations of García Riera, Gary Keller notes in *Hispanics and United
States Film* that "the border functioned in United States film as a no
man's land where Puritan values were severely relaxed and anything
was possible in the way of sex or romance, violence, drugs, conspiracy,
desertion, or hide out" (1994, 84). This analysis is particularly apt when

applied to the plot and structure of *The Pilgrim,* where the comedy of the Chapl(a)in figure depends specifically upon a criminal type posing as a puritan minister and as "the tale of an escaped prisoner who swiped a parson's clothes."[17]

While David Maciel's study *El Norte: The U.S.-Mexican Border in Contemporary Cinema* focuses for the most part on films since 1970, his introductory remarks are relevant for opening up the range of associations that haunt the Texas-Mexico border image and the importance of the cinema in shaping that image:

> Beginning in the late 19th century and continuing throughout the 20th century, writers and media production specialists have portrayed the U.S.-Mexican border as a lawless, rugged, individualistic, and perilous area populated by men and women of action, criminals and crime fighters, settlers, and others who sought a last frontier.... While other cycles or subject matters in North American or Mexican films have come and gone, the depiction of *la frontera* in films has been continuous over time. There is no greater cultural manifestation of the general image and widely held perceptions of the U.S.-Mexican border than the cinema. (1990, 2)[18]

Already in 1909, *On the Border* set the symbolic terms and the cultural stereotypes into motion by depicting how an Anglo "vigilance committee" secured the border from badmen to enforce the formulaic dichotomy of American law versus Mexican lawlessness. Alfred Richard Jr. notes that "it was probably the first production to present Mexico as the refuge for those hardened criminal types of any nationality or breed that required a place to hide out for a while until things cooled off" (1992, 16). Given the peculiar laws prevailing at the time, American law enforcement officers were not allowed to follow criminals across the Rio Grande. In this light, the final scene of *The Pilgrim* must be understood as a comic staging of this historical and film narrative convention that both alludes to and mocks the instantiation of Mexico as criminal refuge. Recall how after the sheriff escorts his charge to the border and encourages him to pick some flowers on the other side, the borderlining Chaplin cannot take the hint or follow the conventional script and comes running back across the border to make his personalized floral delivery. In a similar manner, the scene in which the pilgrim retrieves the Browns' money from Howard Huntington while disguised as a western badman during a robbery already in progress must be understood as a parodic doubling of the cinematic and cultural image of the borderlands as the place where one has to take the law into one's own hands. As Richard notes further, "From the very earliest times, the 'border' came to be associated with all forms of violence. It was a zone in which anything could, and would take place, a place free from the responsibilities and restrictions of North American law" (16).

Interestingly, the cinematic portrayal of the border between the United States and Mexico in *The Pilgrim* as an open frontier without any guards or checkpoints was accurate. Although it might appear delirious today, Chaplin could have charted an unchecked path at the Texas-Mexico border in 1923 like the one that he straddled at the Southern California set where *The Pilgrim* was shot. Indeed, García Riera informs us that such borderlining without reserve was possible until 1924. Thus, *The Pilgrim* is located not only at the tail end of a period of Chaplin's filmic production (at First National), but also at the conclusion of an epoch in the history of frontier relations between Mexico and United States. García Riera's remarks also underline the construct of the Texas-Mexico border as a no-man's-land—an unclaimable and improper site of mix-ups and crossovers that serves quite well as the deterritorialized condition of possibility for the Chapl(a)in signature effect and the comic confusions that are inscribed in *The Pilgrim*:

> The conflict-torn border between Mexico and this territory consisting of the current states of California, Arizona, New Mexico, and Texas would stay open until 1924, permitting free travel on the part of the characters of the Western—vaqueros and cowboys, Mexican and gringo bandits, *rurales* and rangers, Yaqui or Apache Indians, ranchers and cattlemen, fugitives—into a sort of no man's land, sometimes deserted, on other occasions brimming. (1987, 21)[19]

But despite the "open" border maintained between the United States and Mexico, the Mexican authorities unsuccessfully sought to bar *The Pilgrim* from distribution in Mexico on account of its final frontier sequence. It is interesting to note in this specific sociohistorical context that the Mexican government instituted in 1922 a new policy of banning—or at least threatening to ban—films that it deemed to be derogatory to the image of Mexico. Unlike the uproar in Pennsylvania, where *The Pilgrim* was judged to be a mockery of clerical values, the controversy in Mexico focused on the film's negative ethnic stereotyping of that country as a country of bandits and badmen. Although the ban focused for the most part on violent "greaser" movies, a couple of comedies were singled out.[20] An article that appeared in *Moving Picture World* in 1923 reported that the Mexican government had lodged an official complaint against First National's *The Pilgrim* and *The Bad Man* as purveyors of a distorted national image. The sensationalist headline coupled Douglas Fairbanks (who had starred in *The Mark of Zorro*) with his colleague Charlie Chaplin for special mention: "Mexico Bars Any Film of Charlie's or Doug's, Punishing for Kidding Country in Past Pictures."[21]

Such a gesture of censorship on the part of the Mexican authorities misses the ambivalence of stereotypes in a comic film whose implementation mocks negative stereotypes through exaggeration and distortion as much as condoning them.[22] After all, *The Pilgrim* is not some conventional Hollywood border movie that deploys the negative stereotype of the *bandido* or the badman to racialize the border and to spread divisiveness.[23] Its comic vacillation is much more sophisticated. Indeed, Chapl(a)in's straddling of the border in the final image demonstrates that he cannot run away from the *bandido* aspect (or the clerical aspect) of his signature and that he carries that crossroads with him wherever he goes. In this way, Chaplin's comedy of culture deploys a strategy of vacillation along an unstable border that envisions each figure or type in *stereo*.[24] Hence, *The Pilgrim* and its ambivalent use of comic stereotype is perpetually borderlining and remains anathema to the territorial demands and unitary imperatives of the state authorities. Astride the final frontier, the authoritative decree of the Mexican government to police or control the border and to ban the film is challenged by the narrative action of *The Pilgrim* itself and its crossing up of the territorial borders.

The Pilgrim's Signatures

With the plot of *The Pilgrim* and its border straddling in place, it is time to introduce the aliases or the alternative names of the splitting personality in the starring role. The significance of the identities assumed by Chapl(a)in leads *The Pilgrim* seeker to a further unraveling of the narrative structure that follows the twists and turns of the Chapl(a)in's signature. These aliases are embedded into the graphic unconscious of this silent film's narrative and relayed through the modern communications media of posters, telegrams, and newspaper headlines. Each of these assumed names illuminates a constellation of significance reverberating throughout the film.

Escaped Convict

This sign constitutes the first image of the film. It involves the framing of a photographic reproduction of Chaplin by means of a Wild West wanted poster. The film begins with the slapping on and the sticking up of a poster by means of a handheld glue brush, which rubs in and draws extra attention to the trademark of a slapstick mustache that it resembles. This gesture spells out Chaplin loud and clear. Here is a full-frontal mug shot of the pursued in two-toned prisoner's stripes. But the posted announcement registers the view that he will not be pinned down so easily. Above his head, one reads the attributive heading "Escaped Convict."[25] Assuming these words as his own proper reference, one sees that the split of the signature effect in *The Pilgrim* is established from the outset. This defines the difficulties in determining whether *The Pilgrim* has set out in search of a convict who has already escaped or of an escapee who has already been convicted. The wanted poster introduces the quest for identity (and for conviction) that *The Pilgrim* narrates in its hilarious attempt to close this gap and the pseudonymous distance that remains in the trail of its signatures on a wavering border that resists such closure.

When Charles Chaplin, as an older and more neutralized Swiss resident, revived and reedited *The Pilgrim* in 1959 as part of the so-called Chaplin Review (which also included *Shoulder Arms* [1918] and *A Dog's Life* [1918]), he wrote a new sound track for the film that included a country-and-western ballad recorded by popular singer Matt Munro. Chaplin titled this song, in a rather overdetermined manner, "Bound for Texas" (Robinson, 1985, 595). With this musical selection, the question of straddling the (Texas-Mexico) border receives an extra dimension in the song's title and its quadrupled refrain. Adding to the dilemmas of the escaped convict, Chaplin lyricized the adventurer's longing for the wide-open country in terms of the dangers and traps that threaten to tie things up or to imprison him further. "I'm bound for Texas, bound for Texas, bound for Texas land. To hear the moo and rattle of snakes and cattle, I'm bound for Texasland." The double bind of the word *bound* in the title and lyrics of the song articulates "Texasland" as the *pilgrimatic* state of a frontier zone that joins/separates freedom and subjection, nomadic wandering with a captive destiny from which there appears to be no escape.[26]

There are also points in the film where the escaped convict comes up against borders and barriers that recall his problematic position with comic overtones. Early in the film, when he steps up to the counter to buy a train ticket, he impulsively grabs on to the bars that separate customer and ticket seller and that serve as unconscious reminder of the remainder of his other identity. This also links up with the moment when the convict's first blindfolded attempt to select a faraway, "getaway" destination on the board leads to the ironic choice of Sing Sing prison. Later on, he is leaning on a picket fence in front of the Brown residence and flirting with the daughter of the family when Huntington breaks into the romantic scenario. As Chapl(a)in reluctantly shakes the professional pickpocket's hand, he finds that his own gets stuck for a moment between two pickets. Again, this gesture serves as a subtle reminder of the difficulties the escaped convict has in crossing the border to make a clean break and to free himself from a life behind bars.

Lefty Lombard

For any chap in or around London, Lombard is a street paved in pounds. Lombard Street locates the capital of British financial exchange. It is the district formerly occupied by Lombard bankers and still containing many of the chief banks and the money market. For *The Pilgrim*, it is also the site of an exchange. As the quasi parson sits on the train, he catches a glimpse of his shadowy brother and former identity trying to catch up with him. He sees the newspaper headlines and the same incriminating photograph of the prisoner's mug shot staring him in the face. The split of the signature occupies the entire screen, with the chaplain in the cloth on the left and the Chaplin in the prison stripes on the right. Taken aback by this sudden scene of recognition, he spits his drink across the divide, dispensing an expulsive baptism upon his splitting image. At this juncture, the newspaper announces the traces of but one of the signatures left behind in the name of Lefty Lombard:

> Convict Makes Daring Escape: Lefty Lombard Alias Slippery Elm Leaps into Drain Pipe in Dining Hall of Prison and Escapes through Sewer: $1000 Reward Offered: Guards Stand Petrified with Astonishment as Prisoner Makes Leap — Believed to Be Part of Wholesale Escape Plan.

Lefty Lombard might be considered as a left-handed banker, as someone who has taken the left-handed path of banking in bank robbing. But this left-handed path leads *The Pilgrim* to a turnoff where the supposed and suspected thief may have returned to a more sacred practice of saving. The alias of Lefty Lombard might be taken as a key for unlocking the dynamics of the scene, which sets the rates of the Chapl(a)in exchange on a most problematic course. After Nitro Nick has stolen the loot and has left Lefty unconscious in the middle of the floor, the thief flees to the saloon to celebrate. It is here that Chapl(a)in engages in some left-handed banking of his own. First, there is another exchange of identities in the quick transformation of the clerical frock and hat into a western outlaw style that seems more suited to saloon wear. But as he enters the bar, he finds that another robbery is already in progress. Chaplin proceeds to steal from a thief who is being held up by thieves. Lefty Lombard poses a dilemma. Whether posing as one of the bandits, as a thief in his own right, or on the side of the right and just in his thievery, the poetic license taken by Chapl(a)in's signature in the guise of Lefty Lombard leaves open all of these possibilities.

Slippery Elm

Another means to figure a signature gone on pilgrimage comes in the form of Slippery Elm. Assuming this alias, Chapl(a)in slips into the role of the medicinal inner bark of the North American red elm tree. Slippery Elm must be contrasted with the stiffness and paralysis of the stone-faced prison guards who constitute a veritable petrified forest when they stand astonished at the prisoner's daring escape. The curative practice of Slippery Elm lies neither in the *con* (left) nor in the *curé* (right), but in the way that he makes the leaps that mark the space between. Contra Bunyan's, this is the large-soled pilgrim's egress. Slippery's signature already prefigures the uneasy stance during the final but inconclusive Tex-Mex borderline scene. There, the dividing borderline stands out as a vertical marker in the form of a wooden pole labeled "international." This sign provides another way to stage what is at stake in the shifting moves of the Slippery Elm. It marks the no-man's-land that belongs neither to the right nor to the left, neither to Mexico nor to the United States, neither to Chaplin nor to chaplain. As he straddles the line between the United States and Mexico, the Chapl(a)in figuratively becomes a slippery elm — a mobile tree that carves out the middle as a moving border. The pilgrim posits the inter- as the excess or the surplus of the national. If one imagines this post as a moving frontier, it would become the vectorial passage to be cut out by the slippery one or his double. But given that the waddler in the oversized shoes — like the drunkard — always has a problem in walking the straight line, the more appropriate figure for the Slippery Elm lies rather in the zigzag.[27] That is why Deleuze's analysis recalls this passage as the pilgrim's "zigzagging along the frontier between America where the police are on the lookout for him, and Mexico, where bandits are waiting for him" (1986, 170).

This move is not unique to *The Pilgrim,* but returns again and again to the point where this narrative strategy of an ending to evade all endings might be dubbed Chaplinesque in character. Indeed, the borderlining of *The Pilgrim* is packaged carefully between two other open road endings separated by a span of twenty-one years. Having been thrown out of their makeshift and ready-made house, the latter-day tramp and his lady take to a highway divided by a broken stripe. The *Modern Times* (1936) travelers draw the arrow by walking hand in hand and dividing the middle between them. Or, jumping back to the conclusion of *The Tramp* (1915), he departs with his back to the camera, dividing between himself his hobo bag in the left hand and his walking stick in the right hand. Like *The Pilgrim,* both *Modern Times* and *The Tramp* take the pilgrimage in flight as the means to stage an ending.[28]

The slippery dynamics of the final Texas-Mexico border scene and the mistaking of identities in *The Pilgrim* also haunt the narrative structure of *The Great Dictator* in a number of significant ways. It should be pointed out that the climactic moment of *The Great Dictator,* where the accidental yet inevitable switch of identities between the Jewish barber and the German dictator—and, on the metahistorical level in terms of the genealogy of mustaches, between Chaplin and Hitler[29]—takes place, is at the geographic borderline between Tomania and Austerlich. It is on an open road at the crossroads between Tomania and Austerlich where the escaped convicts (the German resister Schultz and the Jewish barber), who have just fled the concentration camp disguised in the stolen uniforms of Nazi officers, are taken by the border guards to be Hynkel and his henchman in the process of leading the invasion into Austerlich. In historical terms, this scene offers a thin disguise of Germany's actual annexation of Austria, or the so-called *Anschluss* of 1938. Meanwhile, on the other side of this mix-up, Hynkel/Hitler is depicted as duck hunting in a pond dressed in Bavarian garb when his boat capsizes, and he is subsequently mistakenly arrested as the concentration camp escapee. This harks back elliptically to the parson in *The Pilgrim,* who is bathing in the river when his clerical outfit is stolen by the escaped convict. Nevertheless, there is a major difference in the use of the border in these two films, and this is related directly to the nature of their narratives. *The Pilgrim* involves the straddling of the Texas-Mexico border because it narrates the zigzagging course of one character mediating between two identities (convict and clergyman). *The Great Dictator* enacts the double cross (which serves as the symbol of Hynkel's political party) because it relies on the crossing up and exchange of two characters and their identities (barber and dictator) even though they are played by the same actor.

The Great Dictator refers to its own double crossing of the borders from the very beginning by means of a satirical disclaimer. The opening title reads: "Any similarity in appearance between the Tomanian dictator and the Jewish barber is purely coincidental." This statement must be viewed as a parody of the conventional line that attempts to maintain a strict border between the inside and the outside of filmic writing. Thus, any similarity between fictional characters on reel and factual characters in the real (whether living or deceased) is said to be mere coincidence. The first subversive thing that Chaplin's disclaimer does is to posit this border as something internal to the filmic text itself. In a film that turns on a case of mistaken identity, this similarity in appearance is a necessary precondition for the comedy. Using the external frame of reference as arbitrator, this disclaimer appears patently absurd given the fact that both the Jewish barber and the Tomanian dictator are played by the same actor—Charles Spencer Chaplin. In other words, coincidence is converted into necessity from the perspective of the real that appears to solve the riddle of the reel. But, unfortunately, the double cross does not stop at this point, because the real is also exposed to the same doubling danger.[30] Chaplin's positing of the internal border is a cover for the existence of another level of simulation whereby life imitates art. The first disclaimer conceals a second one that locates a wavering border in the real itself. Thus, "any similarity in appearance between Adolf Hitler and Charlie Chaplin is purely coincidental." In these ways, the double dealings of *The Great Dictator* expand upon the case of mistaken identity established in *The Pilgrim*.

Philip Pim

The Right Reverend Philip Pim represents the flip side of the coin of Lefty Lombard. This is the prim and proper name of the pilgrim in his religious guise. It is obvious that this name establishes a rhyming resonance with the title of the film—that is, Phil Pim the pilgrim. It is the calling of the theologically inclined parson who has been sent to the border town of Devil's Gulch to fill up its lack of religiosity. But, as *The Pilgrim*'s narrative is (shiftily) constructed, it is the escapee who fills in for Phil by playing at substitute preacher and as a filmic Pim.

While it may sound a bit excessive or may even tempt the evils of anachronism, it is necessary to analyze the proper name of the cleric with the addition of another *p* at the end and as a pimp. This permissive and prophetic reading profits in the scene of the sermon, which draws unseemly connections between the church and the theater. One begins to entertain the proposition of the preacher as panderer who solicits his clients through the collection box, who performs his pulpit theater like a Shakespearean actor or mime, and who returns to take his final bows like curtain calls as he holds on to his performative profits. Between Pim and pim(p)—as between Chaplin and Chapl(a)in—

the split of the signature shuttles between the salvation and the prostituting of souls.

The permissive reading of Pim also finds corroboration when one studies the early scenarios and notes for the film when it was generically titled *Western.* In this early version, the escaped convict, disguised as a minister, arrives in the Wild West town of Hell's Hinges, where he begins to preach a new kind of reform religion that capitalizes upon entertainment values and stresses the need for rather loose adaptations. Satirizing the routines of 1920s radio evangelism in Los Angeles and anticipating the tenets of televangelism, the proto-Pim's program recognizes that the church must appropriate the latest avant-garde tendencies and media technological inventions in order to succeed in modern times. It is a matter of making the rituals of "vice" and "decadence" work in the service of religious rites. Playing the part of Protestant impresario, Phil Pim fills up the church pews. Chaplin biographer David Robinson outlines the radical reforms of the new preacher and their popular success: "His programme for reform is to replace the church organ with a jazz band, to perform the hymns in ragtime and to introduce other attractions such as motion pictures and dice games for the collection. As a result, the saloon empties while the church fills up" (1985, 296). At the end of this warped moral tale, the law manages to catch up with the pseudoevangelist, who is arrested and sent back to prison, to the complete dismay of his totally hooked congregation.

The Pilgrim's Hinges

In Charles Chaplin's personal history as a filmmaker, *The Pilgrim*— which was finished in September 1922 and released in February 1923— resides at a borderline between two periods of his career. It stands as the last film he did for First National Company before he was free to make films for United Artists, the corporation that he founded with D. W. Griffith, Douglas Fairbanks, and Mary Pickford. Given this fact, the final borderline scene takes on added dimensions, and some critics have commented upon this additional biographical connection (Maland, 1989, 62). In fact, one of the working titles for the film, *The Tail End,* offers a humorous commentary on the termination of Chaplin's contract with

First National even as it alludes to the borderline at the end point of the tale (Robinson, 1985, 296). Chaplin's clipped discussion of *The Pilgrim* in *My Autobiography* (1964) pays no attention to the plot or thematics of the film, but instead focuses on the business end of things and on the slippery and successful negotiations involved in terminating his legal obligations to the First National Company. Nevertheless, whether he knows it or not, this procedural review of the negotiations and their give-and-take depicts both a border crossing (i.e., the move from First National to United Artists) and a work of doubling (i.e., *The Pilgrim* taking the place of two feature films) and thereby mimes the central themes of *The Pilgrim* narrative. Furthermore, the focus on monetary rewards (or the more than four hundred thousand dollars that "frees" up Chaplin) might be placed in relation to and in sharp contrast with the first image of *The Pilgrim,* in which a thousand-dollar reward is posted for the capture of the tramp as escaped convict.

> Completing the last three pictures seemed an insuperable task. I worked on *Pay Day,* a two-reeler, then I had only two more films to go. *The Pilgrim,* my next comedy, took on the proportions of a feature-film. This again meant many irksome negotiations with First National. But, as Sam Goldwyn said of me: "Charlie is no businessman—all he knows is that he can't take anything less." The negotiations terminated satisfactorily. After the phenomenal success of *The Kid,* I met little resistance to my terms for *The Pilgrim.* It would take the place of two films and they would give me a guarantee of $400,000 and an interest in the profits. At last I was free to join my associates in United Artists. (Chaplin, 1964, 318)

As mentioned, *The Pilgrim*'s site was set in and on Hell's Hinges in an earlier version of the script, before the name was changed to Devil's Gulch. Indeed, the narrative structure of *The Pilgrim* appears as if it were set on hinges. These are the hinges that connect and divide heaven and hell. It describes the hinged signature effect at the crossroads of Chapl(a)in—what connects and divides hellish sinner and heavenly priest. The story spins its hinges so fast that the poles might no longer be differentiated.[31] They seem to touch one another. *The Pilgrim* poses the possibility of understanding both the outlaw and the preacher as nomadic wanderers and wayfarers on earth who travel the path of nonbelonging. This rapid oscillation produces the consideration of strange exchanges and crossovers. In this way, *The Pilgrim* meditates upon both the sacred action of the clown and the clownish actions of the clergyman.

In the same way that the preacher of conviction keeps brushing up against the law no matter which way he turns, *The Pilgrim* too had its own troubles with the laws of Pennsylvania on account of its derisive and satirical portrayal of the Protestant clergy. Sherwood's review of the film focuses on the irony entailed in this censorship decision by shifting the terms from Chaplin's satire of the ministry to the self-parody always already implicit in the clerical profession itself:

> Perhaps the most hilarously humorous aspect of *The Pilgrim* was provided by the Pennsylvania censors, who barred the picture from the sacrosanct State because, said they, it made the ministry look ridiculous. A number of interested observers have been waiting, since then, to hear that the Pennsylvania censors have suppressed several thousand clergymen on the same charge. (1971[1923], 109)[32]

Nevertheless, *The Pilgrim* hearkens back to a rich pre-Reformation tradition that flourished in French medieval times of the so-called jocular preachers, such as Oliver Maillard and Michael Menot, who understood the usefulness of wit in the service of Christian mass pedagogy and who had no problems reconciling the dual roles of clown and clergyman.[33] In *Curiosities of Literature*, Isaac D'Israeli describes how the sermons of these "pious buffoons" in their rhetorical combination and contamination of "grave declamation and farcical absurdities" sought the widest possible audience. D'Israeli expounds about such "jocular preachers" as follows: "In a word, these sermons were addressed to the multitude; and therefore they show good sense and absurdity" (1839, 91). The aim at mass consumption and the mixture of grave sadness with comic farce establishes interesting parallels with the cinematic arts of this century and the film comedy masterpieces of Charlie Chaplin.

After-Images: Making Chaplin History and Precedent

In *The Writing of History,* the French historiographer Michel de Certeau discusses the proper place of history as located somewhere between "criteriology" and "legend." To illustrate this point, he invokes the final image of *The Pilgrim* as a metaphor for locating the disciplinary site of history as a borderline or a marginal zone that negotiates between the demands of epistemology and the lure of fiction. In this manner, de Certeau's theoretical staging of history gives way to the final image of Chaplin's *The Pilgrim*:

> If history leaves its proper place — the *limit* that it posits and receives — it is broken asunder, to become nothing more than a fiction (the narrative of what happened) or an epistemological reflection (the elucidation of its own working laws). But it is neither the legend to which popularization reduces it, nor the criteriology that would make of it merely the critical analysis of its procedures. It plays between them, on the margin that separates these two reductions, like Charlie Chaplin at the end of *The Pilgrim,* running along the Mexican border between two countries both chasing him in turn, with his zigzags marking both their difference and the seam joining them. (1988, 44–45)

In de Certeau's extended metaphor, Charlie Chaplin stands for history (although, given all the waddling and the zigzagging depicted, the invocation of the straight and the vertical might not be the best way to convey this particular idea). Whereas de Certeau titles this section "History as Myth," it might be alternatively called "Chaplin as History." This involves not merely a consideration of Chaplin making history, for de Certeau literally makes Charlie Chaplin into history — the amusing clown Charlot as somehow the postmodern variant of the ancient historical muse, Clio.

Unlike de Certeau's conversion of Chaplin into the border of history separating legend and epistemology, this essay (and its speculations upon the silent *A*) has explored Chaplin's signature in *The Pilgrim* as a wavering border that moves between convict and chaplain. For it is neither the outlaw to which the tramp would reduce it nor the holy man who would make of it merely sacred law. It plays between them, on the margin that separates these two reductions. In this way, this essay has moved the level of border analysis to some extent from history (or biography) to signature (or bioautography). Whether taking the devilish path of the Biercian serious[34] or taking it lightly, *The Pilgrim* charts the plan of escape and the escaping of plans for a Chapl(a)in's signature. This is the paradox of a "wholesale" signature permanently threatened as a soundproofed simulacrum of itself and on the verge of a head-on collision with what it might or might not take to be its own. But in the meantime, this signature will have generated comic interference patterns in its straddling of the borderline.

It is interesting to consider how the image of the straddling Chapl(a)in at the conclusion of *The Pilgrim* resonates to some extent with the rhetoric of recent borderlands theorists such as Renato Rosaldo and Gloria Anzaldúa, who have advocated the multiple formation of hybridized and hyphenated identities at the crossroads and in the interstices of the territories marked and mapped out as Texas and Mexico. For Rosaldo, this process might be referred to as a process of transculturation. He writes in (and of) "Border Crossings": "Creative processes of transculturation center themselves along literal and figurative borders where the 'person' is crisscrossed by multiple identities" (1989, 216). Meanwhile, in the preface to her autobiographical *Borderlands/La Frontera,* Anzaldúa articulates a position that evokes Chapl(a)in's pilgrim if only he were able to constitute himself as a speaking subject: "I have been straddling that *Tejas*-Mexican border and others, all my life. It's not a comfortable territory to live in, this place of contradictions" (1987, n.p.). Her study advocates a vision of a new hybrid mestiza consciousness cutting across the border of Texan and the Mexican that "depends on the straddling of two or more cultures" (80). Although the present analysis has focused on the straddled staging of the signature effect in "Chapl(a)in" rather than upon lived experience in the production of meaning, there are some connections to be made with Anzaldúa's construct of *los atravesados.* In other words, a tentative alliance might be forged between these crossover characters and the filmic figurations of the little tramp. Thus, it is possible to imagine the referent of the word "here" in the following sentence inhabiting both a Charlie Chaplin film retrospective and Anzaldúa's *Borderlands/La Frontera*: "*Los atravesados* live here—the squint-eyed, the perverse, the queer, the troublesome, the mongrel, the mulato, the half-breed, the half dead; in short, those who cross over, pass over, or go through the confines of the 'normal'" (3). Rather than being blacklisted as the contraband article that must be outlawed from Mexico for negative ethnic stereotyping, Chapl(a)in is hereby reclaimed and reconfigured within the framework of borderlands theory as a "genuine" *atravesado* that crosses up and over.

Later on, Anzaldúa addresses the mortal combat in the borderlands between the dominant and the subjugated cultures as a struggle between "the cop and the criminal." In this way, she figures the contest through the same forces that bisect the pilgrim who straddles the border between Sheriff Byran and the *bandidos*. But this pairing of border characters comes up against its limit when Anzaldúa makes the case for a healing synthesis that will breed a new matrix of reconciliation: "At some point, on our way to a new consciousness, we will have to leave the opposite bank, the split between the two mortal combatants somehow healed so that we are on both shores at once and, at once, seeing through serpent and eagle eyes" (78–79). Despite all the seeming similarities between Chapl(a)in's and Anzaldúa's straddlings, the attempt at synthesis points to an irreconcilable difference. Although there may be an idealistic moment in Chaplin's filmic writing, this tendency is constantly undercut by comic deflation and its release of explosive laughter. The comedy of *El Peregrino* may proceed to the point where violence is deflected into slapstick, but never to where it can be sublated into reconciliation. To see through serpent eyes and eagle eyes is rather to see through the cross-eyed antics of Chapl(a)in's comic gaze. In this respect, his *atravesado* remains a schlemiel peregrinating in a wavering world of comic cutups and trickster antics who fails to cut it as a borderlands theorist.

Outtake

If narrative is considered the pilgrimage undertaken by a film, then *The Pilgrim* narrates the zigzagging pilgrimage undertaken by the Chapl(a)in's signature.

Notes

1. The signature pun is implicit in one recent account of the film. "As the film opens, Charlie has escaped from prison . . . and steals a minister's clothing: Charlie becomes a chaplain" (Maland, 1989, 61). Nevertheless, most commentators do not bother to attend to the signature play at the center of the narrative of *The Pilgrim*.

2. For a penetrating analysis of the "graphic unconscious" in a number of film classics, see Tom Conley's *Film Hieroglyphs* (1991).

3. As far as the geoterritorial coordinates are concerned, the railway board that shows the train's transcontinental passage locates the imaginary crossroads of Devil's Gulch as somewhere between Dallas and San Antonio. The series of stops along the

line run as follows: Dallas, Devil's Gulch, San Antonio, El Paso. This close reading of the train junctions in conjunction with the map of Texas reveals that there has been a taking of cartographic liberties in *The Pilgrim* in that there is a territorial gap of hundreds of miles before one would get to the Texas-Mexico border that provides the film with its final and most famous image. It is also interesting to point out that in his megabiography of Chaplin David Robinson gets the name of the town wrong, substituting a dead man for the duplicitous devil: "Stealing the clothes of a bathing parson, he arrives thus disguised in the town of Dead Man's Gulch, where he is mistaken for a new minister" (1985, 297).

4. According to McCaffrey, the use of "genteel comedy material" is a rare exception for Chaplin and aligns *The Pilgrim* with the comedy of Harold Lloyd in films such as *Grandma's Boy*.

5. Stan Brakhage argues in his essay on Charlie Chaplin in *Film Biographies* that *The Kid* (1921) implicitly deploys the biblical story of the sacrifice of Isaac. Brakhage also alludes to "the slaying of Goliath by David as the greatest pantomime of [Chaplin's] entire career" (1977, 137).

6. Rudolf Arnheim's review of *The Great Dictator* in *Films* (Winter 1940) is quoted by Robinson (1983, 129). To cite another comparison between the two films, Chaplin's final speech takes the place of the David and Goliath sermon in the earlier film.

7. This quote is from Charlie Chaplin, "Nirgends," in Burger's *Charlie Chaplin* (1929). As I am unable to locate the English original, the translation is my own. The same idealistic dream is expressed in Chaplin's speech in *The Great Dictator* in its attempt to shift the terms of debate from the shifty "double cross" to the affirmation of the *inter-*. "Now let us fight to free the world—to do away with national barriers" (Chaplin, 1964, 434).

8. One should notice the structural symmetry in the film, wherein the sheriff's booting of Chapl(a)in across the border (to the right) perfectly counterbalances an earlier kick (to the left) that Chapl(a)in gives to an obnoxious little boy as he is about to enter the kitchen of the Brown residence.

9. At this juncture, it would be useful to recall certain contrasts with a more recent border film that utilizes the Texas-Mexico frontier to stage its opening rather than its ending. Wim Wenders's *Paris, Texas* (1984) begins with the nomadic and lost wanderer Travis (played by Harry Dean Stanton) crossing over the border from Mexico into Texas (to a fictional town named Talingua rather than Devil's Gulch), where he collapses. After he is taken to a hospital, the doctor in attendance begins the dialogue by asking the traveling Travis the following pointed question: "Do you know which side of the border you're on?"

10. This quote comes from Wim van Leer, "Notes to Showing of *The Pilgrim* at Haifa Film Club" on April 22, 1961, file titled "Notes on 'The Pilgrim'" in Jerusalem Cinemateque Film Archives, Jerusalem, Israel.

11. It should be noted that the Nazi propaganda film *Der ewige Jude* (The Eternal Jew), which cast Jewish nomadism as demonic evil, appeared in the same year (1940) as Chaplin's *The Great Dictator* and its attempt to defend both Jewish folk-life and folk against the Nazi onslaught.

12. The scene also recalls a classic Jewish joke of the same period that captures the specific fate of homeless and stateless Jewish wanderers and makes the question of the globe the center of its comic speculations. "It is 1938 and an Austrian Jew, sensing Hitler's imminent takeover of his country, is considering various options for emigration. He goes to a travel agent for advice, and the agent takes out a large globe and begins discussing the entry requirements of various countries. It soon becomes clear that many of the options are beset with difficulties. One country requires a labor permit; the second country does not recognize the Austrian passport; the third has a strict money requirement for new arrivals, while the fourth doesn't want any immigrants at all—especially not Jews. Finally, in desperation, the Jew asks, 'Haven't you got another globe?'" (Novak and Waldoks, 1981, 61).

13. The first chapter of Marcel Martin's biography, *Charles Chaplin* (1966), takes matters at face value and is titled "Le Juif Errant" (The wandering Jew). I personally find it most amusing to point out how Martin speculates in a footnote upon an Anglicizing (or rather "Aryanization") of the proper name of the Chaplin family upon arrival in London: "On songe évidemment a une 'aryanisation' du nom de Kaplan [Obviously one muses upon an 'Aryanization' of the name Kaplan]" (10). In addition, Adolphe Nysenholc (1979) argues explicitly for a Jewish Chaplin, which includes allying his comic art to the schlemiel tradition.

14. The British anti-Semitic writer T. W. H. Crosland spreads the Jewish gospel and gossip as follows: "I suppose the Jews will not take it as an offense if I mention that the most popular living 'Ebrew gentleman is one Charles Chaplin, 'King of the Movies.' Pretty well everybody 'goes to the pictures' nowadays, and everybody knows 'Charlie' though everybody doesn't know that he happens to be one of the Children of Israel" (1922, 155).

15. The biographical entry reads: "Chaplin, Charles Spencer, one of the most famous film actors of our times, born in 1889 in London as the son of an Eastern European Jewish family that moved to England in the middle of the 19th century and that originally bore the name Thonstein" (Davidsohn, 1927, 1329). It should also be noted that the Nazis always referred to this genealogy in their anti-Semitic propaganda against Chaplin. For more details on this front, see Hanisch (1991).

16. For another discussion of the "Jewish question" as applied to Chaplin's enigmatic identity, see Guateur (1969). It is also important to point out that in his exhaustive biography, Robinson (1985) dismisses the Jewish Chaplin legend to the point that he does not even bother to mention it.

17. This is how the advertisement for *The Pilgrim* reads in a two-page spread in *Moving Picture World*, January 27, 1923. *The Pilgrim* is also reviewed in this same issue by C. S. Sewell, who lists among its comic virtues "the final scenes where the sheriff has a hard time getting him over the Mexican border." The film also garners favorable comment in the trade journal in the March 3 (90), March 10 (238), and March 17 (364) issues (there is a publicity still of Chaplin posing as the pilgrim in the last of these issues; 376).

18. Maciel looks at recent Hollywood productions dealing with the issues of illegal immigration and drug smuggling, such as *Borderline* (starring Charles Bronson) and *The Border* (starring Jack Nicholson and Harvey Keitel).

19. The original text reads: "La conflictiva frontera con México de ese territorio, formado por los actuales estados de California, Arizona, Nuevo México y Texas, estaría abierta hasta 1924; eso permitiría el transito libre de los personajes del *western*—vaqueros y *cowboys*, bandidos mexicanos y gringos, *rurales* y *rangers*, indios yaquis o apaches, rancheros y *cattlemen*, fugitivos—por una suerte de *no man's land* desértico en ocasiones y fluvial en otras." The translation is mine.

20. For a full discussion of the administrative dynamics, see Delpar (1984).

21. The purported source of this headline is *Moving Picture World*, January 27, 1923. Although Richard (1992, 279) and Keller (1994, 85) both refer to it in their film synopses of *The Pilgrim*, they see it as a most appropriate and unproblematic action on the part of the Mexican government.

22. This same categorical dismissal of ethnic stereotyping as negative occurs in Maciel's reading of *Three Amigos* and his advocacy of that film's censorship: "Bad comedy and gross stereotyping reached new heights even for Hollywood in *The Three Amigos. . . .* It is no surprise that the Dirección General de Cinematografía in Mexico has barred all of these films. One will never see these border comedies shown commercially in Mexico. For once, a justification could be made for censorship on the basis of quality or offensiveness to the nationality, character, and culture of a country" (1990, 67–68). This approach should be contrasted with Christine List's (1992) excellent study of the contestatory use of comic stereotyping in the films of Cheech and Chong.

23. For discussion of the *bandido* as stock negative caricature, see Pettit (1980).

24. My thanks to Scott Michaelsen for his electronic intervention recalling how in the scripting of *The Pilgrim* "both sides of the border—the *stereo*—are produced as types in the signature."

25. In this regard, *The Pilgrim* is closely aligned to the beginning of *The Adventurer* (1917). As Theodore Huff comments in his *Chaplin* biography, "Significantly, both of these films start *not* with an incarcerated victim but rather with an already escaping Charlie" (1952, 44).

26. Roger Manvell writes of *The Pilgrim*'s paradox that makes the chaplain as imprisoned as the convict: "Charlie is now the prisoner of his disguise" (1974, 125).

27. Chaplin refers specifically to this laughable figure of misaligned mobility (and his attempt at concealment) in the essay "What People Laugh At": "Even funnier however, is the man who, having had something funny happen to him, refuses to admit that anything out of the way has happened, and attempts to maintain his dignity. Perhaps the best example is the intoxicated man, who, though his tongue and walk give him away, attempts in a dignified manner to convince you that he is quite sober" (1971[1918], 48).

28. For a critical discussion of the endings of these films and their quality of theatrical exaggeration, see Tichy (1974, 73–75).

29. For the definitive excursion about the double crosses on the levels of both character and caricature engaged by *The Great Dictator,* see Bazin (1985[1945], 15–19). The essay was originally published in France shortly after the end of World War II.

30. Uwe Naumann's *Zwischen Tränen und Gelächter* reproduces an amazing wartime illustrated comic by Oscar Berger titled "Hitler and Chaplin at 54" that pro-

vides a double reading of their two careers in tandem as "the man who tried to kill laughter" versus "the man who made the world laugh" (1983, 403).

31. This spinning upon hinges provides another way of thinking about why it is impossible to pin down the final straddling scene as any "racializing" of the border between "American law" and "Mexican banditry."

32. David Robinson slightly alters Sherwood's account and adds to the list of religious grievances in *Chaplin: The Mirror of Opinion*: "In some quarters *The Pilgrim* ran into trouble with censors and church authorities. In Atlanta the Evangelical Ministers' Association demanded its withdrawal as 'an insult to the Gospel.' In South Carolina the Daniel Morgan Klan of the Knights of the Ku Klux Klan protested at the showing of the film on the grounds that it held the Protestant ministry up to ridicule. The Pennsylvania Board of Censors eliminated so many scenes that it virtually constituted a ban on the film" (1983, 65).

33. For a full historical account of this phenomenon, see Menache and Horowitz (1994).

34. In an essay that speculates on the pilgrim's path and the centrality of the Texas-Mexico border, the wanderings and the strange disappearance of the American literary wit Ambrose Bierce should not be forgotten. It was Bierce's fate to cross the border in 1913 with the wish to be a part of the Mexican Revolution and never to be heard from again.

Works Cited

Anzaldúa, Gloria. 1987. *Borderlands/La Frontera: The New Mestiza*. San Francisco: Aunt Lute.

Arendt, Hannah. 1944. "The Jew as Pariah: A Hidden Tradition." *Jewish Social Studies* 6: 99–122.

Asplund, Uno. 1976. *Chaplin's Films: A Filmography*, trans. Paul B. Austin. New York: A. S. Barnes.

Bazin, André. 1985. "Pastiche or Postiche; or, Nothingness over a Mustache." In *Essays on Chaplin*, trans. and ed. Jean Bodon, 15–21. New Haven, Conn.: University of New Haven Press. (Reprinted from *Esprit*, November 1, 1945.)

Benjamin, Walter. 1972[1929]. "Rückblick auf Chaplin." In *Kritik und Rezensionen*, vol. 3, *Gesammelte Schriften*. Frankfurt: Suhrkamp.

Brakhage, Stan. 1977. *Film Biographies*. Berkeley, Calif.: Turtle Island.

Burger, Erich. 1929. *Charlie Chaplin: Bericht seines Lebens*. Berlin: Rudolf Mosse.

Chaplin, Charlie. 1964. *My Autobiography*. New York: Simon & Schuster.

———. 1971. "What People Laugh At." In *Focus on Chaplin*, ed. Donald W. McCaffrey. Englewood Cliffs, N.J.: Prentice Hall. (Reprinted from *American Magazine* 86 [1918]: 34, 134–37.)

Conley, Tom. 1991. *Film Hieroglyphs*. Minneapolis: University of Minnesota Press.

Crosland, T. W. H. 1922. *The Fine Old Hebrew Gentleman*. London: T. Werner Laurie.

Davidsohn, Ludwig. 1927. "Charles Spencer Chaplin." In *Jüdisches Lexikon*, vol. 1. Berlin: Jüdischer Verlag.

de Certeau, Michel. 1988. *The Writing of History,* trans. Tom Conley. New York: Columbia University Press.

Deleuze, Gilles. 1986. *Cinema: The Movement-Image.* Minneapolis: University of Minnesota Press.

Delpar, Helen. 1984. "Goodbye to the 'Greaser': Mexico, the MPPDA, and Derogatory Films, 1922–1926." *Journal of Popular Film and TV* 12: 34–41.

D'Israeli, Isaac. 1839. *Curiosities of Literature.* London: Ward, Lock.

García Riera, Emilio. 1987. *México Visto por el Cine Extranjero 1894/1940,* vol. 1. Guadalajara: Universidad de Guadalajara Ediciones Era.

———. 1990. *México Visto por el Cine Extranjero 1970/1988,* vol. 5. Guadalajara: Universidad de Guadalajara Ediciones Era.

Guateur, Claude. 1969. "Notes sur l'énigme Chaplin." *Image et Son* 229: 38–55.

Hanisch, Michael. 1991. "The Chaplin Reception in Germany (Brilliant Comedian and 'Jewish Film Clown')." In *Charlie Chaplin: His Reflections in Modern Times,* ed. Adolphe Nysenholc, 25–33. Berlin: de Gruyter.

Huff, Theodore. 1952. *Charlie Chaplin.* London: Cassell.

Keller, Gary D. 1994. *Hispanics and United States Film: An Overview and Handbook.* Tempe, Ariz.: Bilingual Review.

List, Christine. 1992. "Self-Directed Stereotyping in the Films of Cheech Marin." In *Chicanos and Film: Representation and Resistance,* ed. Chon A. Noriega, 183–94. Minneapolis: University of Minnesota Press.

Maciel, David R. 1990. *El Norte: The U.S.-Mexican Border in Contemporary Cinema.* San Diego, Calif.: San Diego State University.

Maland, Charles J. 1989. *Chaplin and American Culture: The Evolution of a Star Image.* Princeton, N.J.: Princeton University Press.

Manvell, Roger. *Chaplin.* 1974. Boston: Little, Brown.

Martin, Marcel. 1966. *Charles Chaplin.* Paris: Editions Seghers.

McCaffrey, Donald W. 1971. "An Evaluation of Chaplin's Silent Comedy Films, 1919–1936." In *Focus on Chaplin,* ed. Donald W. McCaffrey. Englewood Cliffs, N.J.: Prentice Hall.

Menache, Sophia, and Jenny Horowitz. 1994. *L'rire en l'eglise.* Paris: Labor et Fides.

Naumann, Uwe. 1983. *Zwischen Tränen und Gelächter: Satirische Faschismuskritik 1933 bis 1945.* Köln: Pahl-Rugenstein Verlag.

Novak, William, and Moshe Waldoks, eds. 1981. *The Big Book of Jewish Humor.* New York: Harper & Row.

Nysenholc, Adolphe. 1979. *L'Age d'or du comique: Sémiologie de Charlot.* Brussels: University of Brussels.

———. 1991. "Charles Chaplin and the Jewish World." In *Charlie Chaplin: His Reflections in Modern Times,* ed. Adolphe Nysenholc. Berlin: de Gruyter.

Pettit, Arthur G. 1980. "The Cinematic Degradation of the Mexican, 1894–1947." In *Images of the Mexican American in Fiction and Film.* College Station: Texas A&M University Press.

Richard, Alfred Charles, Jr. 1992. *The Hispanic Image on the Silver Screen: An Interpretive Filmography from Silents into Sound, 1898–1935.* New York: Greenwood.

Robinson, David. 1983. *Chaplin: The Mirror of Opinion*. Bloomington: Indiana University Press.

———. 1985. *Chaplin: His Life and Art*. London: Collins.

Rosaldo, Renato. 1989. *Culture and Truth: The Remaking of Social Analysis*. Boston: Beacon.

Sherwood, Robert E. 1971. "*The Pilgrim*." In *Focus on Chaplin*, ed. Donald W. McCaffrey. Englewood Cliffs, N.J.: Prentice Hall. (Reprinted from *The Best Moving Pictures of 1922–23*, ed. Robert E. Sherwood, 59–62. Boston: Small, Maynard, 1923.)

Tichy, Wolfram. 1974. *Charlie Chaplin in Selbstzeugnissen und Bilddokumenten*. Reinbek bei Hamburg: Rowohlt.

FOUR

The Time of Translation:
The Border of American Literature

David E. Johnson

> What philosophy of translation will dominate in Europe? In a
> Europe that from now on should avoid both the nationalistic
> tensions of linguistic difference and the violent homogenization of
> languages through the neutrality of a translating medium that would
> claim to be transparent, metalinguistic, and universal?
>
> JACQUES DERRIDA, 1992

In the Latin Americas, wherever they are, there are, perhaps still to come,
two steps to the border. These two *pasos* will have been thought under
the auspices of two proper names whose propriety goes unquestioned:
Paz and Borges. They will have taken sides where perhaps there are none.

In any case, the juxtaposition of Paz and Borges, of two relationships
to modernity, has been most recently suggested by Néstor García Canclini in *Culturas híbridas,* in which he poses the problem of their relation as one of the direction of their work, writing of Paz, "Queremos
entender por qué a uno de los promotores más sutiles de la modernidad
en la literatura y el arte latinoamericanos le fascina retornar a lo pre-
moderno [We want to understand why one of the most subtle promot-
ers of modernity in Latin American literature and art is fascinated with
returning to the pre-modern]" (1990, 98; 1995, 68). *Retornar:* return,
step back, turn around. A certain progress will be described in this return. But Borges, according to García Canclini, never steps back, never
returns to a premodernity that would buttress the fictions of modernity:

> Todos los soportes del arte moderno...son ficciones frágiles. Según Borges
> mejor que indignarse por la irrespetuosa demolición que les inflige "la

sociedad de masas," es asumir, mediante este trabajo escéptico, la imposible autonomía y originalidad de la literatura. Quizá la tarea del escritor... sea reflexionar sobre esta situación póstuma de la modernidad. Las paradojas de la narrativa y de las declaraciones borgeanas lo colocan en el centro del escenario posmoderno, en este vértigo que generan los ritos de culturas que pierden sus fronteras, en este simulacro perpetuo que es el mundo. (1990, 106)

[All the supports of modern art... are fragile fictions. According to Borges, rather than becoming indignant at the disrespectful demolition that "mass society" inflicts upon them, it is better to assume, by means of this skeptical work, the impossible autonomy and originality of literature. Perhaps the task of the writer... is to reflect upon this posthumous situation of modernity. Borges's paradoxical narratives and statements place him at the center of the postmodern scene, in this vertigo generated by the rituals of cultures that are losing their borders, in this perpetual simulacrum that is the world.] (1995, 76)

Paz and Borges will be, for García Canclini, the proper names perhaps most exemplary of the two principal strategies for entering and leaving modernity. On the one hand, Paz steps back from modernity in order to reinscribe a certain origin, or point of departure, of modernity; he steps back to step in. On the other hand, Borges doubles the origin of modernity—all the citations and translations—in order to displace its ground; he steps in place, in other words, in order to "leave" modernity behind. Borges writes its obituary, remarks its posthumousness.

Both Paz and Borges conceive modernity as a place and as a place to be left, whether, in Paz, to be left to us, to the future, more secure, or, in Borges, to be left behind, to be left for dead. Both texts thus amount to articulations of the limit, the border; and both can be understood to theorize the possibility of literature and, perhaps, of culture as effects of a certain relation to the border. In this regard, Paz and Borges become important sites (cites) for any attempt to rethink the writing of the borderlands and, perhaps, especially the double writing of Rolando Hinojosa. At stake in Hinojosa's double text, his construction of a county that takes place twice, always in translation, will be the border of American literature and, perhaps, the principle of any possible hemispheric (pan-American) literary production, if not, in fact, that of globality in general.[1]

1

Paz arrives at the border: his entire critical *obra* takes place there, or, more exactly, his critical reflections become possible only after he crosses the border between Mexico and the United States. Only after that step, that first step, will he be able to count (on) another: the return, the re-flection. From the United States, from this side—both *el otro lado* and *este lado*—Paz looks back. In *El laberinto de la soledad*, Paz explains that Mexicans, and thus Mexico as the name of a nationalized entity, as a body and a spirit, can become self-conscious simply by crossing the border into the United States. It is a step he has taken:

> Todos pueden llegar a sentirse mexicanos. Basta, por ejemplo, con que cualquiera cruce la frontera para que, oscuramente, se haga las mismas preguntas que se hizo Samuel Ramos en *El perfil del hombre y la cultura en México*. Y debo confesar que muchas de las reflexiones que forman parte de este ensayo nacieron fuera de México, durante dos años de es-tancia en los Estados Unidos. (1959, 11–12)

> [We can all reach the point of knowing ourselves to be Mexicans. It is enough, for example, simply to cross the border: almost at once we begin to ask ourselves, at least vaguely, the same questions that Samuel Ramos asked in his *Profile of Man and Culture in Mexico*. I should confess that many of the reflections of this essay occurred to me outside of Mexico, during a two-year stay in the United States.] (1985, 12)

The border produces self-consciousness; it enables the reflection that translates without remainder: Mexico will know itself, will find it-self, will see itself reflected in the mirror of North American life; the United States will present Mexico to itself. Indeed, the United States opens the space in which Mexico gives itself to itself, the space in which Mexico is given to itself on account (*se da cuenta*). Such is the "nature" of the border, Paz argues, that it, its crossing, illuminates:

> Recuerdo que cada vez que me inclinaba sobre la vida norteamericana, deseoso de encontrarle sentido, me encontraba con mi imagen interro-gante. Esa imagen, destacada sobre *el fondo reluciente* de los Estados Unidos, fue la primera y quizá la más profunda de las respuestas que dio ese país a mis preguntas. (1959, 12)

> [I remember that whenever I attempted to examine North American life, anxious to discover its meaning, I encountered my own questioning image.

> That image, seen against the glittering background of the United States, was the first and perhaps the profoundest answer which that country gave to my questions.] (1985, 12)

Such illumination, which results from a crossing-over, from a reflection from the other side, and which produces proper Mexicans, Mexicans who "poseen conciencia de sí" (11), who possess themselves, according to Paz, is violent, for this "conciencia de sí," this self-consciousness, he writes, "conquista a México" (11).

The border is essential: it circumscribes, delimits, two entities, describing their respective boundaries. The border in Paz makes a difference; it maintains the difference of cultures, of national identities, and although it allows transgression, a certain trespass, it nevertheless is not open and mandates that one return home. Customs must be passed; in passing, they will be left behind.

The Labyrinth of Solitude thus does not problematize the border, it depends on it. It needs the border's presence in order to guarantee the possibility of its approach, of the step not beyond the border toward the limit of indifference, but rather the step across the border that secures the positivity of difference, of difference's essential import. The border gives difference, gives to us the place of the other. The border corrals the other: "we" approach it safely, protected by all these customs officials.

The lines are drawn before Paz: his articulation—however important and however often imported, despite its nativity, its nativeness, as foreign, coming from the other side—will make no difference. Neither here nor there: these places remain, their juxtaposition, their friction, enabling another discourse, no less positive, of the border, no less productive of self-consciousness and, therefore, of *customs*—and the border patrol.[2]

And such customs, on either side of the border, on both sides of the border, will be the *same*. Thus Paz's crossing over, his translation of the border, does not distinguish two sides of the border, thus two borders; on the contrary, the border produces self-identity—the reflection of the one in/as the other produces identity in difference. This is Derrida's point in *The Other Heading: Reflections on Today's Europe*.

There is no culture or cultural identity without this difference *with itself.* A strange and slightly violent syntax: "with itself" also means "at home (with itself)" (with, *avec,* is "*chez,*" *apud hoc*). In this case, self-difference, difference to itself, that which differs and diverges from itself, of itself, would also be the *difference (from) with itself,* a difference at once internal and irreducible to the "at home (with itself).".....

This can be said, inversely or reciprocally, of all identity or all identification: there is no self-relation, no relation to oneself, no identification with oneself, without culture, but a culture of oneself *as* a culture *of* the other, a culture of the double genitive and of the *difference to oneself.* (1992, 9–10)

Accordingly, Derrida claims that "a culture never has a single origin. Monogenealogy would always be a mystification in the history of culture" (10–11). It is this opening, this difference with itself, that traces the possibility of the other "approach" to the border, but it is always possible, as in Paz's text, not to register the difference this irreducible difference makes.

Mexicanicity, according to Paz, will be given (back) to itself (as such) in and by the United States; Mexico will find itself in this reflection, in its "own," "proper" reflection. In sum, in Paz, the border, though it secures cultural and national differences, produces the same: on either side of the border, on both sides of the border, at the same time and in the same places, the same as such is produced in the same way. There will be no difference between the birth of U.S. cultural identity and Mexican cultural identity: both will depend on the border and its determinations. On either side of the border, on both sides of the border, there is one cultural identity; however it is defined, in whatever terms it is disclosed, it is nevertheless *one*—it is *our* identity. And even if on either side of the border there is more than one cultural identity, each one will be located within the horizon of a certain discretion; each will be found in its own place, bordered by the dream of its proper univocity. Such is the effect of Paz's border, his approach to the border and its crossing. For Paz the other always awaits across the border, always lies on the other side, wherever the border *is,* however it is constituted (historically, geographically, culturally). And while "we" can always cross the border, encounter the other, "we" nonetheless remain (in) ourselves in doing so; "we" do not lose ourselves in this transgression, in this step beyond the "limits" of ourselves, of our horizon; on the contrary, "we" will only find ourselves there, awaiting us on the other side of the border.

The border essentializes "our" identity: its imposition and our crossing over enable us to know who "we" are, to know, then, where "we" are. The border divides us from ourselves, imposing us on ourselves in our reflection: these two, the before and the now, add up to one, to "we," to Mexico and Mexicanicity in Paz. What would appear to be the possibility of plurality is thus the ruse of hegemony: the border, with its two sides, two frontiers, produces one. Far from marking the locus of a heterozone, it is the very site of cultural homogeneity; or, as Jean-Luc Nancy explains of Hegelian metaphysics, a metaphysics both predicated upon the border and definitive of it: "The true *plural* is excluded in principle. The path of self-consciousness can easily lead through desire and recognition to the other, but it is traced beforehand in the circular process of the Self of this consciousness" (1993a, 11). In Paz the articulation of self-consciousness will occur before cognition: the alienation or the step from "home" to the other side, which enables self-consciousness, Paz describes as a feeling: "Todos pueden llegar a sentirse mexicanos" (1959, 11). The arrival at self-consciousness has the immediacy of personal experience, precognitive, emotive: a feeling, but a feeling of the self, of being oneself, or self-conscious. And this feeling, which will produce a certain nostalgia, will be experienced, arrived at, elsewhere, on the other side. And it will send "one" back, guaranteeing the return of the self to itself at home. In every case there will be a movement across the border, through customs, in order to identify, to "know," indeed, to feel (experience) the other. And there *I* will be.[3]

2

There is, however, another "path" to the border, one that remarks its circumference as precisely *inaccesible.* This "approach" — which never crosses the border, but which (always) arrives there — situates "one" at the limit.[4] Unlike Paz's border, which will have been the gift of cultural determinations, the result of customs, this other border, which might be called Borges's, can never be possessed and cannot be determined culturally, geographically, linguistically, politically. It will have no location despite its rigorous specificity and particularity. It is a border that though it could never be called historical, can neither be dismissed as fiction; indeed, its "presence" — which can never be determined — disables the distinction between history and fiction. It is a border that belongs to no one, that occupies no place, that determines nothing. It is a border that produces no relations. *Insondable,* unfathomable, and, therefore, groundless, this border, which is several, cannot be found, nor does it found anything.[5]

Nevertheless this border must be legible in every text as the rule of textuality and, while it leaves a certain mark throughout the entire Borgesian *obra,* nowhere is it closer to arriving than in "La biblioteca de Babel." At the same time, however, the legibility of this unaccountable border in "La biblioteca de Babel" reinscribes reading as subjectless "experience"; it inscribes "experience" within the abyss of its (im)possibility. Reading, then, which no "I" can ever be said to do, situates the subject at the edge of experience.

At the edge, the border (experience) remains unapproachable.[6]

The library is finite, although its arrangement — "En el zaguán hay un espejo, que fielmente duplica las apariencias [In the entranceway hangs a mirror, which faithfully duplicates appearances]" — "produces" "superficies bruñidas [que] figuran y prometen el infinito [polished surfaces (that) feign and promise infinity]" (Borges 1974, 465; 1962, 79). In every case it will be a question of where one stands, of in what place the subject is found, for spatial finitude would enable the approach to the limit of the library, while the structure of abyssal reflection, regardless of the subject's position, displaces it at the center. There will be no identifiable difference between the center and the periphery; it is not that the center will or will not "hold," but that its location will not be known. The principle of the center continues to operate in the library, to govern its structure, but its singularity will have been displaced: every place will be simultaneously at the limit and at the center. In short, the borders of the library remain undetermined: "*La Biblioteca es una esfera cuya centro cabal es cualquier hexágono, cuya circunferencia es inaccesible* [*The Library is a sphere whose precise center is any hexagon, and whose circumference is inaccessible*]" (1974, 466; 1962, 80, translation modified).

The library's infinitely finite space forecloses the possibility of an infinite "content": there, too, the library's limits are rigorously organized, determined, but, again, in such a way that "finally" or "in sum" they remain undetermined. The library's "content" is limited to every possible combination of twenty-five "símbolos ortográficos" (1974, 466) in a required format: "Cada libro es de cuatrocientas diez páginas; cada página, de cuarenta renglones; cada renglón, de unas ochenta letras de color negro [Each book is made up of four hundred and ten pages; each page, of forty lines; each line, of eighty black letters]" (1974, 466; 1962, 80). Further, each of the thirty-two books on each of the five shelves on each of the six walls of each hexagon is marked by letters on the spine, but "esas letras no indican o prefiguran lo que dirán las páginas [these letters do not indicate or prefigure what the pages will say]" (1974, 466; 1962, 80). The books are thus structurally determined without apparent investment in any "content" less material than the possible combinations of a finite set of orthographic symbols. In short, the library makes no sense.

At the same time, however, by virtue of its totality and the principle of each text's singularity—"*No hay, en la vasta Biblioteca, dos libros idénticos* [*There are not, in the whole vast Library, two identical books*]" (1974, 467; 1962, 82–83)—the library encompasses *without repetition* all that is expressible: "todo lo que es dable expressar [everything that it is possible to express]" (1974, 467; 1962, 83, translation modified). The library is governed by this univocity, however plural and heterogeneous, which situates the texts under the order, the rule, of possible—or "given" (*dable*)—expressions. The principle of the voice, the voice of God, perhaps, but a single voice nonetheless, governs the writing in the library, the books contained in it.

There is, then, no writing in the library; or, to put it another way, the possibility of writing in the library is the risk the library runs. For writing is repetition, which threatens the univocity of the voice, its living presence, and thus jeopardizes the totality or self-presence, the absolute plenitude, of the library to itself.[7]

In the library, the scene of writing spells, for the *bibliotecario*/narrator, the demise of the human and the perdurance of the library:

Hablar es incurrir en tautologías. Esta epístola inútil y palabrera ya existe en uno de los treinta volúmenes de los cinco anaqueles de uno de los incontables hexágonos—y también su refutación. (1974, 470)

[To speak is to fall into tautologies. This useless and wordy epistle itself already exists in one of the thirty volumes of the five shelves in one of the uncountable hexagons—and so does its refutation.] (1962, 86–87)

The tautological implications of the "ya existe" define the epistle's uselessness and wordiness, its unproductiveness: this writing, which is "original," *repeats* without copying another no less "original" but no more primary text. There are two identical texts, neither of which will have come first, in a library that denies repetition in principle, indeed, as *the* principle of its existence as voice.

At stake in this writing—that "we" may not understand ("Tú, que me lees, ¿estás seguro de entender mi lenguaje?" [1974, 470])—is the limit or *frontera* of the library: for, on the one hand, if the library contains "todo lo que es dable de expresar" and yet "no hay, en la vasta Biblioteca, dos libros idénticos," then this text, which *ya existe,* cannot be in the library. But, on the other hand, if this text, which already exists in the library, is given as expression, then it must be in the library. This writing, here and now, in its singularity, thus inscribes prohibition and obligation in the same place as the limit that closes the library to useless duplication, to senselessness, in short, to writing; and, at the same time and in the same place, this useless, wordy epistle opens it to the other, to the possibility of repetition without origin, without sense. The library is both constituted and destroyed in this single though heterogeneous and plural gesture: writing without voice.

There is no border *of* the library, no limit *to* it; there is no transgressable border that permits self-reflection, an exit that returns one to oneself with interest. The library, on the contrary, is *at* the border; it is always at, *on,* the border. At the edge of any possible itself, the library *is.* But only *there,* at the limit, neither before nor after; indeed, there will be no before, no after—the border of the library will not describe the limit of an opposition. The library *comes* at the border, the edge or limit that both transgresses and institutes in every case, with every "expression," ad infinitum, without summation, without conclusion: "Such is the logic of the limit in general: the limit has two borders, whose duality can neither be dissociated nor reabsorbed, such that touching the internal border amounts *also* to touching the external border (from the interior,' one could add—which would render the description of the operation infinite and vertiginous)" (Nancy, 1993b, 48). The library is always to come: marked by the repetition that opens the space of its infinity, the library is always before the border, coming to it, arriving without arrival.

The library, its repetitions, will always come as a surprise: "La escritura metódica me distrae de la presente condición de los hombres. La certidumbre de que todo está escrito nos anula o nos afantasma [Methodical writing distracts me from the present condition of men. But the certainty that everything has been written nullifies or makes phantoms of us all]" (1974, 470; 1962, 87). This certainty, which inevitably surprises the *bibliotecario* every single time he speaks, configures the possibility of the end of man, both man's *telos*, particular goal and destiny, and man's demise. The certainty that knows that every possible expression is already written, contained in the library, and is precisely already written at the moment of its first and unique articulation, situates man at the limit of speech and, thus, at the limit of the library. The library will be wherever humankind, "la especie humana—la única" (1974, 470), is, speaks: or, *mejor dicho*, wherever *la especie humana* repeats itself for the first time.

The two will be in the same place without being identified; neither will be without the other:

> Quizá me engañen la vejez y el temor, pero sospecho que la especie humana—la única—está por extinguirse y que la Biblioteca perdurará: iluminada, solitaria, infinita, perfectamente inmóvil, armada de volúmenes preciosos, inútil, incorruptible, secreta. (1974, 471)

> [Perhaps I am deceived by old age and fear, but I suspect that the human species—the unique human species—is on the road to extinction, while the Library will last forever: illuminated, solitary, infinite, perfectly immovable, filled with precious volumes, useless, incorruptible, secret.] (1962, 87, translation modified)

The library survives the extinction of the human species as a kind of pantheon or sepulchre, housing and defining the human being itself. Such would be the risk of the end of humankind, which might well mean its survival — to discover its unique and singular value, a certain worthlessness, and to experience the very end of this singularity, or, in other words, to witness the "closure" of unique experience:

> Si un eterno viajero la atravesara en cualquier dirección, comprobaría al cabo de los siglos que los mismos volúmenes se repiten en el mismo desorden (que, repetido, sería un orden: el Orden). (1974, 471)
>
> [If an eternal voyager were to traverse it in any direction, he would find, after many centuries, that the same volumes are repeated in the same disorder (which, repeated, would constitute an order: Order itself).] (1962, 87–88)

The experience of the library is figured as and, ultimately, is known to be, that of a traveler encountering a certain horizon or edge, a certain limit. This eternal traveler is by definition always on the move, always coming to the border, always there without arriving, without trespassing. Or, rather, this traveler, who will never come to the end, who will never arrive at any destination, trespasses without trespassing, for such trespass transgresses nothing, crosses nothing, and leaves nothing behind without, at the same time, taking anything with it. Every step, every trespass, will be the first step — again.

This, then, is experience: the repetition without origin, without priority or privilege, of every articulation, of every step, of every phrase, for the first time. Experience means to be before the border, to come before the border, for the first time, that has already been crossed. Experience is a two-step in the same place offering itself as one. It is the risk of the traveler: to trespass, to traverse ground already traveled without knowing it; to repeat steps for the first time.[8] Always to be at the border already crossed for the first time. Experience thus names the singular repetition of the unique self-same, the one, as one. Experience, as a result, is always plural, not because there is always more than one experience, but because the one of experience is "itself" plural, heterogeneous. One is multiple and the "itself" — the "self" — is other. The truth of singularity, in sum, is an incalculable plurality.

3

Experience is the step that does (not) take place, that covers (no) ground, that goes nowhere. It is the step without sense, without direction, without meaning. Experience is thus, in Maurice Blanchot's words, "le pas au-delà," the step (not) beyond (1992), that *each time* both opens and closes, as Heidegger would put it, the world. There is a way in which, quite simply, experience marks time, marks a kind of stepping in place: a repetition that goes nowhere and, yet, is nevertheless *each time* the first time, the first step. Each step begins; each marks the first without calculation or accumulation. This plurality of steps (not) beyond will not add up, will be neither accounted for nor held accountable.

The experience of the library is the experience of experience, the experience or risk of what Nancy calls "freedom":

> The experience of freedom is therefore the experience that freedom *is* experience. It is the experience of experience. But the experience of experience is nothing other than experience itself: trying the self at the self's border, the immediate testing of the limit which consists equally in the tearing apart of immediacy by the limit, the passage of the limit, which passes nothing and which does not surpass itself, but which *happens,* in the sense that "*it happens.*". . . Experience is the experience of experience's difference in itself. Or rather: *experience is experience's difference,* it is the *peril* of the crossed limit that is nothing other than the limit of essence (and therefore existence), the singular outline of shared being. (1993b, 86–87)

If, as Nancy suggests, freedom *is* experience, then freedom is also a "founding," for, according to Nancy, "the experience of founding is nothing other than the essence of experience in general. The act of founding is indeed the act par excellence of *experiri,* of the attempt to reach the limit, to keep to the limit" (1993b, 84). "Founding," which is exemplified in "the marking of the outline of the city's limits," "makes nothing" (84). It is not a construction, a base or footing upon which an edifice, for example, a culture, is built. On the contrary, this founding is nothing but a decision that leaves nothing in place: "Here, now, where there is nothing, here and now which are anywhere and anytime, existence is decided for — for example, the existence of a city" (84). It could be any city; it may never be a city at all.[9]

Nancy's rendering of freedom as the unstable foundation of foundation, as experience, amounts to a reading of Heidegger's "Building Dwelling Thinking" that, in a certain way, comes before Heidegger's "bridge," which appears to gather and disclose a world:

[The bridge] does not just connect banks that are already there. The banks emerge as banks only as the bridge crosses the stream. The bridge *designedly causes* them *to lie across* from each other. One side is set off against the other by the bridge. Nor do the banks stretch along the stream as indifferent border strips of the dry land. With the banks, the bridge *brings* to the stream the one and the other expanse of landscape lying behind them. It brings stream and bank and land into each other's neighborhood. The bridge *gathers* the earth as landscape around the stream. (1971, 152)

Nancy pointedly writes that founding or freedom "is experience itself, because it neither gathers nor produces anything: it decides a limit, and thus at the same time — at one *time* — it decides its law and its transgression" (1993b, 85). There is Heidegger's bridge only to the extent there is freedom — that is, there is nothing — before it, at the limit. The limit, the border, doubly interior, doubly exterior, marks freedom's first step.

It will have been at the limit, always at the limit, the border, that the library will be, is, decided for. Always at the limit, the border, always at the site of its transgression, which will have imposed it, situated it, there, for the first time. And yet the library of Babel could never be said to know its own limits. Indeed, it could never be said to have limits. It will never have appeared, will never appear, to itself, at the border. It will simply be there before any reflection.

The border, the site of the step that is (not) one, that is multiple, is the site and originary citing of experience: the origin of experience in citation, in the repetition that will not know itself as repetition, that will never appear to itself transparently as the representation of the first, the original, the one.

4

The border is the site of translation, but as the border is never present to itself, which is to say that the border knows itself — if it ever does — only in translation, then, as Derrida writes in "Des Tours de Babel," "experience is translation" (1985a, 203). We are, no doubt, at this border or limit, a long way from Octavio Paz's comprehension of the border and its effect. With the exception of his remarks on the *pachuco*, remarks that open *El laberinto de la soledad* and thus open Paz's critical project, his text never approaches the border, never comes so close to the limit, again. In Paz there will always be a reservation. It can be argued that the remarks on the *pachuco*'s singularly affirmative negativity, its cultural displacement, its being-on-the-border, haunt Paz's text in ways his understanding of the interred Aztec past cannot.[10] Nevertheless, this border figure amounts to little more than a point of departure for Paz's critical development. There will be no place for the *pachuco* in the labyrinth of solitude, in its determination of Mexican self-consciousness and cultural identity. The possibility of Mexican cultural identity and its relation to *la vida norteamericana* depends on the unity of the origin and the step away from it that amounts to a *return* to itself. A certain indifference to the originary figure of the *pachuco* as double, as marked by the border, the interval between national and cultural entities, foreign to both, that remains unessential to either, regulates Paz's text. The failure to rethink the horizon of national/cultural self-consciousness from the "place" of the *pachuco* is, perhaps, symptomatic of Paz's consideration of the relation of cultural identity and development to translation. In *Los hijos del limo,* remarking Hispanic cultures' lack of an *espíritu romántico,* Paz writes, "El romanticismo español fue epidérmico y declamatorio, patriótico y sentimental: una imitación de los modelos franceses, ellos mismos ampulosos y derivados del romanticismo inglés y alemán [Spanish Romanticism was superficial and declamatory, patriotic and sentimental, an imitation of French models, themselves bombastic and derived from England and Germany]" (1974a, 115; 1974b, 78). Then, Paz quotes the Argentine Domingo Faustino Sarmiento approvingly:

> Al visitar España en 1846, [Sarmiento] decía a los españoles: "ustedes no tienen hoy autores ni escritores ni cosa que lo valga...ustedes aquí y nosotros allá *traducimos.*" Hay que agregar que el panorama de la América Latina no era menos, sino más desolador que el de España: los españoles imitaban a los franceses y los hispanoamericanos a los españoles. (1974a, 116)

> [The Argentinian Domingo Faustino Sarmiento, visiting Spain in 1846, told the Spanish: "You have no authors nowadays, nor writers, nor anything of any value...you over here and we over there *translate.*" One must add that the panorama of Latin America was not less, but more desolate than that of Spain: the Spanish imitated the French, and the Spanish Americans imitated the Spanish.] (1974b, 79, translation modified)

Effectively, Paz argues that translation is derivative and that in the nineteenth century Latin American literary culture was a derivation of a derivation, a translation of a translation that did not amount to a return to and of the original. Preserved in this understanding of translation is the unity, the full self-presence, of the original to itself. The original would have no necessary relation to translation; it would not be marked from the beginning—as the possibility of the origin and the original—by translation, by a certain belatedness.

The Borgesian text appears otherwise, thinking the "origin," or better, the "beginning" and/of experience as translation. Consistent with Nancy's reading of freedom and experience, such translation never appears, never takes place; on the contrary, it simply decides for the original, marking out the limits of the possibility of existence, of being. This "work" arrives without taking place as the "first" of Borges's *ficciones*, the one he claims to have written first,[11] which he has dated chronologically prior to the others in the collection *Ficciones*, but which, nonetheless, comes third in the volume. Third but first, after but before: such would be the rule of "Pierre Menard, autor del *Quijote*."

As Derrida summarizes during a roundtable discussion devoted to translation, Pierre Menard sets himself the task, "the mad project of writing, for the first time, *Don Quixote*. That's all there is to it: He wants to write not a version, not a repetition or a parody, but *Don Quixote* itself" (1985b, 99). Or, as the narrator explains:

> No quería componer otro Quijote—lo cual es fácil—sino *el Quijote*. Inútil agregar que no encaró nunca una transcripción mecánica del original; no se proponía copiarlo. Su admirable ambición era producir unas páginas que coincidieran—palabra por palabra y línea por línea—con las de Miguel de Cervantes. (Borges, 1974, 446)

> [He did not want to compose another *Don Quixote*—which would be easy—but *the Don Quixote*. It is unnecessary to add that his aim was never to produce a mechanical transcription of the original; he did not propose to copy it. His admirable ambition was to produce pages which would coincide—word for word and line for line—with those of Miguel de Cervantes.] (1962, 48–49)

In a letter to the narrator, Menard explains, "El Quijote es un libro contingente, el Quijote es innecesario. Puedo premeditar su escritura, puedo escribirlo, sin incurrir en una tautología [*Don Quixote* is an accidental book, *Don Quixote* is unnecessary. I can premeditate writing it, I can write it, without incurring a tautology]" (1974, 448; 1962, 50). He claims as well that his general memory of the *Quijote*, "simplificado por el olvido y la indiferencia" (1974, 448), is equivalent to the "imprecise" "imagen anterior de un libro no escrito" (448). Menard's memory of the *Quijote* inscribes it, unlike an interjection of Poe or *The Ancient Mariner*, as an effect of chance, of the contingent. Its particular *innecesidad* enables Menard, according to the narrator's reading of Menard's *carta*, to write it without producing tautology, without repeating it. The two *Quijotes*, identical in every way, will nevertheless be marked by difference. They will not be the same. Their identity without sameness forces the narrator to report Menard's *Quijote* as his invisible work, "la subterránea, la interminablemente heroica, la impar" (446), the work, then, without equal, without pair; but also, as the *impar*, as the "odd" work, the invisible text opposes the "even" (*par*) or visible one, and, as Irwin points out in *The Mystery to a Solution* (1994), has a certain temporal privilege or priority, as all odd numbers do.[12]

"Pierre Menard, autor del *Quijote*," remarks, without the narrator's knowing it, the nonessence and nonfoundational ground of the text, the rule of the text that, while it opens the possibility of the subjective production of the text in reading, cannot be read, cannot be named in itself and that never appears, a condition, finally, that keeps it off the narrator's two lists of Menard's work, the visible and the invisible. Indeed, this "work," which is not one, disarticulates the possibility, at the same time that it marks the space, of their decision. This "work" will have the appearance of a translation: in a note pegged to the end of the list establishing Menard's visible *obra*, the narrator reports that

> Madame Henri Machelier [*sic*] enumera asimismo una versión literal de la versión literal que hizo Quevedo de la *Introduction à la vie dévote* de San Francisco de Sales. En la biblioteca de Pierre Menard no hay rastros de tal obra. Debe tratarse de una broma de nuestro amigo, mal escuchado. (1974, 446)

> [Madame Henri Bachelier also lists a literal translation of a literal translation done by Quevedo of the *Introduction à la vie dévote* of Saint Francis of Sales. In Pierre Menard's library there are no traces of such a work.

She must have misunderstood a remark of his which he had intended as a joke.] (1962, 47)

The narrator will not have found this text in the library and, rather than find in its nonappearance the limit or border both of the library in which he seeks it and of reading as a subjective activity, he takes refuge in what Menard's *Quijote* questions: namely, the narrator claims that Madame Bachelier misunderstood a joke, misunderstood, then, Menard's utterance, his intention. Such misunderstanding, which is another way of saying "understanding" or "reading," would be impossible once the possibility of Menard's *Quijote* is admitted. In short, once the intentionality of what remains invisible can be determined, once such invisibility becomes legible, misunderstanding is ruled out, for reading will be comprehended, entirely saturated by the subject of reading. There will no longer be room for the text at the scene of reading.

The literal translation of the literal translation of *Introduction à la vie dévote* points to the *place* of the text, for the literal translation (into French) of the literal translation (into Spanish) of *Introduction à la vie dévote* would *in fact* disappear *as* and *in* the "original." This translation, which would possess no "itself" and which would be called the original the moment it comes into its own, the very moment its double exteriority from the "origin" leaves a trace of the original *as such,* articulates the rule of textuality, the law of the text:

> A text is not a text unless it hides from the first comer, from the first glance, the law of its composition and the rules of its game. A text remains, moreover, forever imperceptible. Its law and its rules are not, however, harbored in the inaccessibility of a secret; it is simply that they can never be booked in the *present*, into anything that could rigorously be called a perception. (Derrida, 1981, 63)

Thus, Derrida writes, "And hence, perpetually and essentially, they run the risk of being definitively lost. Who will ever know of such disappearances" (63). And, elsewhere, writing *on* the place in which the narrator of "Pierre Menard, autor del *Quijote*," loses himself when he cannot find the book in the library, writing on borderlines, Derrida explains:

> A text lives only if it lives *on*, and it lives *on* only if it is *at once* translatable *and* untranslatable (always "at once … and …": *hama*, at the "same"

time). Totally translatable, it disappears as a text, writing, as a body of language. Totally untranslatable, even within what is believed to be one language, it dies immediately. Thus triumphant translation is neither the life nor the death of the text, only or already its living *on*, its life after life, its life after death. The same thing will be said of what I call writing, mark, trace, and so on. It neither lives nor dies; it lives *on*. And it "starts" only with living on (testament, iterability, remaining, crypt, detachment that lifts the stricture of the "living" *rectio* or direction of an "author" not drowned at the edge of his text). (1984, 102–3)

The original no longer takes place before (the) translation; or, it can only take place before (the) translation, facing it, as it were, as nothing present, across a line, a border, an abyss, across, then, a divide that produces no sides, that relates nothing across it. Translation does not determine the original; it simply opens a space — not yet determined as *the* space *for* the original — for the decision of the original, of its presence. Between translation and original there is nothing, and this nothing, which is not determinate, remains, leaves its remains in the *corpus* that lives, in which it lives on or survives.

5

The comments of Gabriel García Márquez notwithstanding, Borgesian translation does not necessarily operate in the service of the state.[13] Nor does it necessarily resist the state's ideological machine in the way Tejaswini Niranjana suggests when she remarks that "the rethinking of translation as un-nostalgic and nonessentialist makes translating a strategy of resistance rather than of containment" (1994, 36). Translation of the sort Borges elaborates comes before any operation comprehended as either a colonial strategy of containment (or "evasion" as García Márquez suggests) or a postcolonial gesture of resistance. Clearly translation can, when thought of as a mode, be accommodated to either of these positions, but to the extent that in much work it would appear to be an either/or proposition, translation remains embedded in questions of the subject that are yet to be interrogated. Borgesian translation comes before, in-decision, any decision of containment or resistance. Such translation is not the result of any subjective agency; it produces no identity, it communicates no meaning to auditors or lectors. Translation of this sort remains entirely unproductive, it makes no difference:

it distinguishes nothing and it is accountable to/for no original, no uni-vocity, no particular sense or direction. This difference, in short, leads nowhere, certainly never forward (back) to self-consciousness. This dif-ference, the difference translation makes without positing, does not give one-self (back) to it-self as subject. The Borgesian difference, which is precisely no difference at all, does not add up to the Pazian difference, which secures for Mexico its cultural identity, its self-consciousness, from the other side. Paz's border enables reflection, enables the return to it-self of Mexican consciousness as self-consciousness: self-consciousness will be, according to Paz, the gift, the present, of the border.

It will also be the possibility of any national literature: Mexican liter-ature, on the one hand, will be written in the shadow of the border; U.S. literature, or so-called American literature, on the other hand, will also take place there, but on the other side, on *our side*. We will have taken sides, occupied and possessed; and while, no doubt, there will be crossing over, in translation and in expatriation, the borders separating these two literatures remain necessarily secure. *The Heath Anthology of American Literature* demonstrates the continued effect, force, of the bor-der in the age of multinational business and free trade agreements. The spirit of internationalism extends only so far: to the border, for with-out the border, with its erasure, there would be no *inter*nationalism be-cause there would be no place for nationalism. A certain international-ism is less the opening of borders than the opening of markets, a certain negotiated and thus highly regulated exchange of the effects, products, of specific national entities. *The Heath Anthology* extends the notion of American literature only as far as English allows it: there will be no text, no "literature," included in the *Heath* that does not appear in English. There will be no text produced on the other side, *el otro lado*, of the border. Columbus's comes closest, it being the text that posits, for Europe, *el otro mundo*. English and, as a consequence, the geographic borders of the United States comprehend American litera-ture: according to the *Heath*, there will be no American literature in any other language, in any other place.[14]

Paz's text respects the border, its force and necessity. Paz would thus know the difference between Mexican and American literatures and, presumably, he would understand and support his exclusion from any anthology of American literature, despite his narrative of the origin of his text, its place within these borders. The exclusion of Paz from American literature points toward the nonrecognition of any dual or hyphenated citizenship: no hyphen bridges the border between Mexican and American literatures; there will be no Mexican-American literature within *The Heath Anthology of American Literature*. Indeed, the politics of inclusion ultimately excludes any plurality: the *Heath* will not be an anthology of American literature, plural and heterogeneous, but of an American literature that inscribes the dream of unity, homogeneity, *e pluribus unum*. Its presentation in one language and its promotion—despite the inclusion of Native, Mexican, Asian, and African American "voices"—of one tradition further homogenizes the literary "representation" of American "experience," as if those who might find their "experiences" or themselves in American literature would do so in only one language. As if that were possible in any place, at any time.

6

What if, for example, there were a body of texts, a *corpus,* for which it was impossible to decide *on any grounds* its place within any national literature? Such an example would explode the limits of national literatures, would, indeed, threaten the border of the example and, thus, of the anthology in general. We could name this example "Hinojosa," but we won't know in what language we pronounce this name or to what side, if any, it belongs.[15]

Hinojosa's *Klail City Death Trip,* the multivolume, collective novel that José David Saldívar (1985) calls a "Chicano border narrative," details "life" in Belken County, a fictional county located in the Rio Grande Valley of South Texas. Like Faulkner's Yoknapatawpha texts and Juan Carlos Onetti's Santamaría series, Hinojosa's *Klail City Death Trip* takes shape within a clearly defined fictional geography that encompasses a certain historical experience. Indeed, for Hinojosa historical experience is conceivable precisely to the extent it is determined by "a sense of place" and by the idea of a life, of *having lived* a life both unique and exemplary, in short, of having lived a life that could be repeated with interest. In "A Voice of One's Own" Hinojosa explains:

I write about what I assume other writers write about: that which they know. I happen to know something about people and about how some of us are. I happen to know some history about the Valley, this country, the state.... Add to this two lifetimes, one of observation and participation, and another of unsystematic but enjoyable reading, ... and you'll be able to read the personal and public voices as well as the voices of those hundreds of characters who populate the works. (1985c, 16).

One life is two; one voice, many. It is, then, a life that bears repeating, but such repetition, according to Hinojosa, is regulated by the laws of lived experience, of history. In "Our Southwest," an interview with José David Saldívar, Hinojosa reports that

with the publication of *Korean Love Songs*, the project title *Klail City Death Trip* first appeared in print.... [*Korean Love Songs*] was written in English: the reason for that was I had originally tried to write about Korea in Spanish, but that experience wasn't lived in Spanish. Army life isn't conducted in Spanish.... So, when I began writing *Korean Love Songs* in narrative prose and in English, it was much easier. But it wasn't what I wanted, either. Eventually, after reading many of the British World War I poets, I got the idea that maybe I should use poetry to render something as brutal as war. That, then, is why I wrote *Korean Love Songs* in verse and in English. (J. Saldívar, 1985, 181–82)

Language's relation to lived experience governs the *Klail City Death Trip*. Explaining how he arrived at Belken County, Hinojosa writes:

I decided to write whatever it was I had, in Spanish, and I decided to set it on the border, in the Valley. As reduced as that space was, it too was Texas with all its contradictions and its often repeated one-sided telling of Texas history. When the characters stayed in the Spanish-speaking milieu or society, the Spanish language worked well, and then it was in the natural order of things that English made its entrance when the characters strayed or found themselves in Anglo institutions; in cases where both cultures would come into contact, both languages were used, and I would employ them both, and where one and only one would do, I would follow that as well; what dominated, then, was the place. (1985b, 23)

"At first" (23), anyway, because later would come an awareness of class, generational, and ethnic differences. But first will have been the place, and that place, which Hinojosa will never refer to as double or multiple, but always singularly as the Valley, will be bordered by languages and lived experience. The Valley names the site of specific, linguistically determined lived experiences.

The *Klail City Death Trip* adds up to this: the repetition of lived experiences bound to the specificity of the language of their origin, of their first presentation. This would be the law of Hinojosa's collective novel: everything will be in its place and every place will be determined by language, even if by "language" is meant the mixture of tongues, a certain babel.

At stake in the *Klail City Death Trip* is the relation between this particular place, here and now, and this particular language—whether Spanish, English, or a mixture of the two—here and now. This relationship defines lived experience and, thus, history; the singularity of this relationship determines the univocity of lived experience and of history—no matter how many stories are told in no matter how many languages and from no matter how many different positions. Further, such determinate univocity makes possible these texts'—and perhaps all texts'—translation: the security and guarantee of lived experience's particular origin—the conjunction of place and language—enables its repetition, its representation, in another language. The relation between place and language remains inviolable; as the veritable kernel of the text, its shell can be moved, changed, without itself suffering any division or fracture. Thus, as with all translations, the translations of the *Klail City Death Trip*'s various installments repeat without repeating the texts, repeat and, as a consequence, leave intact and secure the originals.

The "history" of *Klail City y sus alredededores* is instructive, for though it was written in the United States it will appear here only through a circuit of displacements. As the winner of the Premio La Casa de las Americas, *Klail City y sus alredededores* was first published in Latin America, on so-called foreign soil. Yolanda Julia Broyles's German translation, *Klail City und Umgebung*, based on the already foreign "original," first appeared in former East Germany. This edition would later be adopted by West Germany's "premier publisher, Suhrkamp Verlag" (Broyles, 1985, 109). It is from the position of a certain double exteriority that *Klail City y sus alredededores*, which is American literature, finds its place in the

United States, for its international success apparently leads Justa Publications to offer a bilingual edition bearing the title *Generaciones y semblanzas*. This American literature thus first arrives in the United States doubly, in an "original" Spanish the majority of readers of American literature cannot read and in an English translation whose place within American literature is problematic. The same, no doubt, is true of Julia Cruz's translation of *Claros varones de Belken*: the translation will be excerpted and anthologized, taught in American literature classrooms, thus situating the original within American literature; yet, at the same time, though these translations make possible the canonization of the *Klail City Death Trip* within contemporary multicultural, but still monolingual, American literature, they do so without taking place, without impinging upon Hinojosa's creed: that writing will be determined by experience and that experience is the unique articulation of language and place.

Such translations are necessary for the reading of the *Klail City Death Trip* within American literature, while, at the same time, as with all translations, they remain necessarily unread, absenting themselves before the original, siting the original in its place. The addition of the translation to the original will never add up to two, because the translation does not count. And, despite their inclusion within bibliographies of Hinojosa's work, despite their being cited by various critics writing in English and German, there is, in fact, no question of their being read: these translations will never be included, despite their appearance in canonizing anthologies, in American literature. But this will not be the case only of these translations by others; it will mark the reading of Hinojosa's entire *obra*, a stigma that enables the critical acceptance of Hinojosa's understanding of place and language and, finally, of time. For example, in *Chicano Narrative: The Dialectics of Difference*, Ramón Saldívar lists both the Spanish and English components of the *Klail City Death Trip* in the bibliography, but in the chapter devoted to Hinojosa's work, the English "renditions" appear parenthetically after the Spanish titles, while only the publication dates of the Spanish texts are given. Saldívar thus distinguishes the English original upon which he remarks, *Korean Love Songs,* from those English "renditions" that nevertheless remain subordinated to their "original" Spanish counterparts; and this despite Saldívar's claim that "these 'recastings' and 'renditions' are not translations of the Spanish originals, but different versions of the original narrative." "In recreating the texts in English," Saldívar argues, "Hinojosa foregrounds the question of bilingualism" (1990, 132 n. 1). The question of bilingualism, however, has gone virtually unnoticed: the bilinguality of the *Klail City Death Trip* has to date posed no serious problem for reading.

And yet the question of bilingualism in the *Klail City Death Trip* is precisely the question of reading: How do you, we, read this text, this double and doubling narrative? You, we, will have to decide. Our reading will be the effect of the decision to read, of the decision that is reading. And this decision, in any case, can never be to read *both* at the same time, which is to say, the decision to read one or the other adds up to the decision *not* to read. The *Klail City Death Trip* is not outside the decision to read it; yet the possibility of the decision to read the *Klail City Death Trip*, which is necessary, makes reading it impossible. On the one hand, it must be read; on the other hand, it is impossible to read. This pair, which can never be reconciled, comes together as the particular burden of the *Klail City Death Trip*; it inscribes American literature within the space of an unacquitable debt to an other.

The *Klail City Death Trip* inscribes the limit, the border, not simply of reading and its double necessity, both possible and impossible; it marks and remarks the border of American literature, for the "novel" will be both contained within the horizon of American literature and, *at the same time,* transgressive of it. This because Hinojosa's translations, which both are and are not "simple" translations, do not go anywhere; they carry nothing over; they do not affect any "trans-." These translations, like all translations, are original and originary; they stay in the same place and occupy the same site as the original. They double the ground. Or, they put it in abyss by repeating, for the first time, in the same place and at the same time, the selfsame with a difference. *Dear Rafe* and *Mi querido Rafa,* for example, are not the same, but within the *Klail City Death Trip* they occupy the same narrative place and time. They thus double it, repeat it, but in each case for the first time, without any relation to the other.

The principle of Hinojosa's narrative, what he calls "the sense of place," cannot tolerate such repetition, the effect of which is to displace the singularity of place, the jurisdiction of language and the borders that would determine the unique, the univocal. Bilingualism, or the so-called bilingual text, in no way threatens the security and guarantee of the sense of place; on the contrary, bilingualism is productive of it: it takes place, according to Hinojosa's narrative principle, only where it would "naturally" occur. Thus while bilinguality may well result from the friction of cultures, from their proximity, it does not take place *between* cultures; rather, it insinuates itself, as a third culture, but one nonetheless, in the interval of cultures that maintain the ruse of monolinguality. So-called border cultures, then, do not amount to the future possibility of cultural development that could be called a common ground; instead, they multiply borders. Culture will be found within borders, never between them, for what is within borders will in every singular case be determined by a particular configuration of language, space, and time. Gloria Anzaldúa, for example, identifies herself as "a border woman," writing, "I grew up between two cultures" (1987, pref., n.p.), but what she ultimately describes is the site of a culture, the site of the new mestiza, a place determined by its own language:

> The switching of "codes" in this book from English to Castillian Spanish to the North Mexican dialect to Tex-Mex to a sprinkling of Nahuatl to a mixture of all of these, reflects my language, a new language — the language of the Borderlands. There, at the juncture of cultures, languages cross-pollinate and are revitalized; they die and are born. Presently this infant language, this bastard language, Chicano Spanish, is not approved by any society. But we Chicanos no longer feel that we need to beg entrance, that we need always to make the first overture — to translate to Anglos, Mexicans and Latinos, apology blurting out of our mouths with every step. Today we ask to be met halfway. This book is our invitation to you — from the new mestizas. (pref., n.p.)

This is writing from the inside, sent "to you" — to us? — on the outside: you'll (we'll) be met halfway, at the border. There customs will be passed.

The border would be that which absolutely separates whatever occurs within this spatiotemporal-linguistic horizon from whatever does not. Because everything that is takes place within a particular spatiotemporal-linguistic horizon, however, the rule of the border, which is the rule of place in general, determines that nothing is between places, between the sites of culture. Thus while no two spatiotemporal-linguistic places will be the same, all of these places will be organized by the same principle, the principle of singularity, of univocity, of the one. This rule leaves no room for any remainder; nothing lies outside some unique place.

The *Klail City Death Trip* opens the space of an exteriority that is not between two places, but that remains absolutely outside in the same place. This difference does not result from any incommensurability of the content of the Spanish and English "renditions" of the same; it is quite simply that both narratives occupy necessarily and impossibly the same place. The Spanish and English "originals" are different, but the place of their singular articulations remains the same: for example, in the case of *Los amigos de Becky* and *Becky and Her Friends,* the same "informant" talks to the same "ethnographer" in the same place in both texts; in the case of *Dear Rafe* and *Mi querido Rafa,* the same "Jehú" writes the same letters to the same "Rafe"/"Rafa"—which is not to say that the letters do not differ semantically, perhaps even structurally; rather, the context or spatiotemporal configuration remains exactly the same in both texts. The idea of place articulated by Hinojosa cannot support this repetition of the same, not without subordinating one text to an other, not without relegating one text, or an other, to the position, the place, of the translation, which is no place at all. This the *Klail City Death Trip* does not do, and such nonsubordination disables the possibility of any relation between the texts at all in the same place. The indecision over which text comes first, a decision that cannot be made, makes reading the *Klail City Death Trip* impossible, for we cannot read the same text twice at the same time. Any reading of the collective novel must decide where to begin, which originals to read; yet any decision, which necessarily excludes other texts, the same texts, adds up—by subtraction—to the impossibility of reading. There will always be an other *Klail City Death Trip,* but it will not be an other against which the one, whichever one it might be, defines or knows itself. Neither *Becky and Her Friends* nor *Los amigos de Becky,* neither *Mi querido Rafa* nor *Dear Rafe* indicates the place, the presence of the other. They will not be in relation, these two others, if relation assumes knowledge of the other, a dialectic of difference, in short, the colonization of the other as the means of *self*-production. They will simply be together in the same place *without* the other, *before* it. There will be no reflection here, wherever these two others happen to be, together; no longing looks across the border that would recall one to oneself, that would return one to oneself, leaving the other behind, there, across the border, on the other side. Rather, these two texts edge one another in-decision. Indeed, there are two texts only in-decision: the decision to read the *Klail City Death Trip* reduces plurality to the discourse of one, of pluralism, perhaps, of bilingualism and biculturalism, but of one nonetheless.

Plurality, the plurality of the radically singular, of a togetherness without reflection, without return, cannot be read: there is no time, no place for it. But one will never have come temporally before an other; there will be no one without an other, no singularity, no univocity, no unique one, without an other. One does not come first: they will come together, one (before) an other. The double texts of the *Klail City Death Trip*—*Dear Rafe/Mi querido Rafa, Becky and Her Friends/Los amigos de Becky, Estampas del valle/The Valley*—come together in a nonintimate relation of neither inside nor outside; they come together, before each other, across a *frontera* that does not exist, a break that neither separates nor combines. There is, then, a limit between Spanish and English, one is (not) other, but we cannot determine the place of this difference. We could never site it. It will not be posited. Or, more precisely, in deciding the border between them, we already cross it, transgress it, even as it withdraws before us. We will always be at the limit of this (in-)difference; American literature, if there is one, will always be before an other to which it is not related, which it cannot comprehend, but which nonetheless haunts it.

In Hinojosa's *Klail City Death Trip* the border between Spanish and English, between *deste lado* and *el otro lado,* is the Rio Grande, *el río bravo del norte.* But the river, which must be crossed only by passing through customs on both sides, thus by formally leaving the one culture and entering the other, has not always been understood as a barrier. In *Claros varones de Belken,* Esteban Echevarría II claims, "Y ese Río Grande que era para beber y no pa' detener los de un lado contra el otro . . . no . . . eso vino después: con la bolillada y sus ingenieros y el papelaje todo en inglés" (Hinojosa, 1986, 207). And later, Esteban Echevarría III asks, "¿Quién inventaría eso del 'otro lado' y 'deste lado'?" (211). The arrival of *la bolillada* and their English, the myth would have it, fractures the south Texas Rio Grande Valley and institutes the possibility of cultural diversity as an aftershock of ideological homogeneity. Anglos brought "deste lado" and "el otro" with them—as if Hispanic culture had been homogeneous, one. Before the gringos arrive, the myth would have it, there was no difference between this side and the other, no need for translation. Before the arrival of Anglo settlers, there would have been no customs, no border patrol, and without them, perhaps, no culture.

7

Translation does not operate only between languages, between Spanish and English, for example; rather, as Borges suggests, within any one language translation is at work, inscribing illegible difference at the origin, in the place of the original.

Partners in Crime is one of the three installments of the *Klail City Death Trip* to have been published first and, to date, solely in English. *Partners in Crime* is a detective novel, "a Rafe Buenrostro mystery," that, like Borges's "Garden of Forking Paths," is about time. The narrative concerns the time of detective work: the time it takes detectives to solve crimes. This is not simply because it takes a while to find the criminal, as if time were something one fills up and nothing more, as if it were something one saves or kills. Early on, the unnamed narrator remarks that "the second ingredient that led to the solving of cases was dedication to detail, to the job at hand, and to the amassing of hard facts, which would then be translated into evidence" (Hinojosa, 1985a, 7). Translation makes facts evident, makes them appear: "And then, as The Lab Man promised, the evidence revealed itself (as it usually does when it is there). It wasn't in plain sight, of course, but it *was* there" (206). Facts are amassed, but they lead nowhere; they determine nothing: "A lot of facts, but no killer" (65). Their presentation translates them into evidence. Such translation is not the result of the labor of any subject. Rather, it simply happens and the evidence, what is evident, reveals itself. Thus while evidence can be new it is always the repetition of that which withdraws in its presentation. Time, then, is not the law of chronology, of sequence, or addition: time is another name for the operation of translation, that which happens by chance. Time, which, according to *Partners in Crime*, "is the one element that policemen everywhere count on" (206), does not necessarily add up; it accumulates without calculation.

Nothing happens because of time. Time, or translation, what Rodolphe Gasché calls "the operator of differánce" (Derrida, 1985b, 114), opens the space for the repetition that appears for the first time. Translation or time—a certain doubling at and of the origin—makes possible, without determining, the "step" from space to place. Translation, then, which can never be read because it, having no essence, does not appear, makes possible—at the same time it makes impossible—reading and the subject of reading. In other words, there is culture, if there is any, only in translation.

It is easy to imagine *Partners in Crime* in the American literature classroom playing the role of the exemplary South Texas Chicano novel. Written in English and obedient to the protocols of the detective novel, it nevertheless remarks on a multicultural, multinational society.[16] And unlike other texts in the *Klail City Death Trip, Partners in Crime* appears to need no translation; we will not have to decide "where" to read it. There will thus be no in-decision that would jeopardize the singularity of its here and now, of its originality—except by chance, for chapters 12 and 13 must be read twice. *Partners in Crime* "repeats" chapters 12 and 13, in order, though continuously paginated, thus forcing the reader to read chapters 12 and 13 after having read chapters 12 and 13 before reading chapter 14. The text produces a literal loop that repeats without reflection, without apparent difference, two chapters, the second (and fourth) of which, chapter 13, records and plays back, more than once, a phone conversation. The call comes from the outside to an inner office of the Klail City First National Bank. The bank is the site par excellence of capitalism, the place in which "time is money, Zeit ist Gelt" (81). The caller wants to know if the banker, if the bank, is "interested" (79). To the bank nothing is without interest.

What interest do chapters 12 and 13 earn? Who or what gains or profits by their return? Or do they simply accumulate, add up, without interest, come back without return? What difference do they make? It would appear they make no difference: they add nothing to the text. Except time. The repetition of chapters 12 and 13, which amounts to nothing more, nothing additional in the narrative (*Partners in Crime* could never be said to know, to be aware, *darse cuenta*, of the repetition or addition), nevertheless adds time. But *Partners in Crime* cannot capitalize on this time, this accumulation that adds up to the incalculable. A doubling without reserve that neither gains nor loses, the repetition of the chapters is inscribed within the conceptual possibility in Spanish of consciousness, the colloquial phrase *darse cuenta*, which, translated, means, "to give oneself account/bead/bill."[17] Self-consciousness, in Spanish, remarks the scene of an exchange, an economy, that, in the same place and at the same time, invests the subject with a net gain (consciousness) that is nevertheless a net loss (a bill, an invoice, an IOU). There is, then, never any reserve of identity, never a storehouse or stockpile: identity, self-consciousness, at the very moment of its articulation is always already spent, exhausted, owed to an other.

There is no more economical translation than the translation, the literal movement, of one text from one place to another that occupies the same place within the same narrative. This would be, as Borges would have it, the literal translation of the literal translation that leaves no trace, a doubling without reserve. Chapters 12 and 13 thus translate chapters 12 and 13, but there will be no difference between them and none within them either. One could never tell the difference.

On the one hand, we must read them both: the narrative requires it. Chapters 12 and 13 follow chapters 12 and 13: those pages, their particularity, must be accounted for. On the other hand, we cannot read them both, for they are not presented as the repetition, the strategic replay of earlier events: these chapters simply come back; they remark for the first time what has already been narrated before in the exact same place within the narrative. We must read them; we cannot read them. We must decide. Such is our responsibility, our obligation to the text and to the border effect that sustains it. It is, of course, an impossible possibility, this debt to the text: it is impossible to read *both* sets of chapters without recourse to repetition, to read both as original and originary, to read both for the first time. It is impossible to do so. Yet it is impossible to read the *Klail City Death Trip* without the possibility of reading *both* for the first time, and to do so without recourse to the other, without recourse, in other words, to any *as if*.[18]

American literature takes place at this limit. It will never be located, found, on either side, in either decision, whichever chapters — 12 and 13 or 12 and 13 — we choose to read. American literature, which is to say "America," for whatever interest it holds, for whatever its worth, arrives in-decision, at the limit, if there is one, of decision. In any language, even in this one.

The border, then, is not a place, however singular it seems; it is, rather, the excessive citation of any place in "its" place: a literal taxing of the proper. The border is not a place that could be "itself" of interest. There is nothing to be gained "there." And, at the same time, there is nothing to be lost. The border, which does not exist as such, is always and only the limit of decision. We cannot and we cannot not decide. Such being-in-decision, which might be called translation or, simply, reading, takes time. It is the time of an other, the time, then, of our responsibility to an other, the time of any possible ethics, of any possible politics that is not simply and from the start an identity politics. Rather than being a politics that assumes the border and the sides it separates, this politics is always on the border, at the limit, of any possible relation to an other.

Notes

1. This is the most important shortcoming of José David Saldívar's *The Dialectics of Our America: Genealogy, Cultural Critique, and Literary History* (1991), to date the major articulation of a pan-American or hemispheric-American literature. Saldívar never considers the question of translation, never remarks the translation effect that both enables a certain hemisphericity at the same time that it perhaps precludes it in the name of the originality granted by national and cultural idioms. Saldívar's thematic constellation of identities across borders (resistant cultural identities versus dominant cultural identities, for example) must assume translation, must assume its possibility without in any way accounting for its effects, one of which is, perhaps, the border and the borderlands culture Calderón and Saldívar's *Criticism in the Borderlands* (1991) promotes; another, perhaps, the unproblematized notion of experience that governs his identity politics.

2. See Gloria Anzaldúa's *Borderlands/La Frontera: The New Mestiza* (1987) and D. Emily Hicks's *Border Writing: The Multidimensional Text* (1991) for recent and oft-cited attempts to determine the "culture" of the "borderlands." See the intro-

duction to this volume for a reading of the problems of Anzaldúa's and Hicks's notions of border cultures.

3. Much recent anthropology, in its efforts to liberate the other from the position of the object and to incorporate it as a subject, is grounded in this gesture. Such epistemological progress leads nowhere anthropology hasn't already been. For examples of anthropological narratives that identify themselves against an older form of anthropological discourse that took its subject for an object, see Rosaldo (1993), Behar (1993), and Tedlock (1992). For an attempt to think through in a more theoretical way the problems of feminist ethnography, see Visweswaran (1994), but she doesn't handle the question of the positioned subject any better. None of these texts adequately addresses itself to Tzvetan Todorov's claim that "we are like the conquistadors and we differ from them; their example is instructive but we shall never be sure that by *not* behaving like them we are not in fact on the way to imitating them" (1992, 254).

4. This change of direction, which attempts to relieve direction of its sense, follows a suggestion of Derrida's in *The Other Heading*: "Indeed it can mean to recall that there is another heading, the heading being not only ours but the other, not only that which we identify, calculate, and decide upon, but the *heading of the other*, before which we must *remember, of which* we must *remind ourselves,* the heading of the other being perhaps the first condition of an identity or identification that is not an egocentrism destructive of oneself and the other. But beyond *our heading,* it is necessary to recall ourselves not only to the *other heading,* and especially to the *heading of the other,* but also perhaps to the *other of the heading,* that is to say, to a relation of identity with the other that no longer obeys the form, the sign, or the logic of the heading, nor even of the *antiheading*—of beheading, or decapitation" (1992, 15). It is perhaps at the site of the "other of the heading" that one begins to locate the possibility of Jean-Luc Nancy's (1991) notion of community.

5. Jean-Luc Nancy writes: "What is your foundation? What will it be? It is, will be, more than America's foundation or opening—cleavage, wound, open mouth— to its own absence of foundation. You make a Founding Fathers *mestizaje,* showing that all foundation is itself unfounded, and it is well founded to be unfounded" (1994, 116).

6. Giorgio Agamben opens *Infancy and History: Essays on the Destruction of Experience* in exactly this way: "The question of experience can be approached nowadays only with an acknowledgement that it is no longer accessible to us" (1993, 13).

7. See, among other texts, Derrida (1973), but also *Of Grammatology* (1976), where Derrida explains the phrase "il n'y a pas de hors-texte": "What we have tried to show by following the guiding line of the 'dangerous supplement,' is that in what one calls the real life of these existences 'of flesh and bone,' beyond and behind what one believes can be circumscribed as Rousseau's text, there has never been anything but writing; there have never been anything but supplements, substitutive significations which could only come forth in a chain of differential references, the 'real' supervening, and being added only while taking on meaning from a trace and from an invocation of the supplement, etc." (158–59). Writing, then, as the supplement of voice, as the play of differance "that ... makes the opposition of presence

and absence possible" (143), that thus makes possible the difference between life and death, it is, then, a certain play of differance that makes possible the two, opposed, sides of the border.

There has been, however, a recent attempt to situate Derrida's grammatological intervention within the horizon of metaphysics, as the effect of the withdrawal of the Voice. In *Language and Death*, Giorgio Agamben writes, "Although we must certainly honor Derrida as the thinker who has identified with the greatest rigor . . . the original status of the *gramma* and of meaning in our culture, it is also true that he believed he had opened a way to surpassing metaphysics, while in truth he merely brought the fundamental problem of metaphysics to light. For metaphysics is not simply the primacy of the voice over the *gramma*. If metaphysics is that reflection that places the voice as origin, it is also true that this voice is, from the beginning, conceived as removed, as Voice. To identify the horizon of metaphysics simply in that supremacy of the *phone* and then to believe in one's power to overcome this horizon through the *gramma*, is to conceive of metaphysics without its coexistent negativity. Metaphysics is always already grammatology and this is *fundamentology* in the sense that the *gramma* (or the Voice) functions as the negative ontological foundation" (1991, 39).

8. See Philippe Lacoue-Labarthe, *La Poésie comme expérience*: "Ce dont il est la traduction, je propose de l'appeler l'*expérience*, sous la condition d'entendre strictement le mot — l'*ex-periri* latin, la traversée d'un danger" (1986, 30); see also his etymology of *expérience* (30 n. 6).

9. In *Speech and Phenomena*, writing of the "perfect incorporation" of "pure psychological experience" in Husserl, Derrida points out that "a radical difference remains, one having nothing in common with any other difference, a difference in fact distinguishing nothing, a difference separating no state, no experience, no determined signification — but a difference which, without altering anything, changes all the signs, and in which alone the possibility of a transcendental question is contained. That is to say, freedom itself. A fundamental difference, thus, without which no other difference in the world would either make any sense or have the chance to appear *as such*" (1973, 11).

10. See Johnson (1992) for a reading of the place of the *pachuco* in Paz's critical work.

11. See Irwin on the "history" of Borges's "Pierre Menard, autor del *Quijote*" (1994, 122). Also see Sarlo, who writes that in "Pierre Menard," "the idea of the fixed identity of a text is destroyed, as are the ideas of authorship and of original writing. With Menard's method, original writings do not exist and intellectual property is called into question. Meaning is constructed in a frontier space where reading and interpretation confront the text and its (always ambiguous) relationship to any claim to literal meaning and objectivity" (1993, 32). Further, Sarlo argues that "Borges lays claim to the productivity of reading and demonstrates the impossibility of repetition; although every text presents the variation of a few topics, it also reveals the radical difference between them. There is no way, Menard says or Borges says, that a text can be the same as its double or as its exact transcription. All texts are, from this point of view, absolutely original, which amounts to saying that none can

aspire to this special quality. Borges is fascinated by translations (which are another mode of transcription, more arduous, perhaps, and ultimately impossible)" (33).

12. "The advantage white is given at the start of the game consists in what might be called temporal odds (precedence in a series of alternating moves)" (Irwin, 1994, 117).

13. García Márquez remarks in a conversation with Mario Vargas Llosa that despite his nightly reading of Borges, he nonetheless dislikes Borges's work, considering it, he claims, "una literatura de evasión.... es pura evasión" (1968, 36). This remark comes on the heels of Vargas Llosa's question concerning García Márquez's identity: "¿En qué sentido te consideras tú un novelista latinoamericano? ¿Por los temas que tocas? Te hago esta pregunta porque podría citarte un ejemplo, el de Borges, digamos. La mayor parte de su obra toca temas que anecdóticamente no podrían ser considerados temas argentinos" (35). García Márquez responds: "Fíjate, yo no veo lo latinoamericano en Borges" (35). He admits that he once had the same problem with Cortázar, but that after having spent time in Buenos Aires after reading Cortázar, he could understand Cortázar's Latin Americanness ("Ahora, yo tuve la impresión en Buenos Aires de que los personajes de Cortázar se encuentran por la calle en todas partes. Pero así como me doy cuenta de que Cortázar es profundamente latinoamericano, no encontré en Borges ese aspecto" [36]). Borges fails not only to represent the lived reality, however fantastic or magical, of Latin America in his work, according to García Márquez, he also fails to represent Latin American irreality: "Yo creo que la irrealidad en Borges es falsa también; no es la irrealidad de América Latina" and this because, for García Márquez, "la irrealidad de la América Latina es una cosa tan real y tan cotidiana que está totalmente confundida con lo que se entiende por realidad" (40). Despite the difficulty such indifference, indistinguishability, presents for representation, García Márquez nonetheless has recourse to a notion of an essential intentional structure that governs narrative, arguing that although a writer's first obligation is to write well, it is nevertheless impossible for the writer's "formación ideológica y [su] posición política" (41) not to be implicated in the text. In short, it is impossible for the writer's politics to hide in the narrative. And yet García Márquez notes in the same response the necessary possibility that the reader will miss this politics. But when Vargas Llosa explains that when he reads Borges he locates no traces of Borges's profound political conservatism ("En cuanto creador no es un reaccionario, no es un conservador; yo no encuentro en la obra de Borges... nada que proponga una concepción reaccionaria de la sociedad, de la historia, una visión inmovilista del mundo, una visión en fin que exalte, digamos, el fascismo o casas que él admira como el imperialismo. Yo no encuentro nada de eso" [42]), García Márquez responds, somewhat problematically, given his understanding that if a writer has an ideological formation and a political agenda, that position will necessarily reveal itself in the text, "No, porque es que se evade inclusive de sus propias convicciones" (42). At stake in García Márquez's rejection of Borges—and that of José David Saldívar in *The Dialectics of Our America* (1991), in which Saldívar cites fragments of this conversation—is the politics of opposition. What is precisely troubling about Borges, however, is the impossibility of definitively situating his text on either side of the border; it is, rather, a text that

challenges the decisiveness of any politics of representation, of any mimetic politics inscribed within the horizon—as every politics of representation will be—of presence, of identity, then. It is, in short, always possible that in an effort to appear responsible, committed, to a certain politics, writers like García Márquez respond irresponsibly to, decide perhaps too quickly the case of, Borges. Borges, of course, addresses the question of national identity in "El escritor argentino y la tradición"; see also González Echevarría (1990, 161–65) on Borges's "regional novel," Sarlo (1993) on Borges's relation to Argentine letters in the 1920s, and García Canclini (1990, 105–6) on Borges's status as a cosmopolitan writer of the periphery, as a Third World writer of the metropolis.

14. A move is afoot to change all this: Harvard established the Longfellow Institute in 1994, directed by Marc Shell, Doris Sommer, and Werner Sollers. The institute, with funding from the Andrew W. Mellon Foundation, runs a seminar, "Languages of What Is Now the United States" (LOWINUS), and offers postdoctoral, doctoral, and other research fellowships. The first publishing project of the institute will be an anthology that will include bilingual versions of texts never before available in English, all of which would have been published in what is now the United States in languages other than English.

15. Yolanda Julia Broyles writes that "the novel's firm footing in both Latin American literature and United States literature defies the arbitrary political borders and the corresponding categories of national literatures. *Klail City* is a prime example of the type of Chicano literature which is *sin fronteras*. It is born as the spiritual, political and economic intersection of the Anglo and the Mexican worlds" (1985, 109).

16. Although the novel's protagonist is Rafe Buenrostro, a Chicano detective, its hero is Capitán Lisandro Gómez Solís of the Barrones, Tamaulipas, *Cuerpo de policía estatal; Sección del orden público* (128), who commits a crime in the United States and then helps the Homicide Squad of Belken County solve the crime without implicating himself. He is found out, but too late, and the novel ends with Gómez Solís uncaptured, "free," having crossed the border, about to take up residence in the United States. *Partners in Crime,* then, is a detective novel that names but never cites the bad guy, never catches him, not because he flees across the border to lawless Mexico, but because, having crossed (back) to this side, he disappears in his new home.

17. This is an impossible translation, a literal one, as it were. *Darse cuenta* means most often "to realize," in the sense of "to become aware."

18. See Readings (1989), who remarks the necessity of deconstructing the metaphoricity of the *as if,* which is a symptom of the intransigence of the distinction between the literal and the figural, between action and thought.

Works Cited

Agamben, Giorgio. 1991. *Language and Death: The Place of Negativity.* Trans. Karen E. Pinkus et al. Minneapolis: University of Minnesota Press.

———. 1993. *Infancy and History: Essays on the Destruction of Experience.* Trans. Liz Heron. London: Verso.

Anzaldúa, Gloria. 1987. *Borderlands/La Frontera: The New Mestiza*. San Francisco: Aunt Lute.

Behar, Ruth. 1993. *Translated Woman: Crossing the Border with Esperanza's Story*. Boston: Beacon.

Blanchot, Maurice. 1992. *The Step Not Beyond*. Trans. Lycette Nelson. Albany: State University of New York Press.

Borges, Jorge Luis. 1962. *Ficciones*. Ed. Anthony Kerrigan. New York: Grove.

————. 1974. *Obras completas*. Buenos Aires: Emecé.

Broyles, Yolanda Julia. 1985. "Hinojosa's *Klail City y sus alrededores*: Oral Culture and Print Culture." *The Rolando Hinojosa Reader: Essays Historical and Critical*. Ed. José David Saldívar. Houston: Arte Público.

Calderón, Héctor, and José David Saldívar, eds. 1991. *Criticism in the Borderlands: Studies in Chicano Literature, Culture, and Ideology*. Durham, N.C.: Duke University Press.

Derrida, Jacques. 1973. *Speech and Phenomena and Other Essays on Husserl's Theory of Signs*. Trans. David B. Allison. Evanston, Ill.: Northwestern University Press.

————. 1976. *Of Grammatology*. Trans. Gayatri Chakravorty Spivak. Baltimore: Johns Hopkins University Press.

————. 1981. *Dissemination*. Trans. Barbara Johnson. Chicago: University of Chicago Press.

————. 1984. "Living On * Borderlines." Trans. James Hulbert. *Deconstruction and Criticism*. Ed. Harold Bloom et al. New York: Continuum.

————. 1985a. "Des Tours de Babel." *Difference in Translation*. Ed. Joseph F. Graham. Ithaca, N.Y.: Cornell University Press.

————. 1985b. *The Ear of the Other: Otobiography, Transference, Translation*. Trans. Peggy Kamuf. New York: Schocken.

————. 1992. *The Other Heading: Reflections on Today's Europe*. Trans. Pascale-Anne Brault and Michael B. Naas. Bloomington: Indiana University Press.

García Canclini, Néstor. 1990. *Culturas híbridas: Estrategias para entrar y salir de la modernidad*. Mexico City: Editorial Grijalbo.

————. 1995. *Hybrid Cultures: Strategies for Entering and Leaving Modernity*. Trans. Christopher L. Chiappari and Silvia L. López. Minneapolis: University of Minnesota Press.

García Márquez, Gabriel, and Mario Vargas Llosa. 1968. *La novela en América Latina: Diálogo*. Lima: Carlos Milla Batres/Ediciones Universidad Nacional de Ingeniería.

González Echevarría, Roberto. 1990. *Myth and Archive: A Theory of Latin American Narrative*. Cambridge: Cambridge University Press.

Heidegger, Martin. 1971. *Poetry, Language, Thought*. Trans. Albert Hofstadter. New York: Harper & Row.

Hicks, D. Emily. 1991. *Border Writing: The Multidimensional Text*. Minneapolis: University of Minnesota Press.

Hinojosa, Rolando. 1985a. *Partners in Crime: A Rafe Buenrostro Mystery*. Houston: Arte Público.

————. 1985b. "The Sense of Place." *The Rolando Hinojosa Reader: Essays Historical and Critical*. Ed. José David Saldívar. Houston: Arte Público.

————. 1985c. "A Voice of One's Own." *The Rolando Hinojosa Reader: Essays Historical and Critical*. Ed. José David Saldívar. Houston: Arte Público.

————. 1986. *Claros varones de Belken/Fair Gentlemen of Belken County*. Trans. Julia Cruz. Tempe, Ariz.: Bilingual Press.

Irwin, John T. 1994. *The Mystery to a Solution: Poe, Borges, and the Analytic Detective Story*. Baltimore: Johns Hopkins University Press.

Johnson, David E. 1992. "Excavating Spirit on the *American* Border: Hegel, Paz, *La Crítica* and the *Pachuco*." *Siglo XX/20th Century: Critique and Cultural Discourse* 10.1–2: 49–80.

Lacoue-Labarthe, Philippe. 1986. *La Poésie comme expérience*. Paris: Bourgois.

Nancy, Jean-Luc. 1991. *The Inoperative Community*. Trans. Peter Connor et al. Minneapolis: University of Minnesota Press.

————. 1993a. *The Birth to Presence*. Trans. Brian Holmes et al. Stanford, Calif.: Stanford University Press.

————. 1993b. *The Experience of Freedom*. Trans. Bridget McDonald. Stanford, Calif.: Stanford University Press.

————. 1994. "Cut Throat Sun." *An Other Tongue: Nation and Ethnicity in the Linguistic Borderlands*. Ed. Alfred Arteaga. Durham, N.C.: Duke University Press.

Niranjana, Tejaswini. 1994. "Colonialism and the Politics of Translation." *An Other Tongue: Nation and Ethnicity in the Linguistic Borderlands*. Ed. Alfred Arteaga. Durham, N.C.: Duke University Press.

Paz, Octavio. 1959. *El laberinto de la soledad*. Mexico City: Fondo de Cultura Económica.

————. 1974a. *Los hijos del limo*. Barcelona: Seix Barral.

————. 1974b. *Children of the Mire: Modern Poetry from Romanticism to the Avant-Garde*. Trans. Rachel Phillips. Cambridge: Harvard University Press.

————. 1985. *The Labyrinth of Solitude*. Trans. Lysander Kemp et al. New York: Grove.

Readings, Bill. 1989. "The Deconstruction of Politics." *Reading de Man Reading*. Ed. Lindsay Waters and Wlad Godzich. Minneapolis: University of Minnesota Press.

Rosaldo, Renato. 1993. *Culture and Truth: The Remaking of Social Analysis*, 2d ed. Boston: Beacon.

Saldívar, José David, ed. 1985. *The Rolando Hinojosa Reader: Essays Historical and Critical*. Houston: Arte Público.

————. 1991. *The Dialectics of Our America: Genealogy, Cultural Critique, and Literary History*. Durham, N.C.: Duke University Press.

Saldívar, Ramón. 1990. *Chicano Narrative: The Dialectics of Difference*. Madison: University of Wisconsin Press.

Sarlo, Beatriz. 1993. *Jorge Luis Borges: A Writer on the Edge*. London: Verso.

Tedlock, Barbara. 1992. *The Beautiful and the Dangerous: Encounters with the Zuni Indians*. New York: Viking.

Todorov, Tzvetan. 1992. *The Conquest of America: The Question of the Other*. Trans. Richard Howard. New York: HarperPerennial.

Visweswaran, Kamala. 1994. *Fictions of Feminist Ethnography*. Minneapolis: University of Minnesota Press.

Part II

Other Geographies

FIVE

Run through the Borders: Feminism, Postmodernism, and Runaway Subjectivity

Elaine K. Chang

Life Writings/Writing Lives: Feminist and Postmodern Approaches

As Anglo-American theorists of women's autobiography have shown, female subjectivity is characterized both by women's experiences in social contexts not of their own making and by their lack of access to means through which to represent the specificity of these experiences (Jelinek, 1980; Personal Narratives Group, 1989; Bell and Yalom, 1990; Smith and Watson, 1992). Women's "life writing," by these accounts, entails and encodes a double marginalization: an alienated relationship to the material conditions of existence on the one hand, and an estrangement from the cultural practices through which these conditions are mediated and understood on the other. Postmodern strategies of "textualization" — decentering, difference, the "play" of signification — have had several controversial consequences for this kind of inquiry into women's lives and women's texts. A dialectics of "life and text," in fact, appears as one of the more congested intersections — a zone of both contact and combat — at which feminism makes its "postmodern turn." In this essay I will be examining one such intersection, among other locations, at the corner of Broadway and Commercial Drive — transiently populated by Vancouver's prostitutes and their customers, and one of the sites in which a young woman's life-and-text struggle plays itself out.

Evelyn Lau's *Runaway: Diary of a Street Kid* (1989) is, in the author's own terms, "a story of survival" (5): it is the memoir of a gifted teenager's struggles, from the ages of fourteen to sixteen, to survive and to write in the margins of dominant social formations and discourses.[1] To look at her face, emblazoned on the paperback cover and again on the book's spine, we might not recognize the "street kid" who relays in detail her experiences with drugs, prostitution, and multiple suicide attempts: "I'd been," Lau writes, "the good little Chinese girl all my life, jumping through every hoop my parents had set up" (31). Nor might those of us familiar with Vancouver recognize the city Lau both hits and misses throughout her *Diary*: "I miss Vancouver," she writes while in Boston, "the men with glazed eyes slipping me grams of hash at bus stops" (66). The Vancouver Lau has lived and rewritten might evoke what Fredric Jameson has called the "underside of culture" (1984, 57), overlooked by celebratory logics of late capitalism. A suburban house, possibly indistinguishable from the rest of the block on the outside, but internally destroyed by violence, repressive discipline, and economic uncertainty. A labyrinth of "social services": its psychiatric wards, group homes, food banks and jails, and "rehabilitation" programs that go by names like Changes, New Beginnings, and Independent Living. Back alleys and all-night restaurants. The literal and metaphorical fringes of Expo 86. A world in which "sexual favors for money and the availability of drugs" are "normal" (317), Lau demonstrates, coexists alongside all that might glitter in the western Canadian metropolis.

Yet while *Runaway* invites us to look beyond the appealing surfaces of "official" images, it offers more than a view of the city from the underside; it is more, in other words, than "A Street Kid's Guide" or "How to Have a Really Bad Time" to/in Vancouver. And it would also be reductive to read Lau's book as a personal foray into something like Vancouver's "heart of darkness," whereby the narrator-protagonist, cast as an either abject or heroic individual, is seen to come to consciousness and to mobilize her own (storytelling) skills against a recalcitrant, menacing, but otherwise inert environment. The former approach confers an illusory stability on highly contingent urban configurations,[2] and implies, simply, that places characterize or exert power over their human "fixtures." The latter approach suggests something of the same and something of the reverse: that there are bad places out there, frequented by the poor, the tired, the hungry and/or the depraved; but at the same time, individuals exist prior to place, and are invested with the ability either to conquer or to succumb to the predicaments they wander into.

Both of these approaches are inadequate in that they oversimplify relations between subjectivity and place; one category is posited as mobile and operative, while the other is presumed immutable, if portable, and subordinate. Lau and the city in relation to which she is both an insider and an outsider seem to devise and destabilize each other in much more dynamic, participatory, and antagonistic ways. To be precise, Lau *runs*—in, out of, to, and away from the city—and she is not always sure why she is running, what she is leaving, or where she is going. Her running serves to situate Vancouver as a paradoxical place, at once home and not-home, "here" and "there." And by running, her own location—as a subject multiply determined by gender, race, class, and age, compelled by the competing imperatives and promises of writing— is rendered similarly, if not symmetrically, ambiguous. In the process of problematizing subjective and sociospatial identity, Lau introduces an as yet largely underrepresented "runaway subject" to discourses of feminism and postmodernism and their preoccupations with the borders between life and text.[3]

Donna Haraway has described the encounter between postmodernist and socialist-feminist strategies in terms of an "ironic alliance": "The acid tools of postmodernist theory and the constructive tools of ontological discourse about revolutionary subjects might be seen as ironic allies in dissolving Western selves in the interests of survival" (1991, 157). By Linda J. Nicholson's account, Western feminists are called upon around the mid-1980s to engage in collective self-criticism, to account for the "problematic universalizing tendencies" in their scholarship (1990, 1). Through its primary emphasis on gender oppression, Anglo-American feminism has "ironically" silenced and excluded entire groups of women, eliding into the category of "all women" those for whom racism, colonialism, and/or class conflicts may be more or equally constitutive of their conditions than their gender.[4] Gender can thus no longer be posited as an essential and universal category, prior to other social relations, or unifying all subjects of the same sex; hence the appeal of postmodernism's critique of the "God's eye view" of subjectivity, history, and art (Nicholson, 1990, 3).

From a perspective both within Western feminism and without, Chandra Talpade Mohanty has also challenged the ethnocentric myth of "global sisterhood" and stressed the necessity of decentralizing feminist movements. According to Mohanty, "the complex *relationality* that shapes our social and political lives" enables and requires feminists to rethink static notions of history, consciousness, and agency that have been especially inadequate in evaluating the conditions and experiences of Third World and postcolonial women:

> The relations of power... are not reducible to binary oppositions or oppressor/oppressed relations. I want to suggest that it is possible to retain the idea of multiple, fluid structures of domination which intersect to locate women differently at particular historical conjunctures, while at the same time insisting on the dynamic oppositional agency of individuals and collectives and their engagement in "daily life." (1991, 13)

As a concept-metaphor for the questioning and complication of Manichaean dichotomies — oppressor/oppressed, good/evil, truth/falsehood, speech/writing — "relationality" might be considered the operating mode of postmodernist theory.[5] Although Mohanty does not align herself with the postmodernist project — and emphatically, as will be discussed shortly — her concept of relationality cautions against the abstract "man/woman," "villain/victim" dualisms from which feminists have derived overly narrow explanations of women's subjection and resistance; opposition, she argues, is never strictly or merely binary.

A theory of relational, oppositional agency — born of and responsive to the exigencies of "daily life" — rewrites oppression so as to particularize the struggles of fragmented and interstitial subjects, subjects whose location-specific knowledges interrupt the "grand narratives" of teleological progress and autonomous individuals that constitute "History" from a sedentary point of view. Evelyn Lau can be read as this kind of subject in action. Lau's parents, psychiatrists, surrogate caregivers, johns, dealers, editors, and readers — the categories and their corresponding institutions overlap — wield over her various powers: of judgment, confinement, invasion, violence, and the panoptic gaze. Yet we cannot regard Lau as one victimized according to a single overriding determinant (e.g., her gender, age, or ethnicity). To *Vancouver Sun* headlines that would sensationalize her situation as that of a "Young Woman Hunted," Lau eloquently objects (1989, 21). She is a multiply marked subject who interacts with "fluid structures of domination," whose identity is enacted, and en-gendered, in the breaks left open in the fabric of social relations and discourse.

Evelyn Lau's running—to and away from safety, danger, and writing—problematizes assumptions about agency, authorship, and the integrity of the self while it literalizes the "in-between" and "back-and-forth" dynamics of relationality. The teenage runaway in advanced industrial societies may be an exemplary relational subject, in that he or she oscillates between childhood and adulthood, dependence and independence, anonymity and visibility, social pity and contempt, home and homelessness. Evelyn Lau may be "no ordinary runaway"—at least in the estimation of the book-jacket blurbists who've packaged her story—but she resembles her counterparts in this intermediary capacity. In running from one uninhabitable place or condition to another, she mediates among identifications that resist aggregation into a unified whole. She occupies, instead, many discontinuous locations, as an honor roll student "turned" junkie and prostitute, a native Vancouverite, a Westernized daughter of Chinese immigrants, a psychiatric patient, an activist, and "some bum sustained by the state" (Lau, 1989, 143). By writing as she runs, Lau manages to inscribe herself into her own chaotic text, complying with and escaping from these identifications, and in turn conforming to and exceeding several formal categories. The *Diary* contains elements of the confessional, travelogue, social polemic, *Bildungsroman*, family melodrama, and "juvenilia," but cannot satisfactorily be classified as any one of these subgenres.[6]

The constraining power of identificatory labels is one of the factors prompting Lau to run and to write in the first place: labels such as "the hidden-away Chinese Girl" (308), "hooker" (205), and "street kid" (129) may vary in their connotations, the conditions of their enforcement, and the identity crises they precipitate, but they are equally anathematic to her, serve equally to name hierarchical relations between labeler and labeled, and are equally impossible to shake. In the epilogue to *Runaway*, Lau expresses her concern that she will ultimately be commodified as "'the ex-hooker turned writer'" or "'the recovered street kid,'" and muses: "I hope that with the publication of this book at least no one will ever look me up and down and ask me what it was like to be a prostitute. However, I know I might get a lot more of that" (339). The implicit challenge she poses to her readers involves how the border or suture between Lau-the-living-person and her book is to be construed.

Donna Haraway describes intersections between postmodernism and feminism in terms of a "necessary multiple desire": a balancing act between "an account of radical historical contingency for all knowledge claims" on the one hand, and "a no-nonsense commitment to faithful accounts of a 'real' world" on the other (1991, 187). Perceiving an untenable contradiction in this kind of formulation, activists of many different persuasions have condemned postmodernist interpretive techniques for relativizing relations of power. Against the threatened elision of everything into "discourse" and "text," some feminists have countered, in different intensities, with appeals to the primacy of "lived experience" and "the real world." Marnia Lazreg, for example, has argued against adapting Michel Foucault's decentralized analytics of power toward feminist projects; such a move can only reproduce the "power of interpretation" exercised first by "male-centered society" and subsequently by the academy: "Subsuming all reality under discourse, as Foucault does, has resulted in a shift of focus from women's lived reality to endless discoursing about it" (1988, 96).

"Who am I if not a writer?" Writing on the Run

But even if we choose to focus on the dynamics of the "real world," equating "text" and "discourse" rather narrowly with the elite practices of literature and moving them all to the side, I would object that we do not necessarily circumvent the reproduction of unequal power relations in our own critical practice. Evelyn Lau is compelled on several occasions to throw stashes of her writings into garbage cans; such an act of writerly self-dispossession, as a matter of practical necessity, marks her initiation as a "runaway" and is commemorated in the *Diary*'s first entry (9). This is an example of textual abandonment under duress — which some critics imitate, or so it would seem, at the risk of flaunting their considerable privileges in the process of flouting them. Activist scholars, to put it bluntly, are not forced to discard texts to save their lives, or the lives of the subjugated "others" in whose interests the gesture is often made.

Speaking for herself, Lau asks: "Who am I if not a writer? It's all I have—this pile of crumpled paper that follows me everywhere in my backpack, words breathing life, my existence" (1989, 146). And to the kind of pronouncements on world-text distinctions that feminists have made, Lau the writer offers some especially challenging questions. Mary E. Hawkesworth, for instance, condemns postmodernism for disregarding "realities . . . circumscrib[ing] women's lives" that do not "admit of the free play of signification": realities such as "rape, domestic violence, and sexual harassment" (1989, 555). "The victim's account of these experiences," Hawkesworth continues, "is not simply an arbitrary imposition of a purely fictive meaning on an otherwise meaningless reality" (555). It has become almost a procedural requirement, in a great many activist-academic discussions, to oppose deconstruction with the unimpeachable authority and authenticity of victims' testimonials. According to Hawkesworth's version, the victim's testimony in court cannot be submitted to a deconstructive reading; one cannot conclude "that all other accounts (the assailant's, defense attorney's, character witness's for the defendant) are equally valid or that there are no objective grounds on which to distinguish between truth and falsity in divergent interpretations" (555).

I would agree that we must not enter the scenario described here with the presumption of "equal validity" among all accounts. But if one insists on the self-evidence of "the victim's" truth in exactly the way the example suggests, one implicitly vindicates the court system as a given or transparent conduit to reparation or relief. Victims of rape and battery who have had the dubious privilege of bringing their attackers to trial, and who report feeling additionally violated by the process, in a concrete sense attest to the "textualization" of the law and the real capacity of legal "discourse" and institutions to act on them and inflict suffering. These victims' participation in legal proceedings is a series of interactions with powerful codes and those who speak and manipulate them. These codes, moreover, are complicitous with a broader "social text" that normalizes violence as a mechanism by which to preserve hierarchical relations among its constituents.

And some victims never make it to court. One of the most disturbing aspects of *Runaway* is its representation of legal and welfare systems cooperating to return children to abusive parents, literally at all costs, before consenting to adopt these "minors" symbolically as public charges and wards of the court. Early in this protracted process, Lau comments: "Social services would take me in if I ran away another fifteen times or so — oh sure, sounds like great fun" (34). Even when social services does agree to "take her in," this last resort, Lau reveals again and again, is a problematic solution at best. Lau is interpellated as dependent and as property in a normalizing *fiction* of "functional" families authored and reproduced by the state. After her forced stay in a psychiatric ward, Lau recounts a meeting orchestrated among doctors, social service workers, and her parents, in which the decision is announced to "release [her] into [her] parents' care again" (32). Fighting against the emotional, as well as legal and medical, appeal of the metaphor "parental care," Lau leaves her family in the medical building's coffee shop and runs "along Broadway Street, dashing past the open-mouthed, wide-eyed passersby — what fragile hope that I would not be stopped" (33).

Running in this and other instances is an inaudible speech act, a protest on the part of a subject rendered voiceless by and in the codes that determine and enforce her "best interests." And one cannot spirit away the power of codes without relying on other codes; clearly, the issue is not whether Lau should have been granted the opportunity, like the celebrated "Gregory K." here in the United States, to formally divorce her parents before judge and journalists. Rather, the truths, realities, and lived experiences *Runaway* records are compelling precisely because they — inseparable from the specific ways and forms in which Lau (re)-writes them — constitute testimony inadmissible in a court of law. Lau can neither make use of such a forum nor assume its kind of audience.

As for what Hawkesworth and others have accurately put forward as "realities that circumscribe women's lives," Lau's book relays and attempts to make sense of almost countless incidents of rape, domestic violence, and sexual harassment. But she is not always able or willing to "testify" to their occurrence, much less, at times, to their "genuine" significance. Lau is sexually initiated through an act of rape. A hippie and fellow anarchist, by Lau's description, agrees to house the then fourteen-year-old girl in his cabin on the coast, her first refuge after running away from her parents; he rapes her the night after her arrival. Joe's attack is chronicled on the day of its occurrence (March 25, 1986) in a journal entry that deals primarily with Lau's mixed feelings of guilt and gratitude toward the friends who have arranged her escape:

> Then Don and Crystal, how I'd almost forced myself on them, and now Joe. . . . I cried for hours, the first time since leaving home. Joe came into the kitchen, held me, rocked me like a baby, guided me to bed. He was silent except for when he murmured hypnotically that everything would be all better, it would. He repeated this over and over until I stopped shaking, then he kissed me good night and left, and I fell asleep exhausted under twisted covers. (12–13)

The rape is signified both by marks of ellipsis and by Lau's layered revision of the event. Language thus calls attention to itself for its interference with "the facts." Lau crafts a domestic scene, re-creating her assailant as a paternal figure and his cabin as her home. It is not until the journal entry for the following day that Lau admits: "I *feel* like I've been raped. Feelings of self-hatred, disgust and hatred of men, unfamiliar, are racing through me" (13; emphasis added). Lau then discloses details of the previous evening based relatively more on fact than on "feeling": that she and Joe had been drinking, that Joe proposed she sleep in his bed and she "naively" accepted, that "it hurt, and with panic I rose out of my stupor and told him to stop, but he wouldn't" (13).

In the space of two or three pages, then, we are presented with overlapping fragments of several discourses: a factual recounting of events, the vocabulary of denial and self-blame common among victims of sexual assault, and an interruption of sentimentalized familial discourse, possibly attributable both to a young girl's desire to replace the parental home she has just fled and to the predatory tactics of a child molester. Furthermore, the codes of the diary — a form that pretends toward "to-the-moment" reportage — in this instance thematize and interrupt themselves. Immediately after having been attacked, it would seem "experientially" unlikely that Lau could have composed the paragraph on the fatherly Joe tucking her in. *Runaway* is shot through with jarring textual moments like this one, in which it appears that Lau (and/or her editor) has revised and embellished certain sections of the original diary with the qualified advantage of hindsight.[7] By remarking these kinds of seams and fractures, we are not, as Hawkesworth might argue, substituting for the world a "text" upon which we perform mere "literary criticism" (1989, 555–56). Nor are we rejecting recourse to existing institutional channels for redress. Rather, we are underscoring once again the inseparability of "life" and "text."

Liberal feminists often seek to defoliate the narrative layers and competing codes of stories like Lau's in order to uncover and give expression to truths subtending the surfaces of texts: that is, the ontology of the "real woman" and her experiences of victimization. The subjects distilled by this kind of interpretive procedure — and it *is* an interpretive procedure — come to resemble the norm of the white, middle-class, adult woman that is currently under such widespread feminist reinvestigation; to understate the case, Lau is not this "woman." If one unilaterally sacrifices text for life, one rules out the processes by which Lau's identity — including her identity as a woman and as a victim — is being negotiated. Some of these processes happen to appear on the page, as the slippery textual mediations that render self-awareness and testimony both possible and impossible.

The truth of victimization is rarely open and shut. Lau does not once openly "confess" that Joe has molested her, and this silence is a palpable sign of her marginalization from the dominant institutions and discourses that promise her protection. To read Lau's silences requires close attention to the often ambiguous text she provides, and not with an eye or ear to recovering some buried factual substrate or muted "voice." Reader-advocates who selectively sift through contradictions and mediations such as those Lau produces in her own text can compound the problem of victimization by stripping the subject in question of her defenses, secrets, and distinguishing marks.[8] In the act of ventriloquizing on behalf of silenced "victims," critics can, in other words, rob these subjects of their own agency. Gayatri Chakravorty Spivak has argued against this tendency to "patronize and romanticize" the disprivileged or silenced "other": "The academic feminist must learn to learn from [these women], to speak to them, to suspect that their access to the political and sexual scene is not merely to be *corrected* by our superior theory and enlightened compassion" (1988, 135). Lau has experienced this sort of critical intervention as a personal violation: "They stole my words and bled them limp, beat them with truncheons" (1989, 21). She appeals to writing as her preferred form of protection, and that which best defines her individual identity: "Don't you see: I don't fit in anywhere. All I have in the world that is precious is my writing, which I clutch and shove in front of my vulnerabilities like a shield. Evelyn isn't alive at all, it's always her writing, her writing" (156).

Autobiography as Self-Knowledge

However, given this construction of the tension between "text" and "life" — and Lau consistently sees her writing as more "alive" than herself — to celebrate illegibility is an equally reductive critical procedure, if what is being posited instead of plain-speaking, truth-telling subjects are indecipherable, inscrutable (or "dead") ones. In order to refine how opaque "textuality" might materially contribute to Lau's constitution as a subject, we must press further into issues of self-representation, in both the political and the aesthetic senses of the term. It is a normative assumption, within and beyond feminist theory, that autobiographical writing facilitates subjective self-knowledge, re-presenting the writer in legible form to and for herself. Lau runs up against this edict from several different directions, which we might track through another series of cross-theoretical comparisons. Like *Runaway*, Minnie Bruce Pratt's autobiographical essay "Identity: Skin Blood Heart" (1984) traces movements to, away from, and among various homes, and the ways in which these trajectories complicate notions of historically continuous self-development. In their interpretation, Biddy Martin and Chandra Talpade Mohanty attend to the nuances and broader implications of Pratt's text; at the same time, they locate the text in the feminism/postmodernism debate over categories of life and text. Contending that the form of Pratt's text would be dismissed by deconstructivists on the basis of its "conventionality," Martin and Mohanty proceed in their reading to rescue the text from postmodernism's fetishization of "abstract indeterminacy" and "self-referential language" (1986, 194).

Although they apply themselves as "literary critics" to Pratt's narrative complexity, Martin and Mohanty thus share Hawkesworth's suspicion of "textuality," taken as a series of language moves remote from the *Realpolitik* of lived experiences. Whereas Hawkesworth champions the transparency of spoken testimony, Martin and Mohanty base their reading on the assumed transparency of the autobiographical writer's motives to herself. Pratt is seen to "reanchor herself," to "work to expose the illusory coherence" of the positions from which she speaks, and is in this way repeatedly congratulated by her readers for her self-awareness and control (Martin and Mohanty, 1986, 194). Pratt's consciousness is interpreted as emerging from, if not transcendent over, her text as it unfolds. The self-inventing, self-directed subject of Enlightenment humanism is thus recuperated, albeit in attenuated or "incoherent" form, as the critical subject of feminist politics. Reading Lau against Pratt, I want to ask whether Pratt's narrative strategies, and her critics' priorities, may serve to reproduce in a different context the power dynamics embedded in the reworked conventions of traditional self-representation.

Beyond certain thematic commonalities, Pratt's engagement with multiply charged "homes" departs from Lau's, especially regarding the emergence of self-consciousness in and through writing. Pratt begins her life in privileged surroundings: a white, middle-class, familial home in the (de facto) segregated American South. Although there is no "linear progression" to these life events (Martin and Mohanty, 1986, 196), Pratt moves chronologically through roles as a sheltered daughter, married woman, "out" lesbian, activist against racism and other forms of oppression, and finally an "alien" white person residing in a predominantly African American district of Washington, D.C., called "the jungle" by white suburbanites (Pratt, 1984, 11). Over the course of these events and displacements, Pratt calls into question the "familiarity" of a "home" built on exclusion and exploitation and the deliberate concealment of these realities from those who benefit from them; at the same time, she finds she cannot divest herself of the "growing up places" she carries with her. Each of these places — Alabama, North Carolina, and Washington — is marked, in Pratt's narrative, by a moment of extended self-reflection. Martin and Mohanty punctuate these moments by calling attention to Pratt's "acute awareness," her "realiz[ation] that home was an illusion of coherence," and her conferral of "meaning and function" on otherwise discrete and meaningless locations (1986, 197).

Like Pratt, Lau's running defamiliarizes "home" and normative ideologies of family and community. Yet whereas Pratt's definition of home issues from the space in which she was first pampered and protected, Lau's familial home is from the beginning and throughout a space of danger. As is the case with Pratt, Lau's "original" and subsequent homes remain with her as traces, regardless of the physical distances she imposes between them. But whereas Pratt's former homes represent mainly the race- and class-bound advantages to which she has grown accustomed, Lau's "growing up places" continue to haunt and subject her. Vancouver becomes materially and symbolically consonant, not with Lau's own privileges, but with those of her parents: "I CAN NEVER BE FREE OF THEM IN VANCOUVER. How can two small human beings wield this much control?" (Lau, 1989, 105). Lau thus serves to unsettle the value-laden "tension between two specific modalities . . . being home and not being home" (Martin and Mohanty, 1986, 197) assumed by Pratt and rehearsed by a number of feminist writers dedicated to location or situation theories of subjectivity.[9] Lau does not maintain that the opposite valorization applies so much as she suggests that the categories are relative and restless. Movements away from "home" to Calgary, to Boston, and elsewhere—it's hard to keep track—are in *Runaway* as short-lived and ambiguous as her decisions, once "there," to return to Vancouver. Invoking "here" as the present and scene of writing and "you" as an unspecified interlocutor, Lau asserts her longing for the traditional home that Pratt rejects: "Here I am. I want to go home. I want to have friends. I want to be loved by someone. Is that naked enough for you?" (152).

Of course, a teenage runaway and an experienced writer/activist occupy markedly different locations in networks of power and subordination. But attention to age and status discrepancies between Lau and Pratt again underscores the persistence of textuality. To what extent might "maturity," for example, be accomplished or commemorated through writing? Lau poses and responds to this question whenever she acknowledges in the *Diary* her inexperience: "I know that much of my writing is immature and self-absorbed, and that alone is enough to depress anyone. Depression is a brick sitting on top of your head, weighing down and compressing your thoughts into nuggets of lead" (151). Lau's "depression" over her self-perceived "immaturity" yields immediately to an exercise in metaphor making, foregrounding (poetic) language as that which both facilitates and antagonizes the writing subject's self-development. Pratt, in contrast, does not — perhaps need not — reflect on her social location or abilities as a writer; the struggles she documents are not with the language she uses to represent them.

I would venture that the "politicized" moments Martin and Mohanty locate and reinforce in "Identity: Skin Blood Heart" coincide with gestures that effect Pratt's maturation process — that is, her ascension to self-knowledge — in writing; Pratt's readers are reluctant to examine her rhetorical strategies critically, and they justify this reluctance in the name of a feminist critique of postmodernism. With the "self-referential" operations of language rejected as irrelevant to political analysis — or worse, as a depoliticizing smoke screen over the "real world" — Pratt can be commended for her ability to re-cognize her own location, however often she chooses to change neighborhoods, and to endow her experiences with meaning. Held up as a nonunified subject, Pratt is thus nevertheless able to re-create and comprehend her own past; select which locales and experiences to "revisit," and for how long; and acquire both a mobility and a stability relative to the places and populations she describes. These moves are simultaneously experiential and textual privileges, which the narrator-protagonist of *Runaway* either lacks or attempts to exercise with varying degrees of success. So long as "politicization" is equated with transparent or transcendent self-knowledge, runaway subjects — who may not have the time or distance to narrativize and reevaluate their own locations — are denied participation in political discourse.[10]

Given this tendency to equate lack of self-knowledge with prepolitical consciousness (or childishness), it is not surprising that Lau aspires to the model of self-conscious writing exemplified by Pratt. Lau's aspirations not only correspond to her desire to "mature" and to make sense of her own history, but also manifest themselves in the form of aggravated mind/body splits. When her dependence on drugs is at its most severe, one of Lau's psychiatrists hopes to elicit a reaction by calling her a "junkie whore." Lau reflects:

All that mattered was drugs, and even those weren't as good as they used to be—my body was becoming more tolerant of the chemicals. And I had thought I was immune! Simply a reporter standing by with her journal, perched on the very fringe of the drugs and the streets, tampering with them a little, just experimenting—I'd never thought I had a normal body, a normal mind, that could be sucked in as easily as any other human being's. Never thought that. (251)

In a manner of speaking, Lau here comes to the "acute awareness" that she has taken the autobiographical ideal too literally. She had assumed she could transcribe her own life events as so many "experiments"; as it turns out, the paradigm of writing in which Lau has invested depends on the illusion of separation between "reporter" and reported—that is, between textual producer and "real world." The allure of writing as an instrument for self-reflection has extended a false promise of immunity, of mental and bodily transcendence over (potentially life-threatening) experiences; and while exercising her "freedom" as a writer, Lau has become "enslaved" to drugs.

Yet Lau's insight into the irony of her predicament does not give over to a deconstruction of traditional models of self-representation, nor even an overall comment on the strategies of *Runaway*. Lau more often than not accepts autobiographical writing's claims to self-apprehension in good faith, at times in desperation; her primary identification as a writer continually promises to save her, or offer special dispensation, from other reifying assessments—in this case, as "junkie whore."[11] Lau's relationships to the autobiographical protocol—her striving toward and loss of control over her chosen form—might therefore be considered in both ideological and stylistic terms. This kind of reading is possible without reinfantilizing Lau, or inscribing her anew as "no ordinary runaway" in some other narrative of self-improvement.

Lau can be seen to have adopted dominant (middle-class, Anglo-American) ideology, to the extent that she accepts the values of introspection, self-analysis, and will to success embodied by bourgeois autobiography (Gagnier, 1991, 11–54):

I...want to be myself, turning to my journal...when I have a problem, writing it out instead of muffling it further into my subconscious with dope. I want to feel whole, healthy and happy, and able to deal with things straight. I want to eliminate my compulsive attitude towards drugs so that it won't deter me from progressing as a human being with potential. I want the very best for myself. (Lau, 1989, 262)

But like the British working-class autobiographers of Regenia Gagnier's study, Lau's "experience cannot be analyzed in the terms of [her] acculturation," and a "gap between ideology and experience leads not only to the disintegration of the narrative the writer hopes to construct, but . . . to the disintegration of personality itself" (Gagnier, 1991, 45). The specifically literary standards Lau has internalized wield even more authority than do the standards of health, happiness, and human "wholeness" (Lau, 1989, 275) idealized by dominant autobiographical forms. And when Lau fails to "live up" to her own notion of her promise as a writer — and to the (both formal and behavioral) expectations of conventional autobiographical narrative — she experiences her most devastating bouts of uncertainty and depression. These register, as I have already discussed, in some of *Runaway*'s most layered, fractured, and "poetic" moments, accentuating Lau's own sense of multiple personality disorder, of compound mind/body, body/text splits. "My writing isn't moving. . . . I had never thought that prostitution would become a substitute for writing" (Lau, 1989, 330). "I want to disown this body now, cast it forever into the winds. It is too gross to be mine, it will always be scrawled with oozing white semen" (260).

There apparently can be no more or less "transparent" forms of self-expression, given their imbrication and complicity in stratified social relations. In her discussion of persuasive rhetoric, particularly its emphasis on "clear expression," Trinh T. Minh-ha suggests a different evaluation of transparent discourses than I have so far taken into account:

> Clarity as a purely rhetorical attribute serves the purpose of a classical feature in language, namely, its instrumentality. To write is . . . at any rate to *mean* and to send out *an unambiguous message*. Writing thus reduced to a mere vehicle of thought may be *used* to orient toward a goal or to sustain an act, but it does not constitute an act in itself. (1989, 16)

As *Runaway* demonstrates (at times by counterexample), codes of writing succeed in convincing readers of their clarity or pure instrumentality to the degree that their users are "at home" with them: able to focus on the projected goal of writing and only incidentally on the "vehicle" that gets them there. For all that the modalities of home and homeless-ness may be represented through writing, it may be the case that language offers itself most intimately to issues of place and displacement when at its most indirect and "foreign." In *Runaway*, words often appear as traffic in runaway vehicles of thought, licensed to carry their cargo where they will:

> I'm writing because it's 3:00 a.m. and I'm cold, dizzy with exhaustion; things are beginning to waver. I'm writing to keep myself awake. I don't know who, if anyone, to trust anymore, because men take advantage of you if you're downtown late at night looking like you're not going any-where. (90)

Writing as an act in itself provides Lau with emergency shelter, en route to some deferred destination — perhaps just as the planes, buses, and automobiles Lau gets herself into offer "freedom" and security only in transit.[12]

Unlike more culturally authoritative writers — a category that, in re-lational terms, might include Minnie Bruce Pratt — Lau is prevented from feeling "at home" with the activity to which she looks for suste-nance and support. She begins to "politicize" her experience on the basis of this alienation from writing. Defying her parents' injunctions against her poetry and journals, Lau gradually learns to use writing as a way to circumnavigate a succession of dead ends and locked doors, to "yo-yo" from one temporary or inadequate refuge to the next. This destination-less journey takes place in the immediate context of her running text and the wider context of an urban-social text in the process of being writ-ten and read.

"Streetwalking" in the City

Lau activates the city like a private language and is also inscribed — at times anonymously, at times conspicuously — into its densely woven signifying fabric. What *Runaway*'s readers see of Vancouver is not its geomorphology, architectural attributes, and street patterns, worked into a composite whole, but the city's micrological texture in a succession of "close vision-haptic" snapshots. "Granville Street at night. Men walk up out of the blackness; their hands dart out to grab my breasts; they lead me into their cars" (88). A deceptively depopulated Vancouver on

Christmas Day, 1986: "The buses were empty except for one or two people; the streets were pearly gray and silent except for Skid Row, where
the street people nodded on their benches like pigeons on a line" (150).

The annual Walk for Peace, April 1987, presents an occasion for Lau
to train this kind of microperception on the phenomenon of crowds, and
on her alienation from and absorption into several larger populations:

> Out on Broadway, in the brilliant sunshine. The traffic is heavy, but nearly
> every car going past is full of families or couples. The buses are loaded
> with the peace marchers. Friends had called me several days ago, hoping
> I would help organize a youth demonstration inside the Walk because
> they felt that young people weren't being represented properly. They also
> felt . . . that there were larger issues at stake such as discrimination against
> women, racism, etc. I agreed perfectly, but I no longer felt comfortable
> with politically active people. I belonged on Broadway more than at the
> Walk for Peace. (204)

Lau reads the Walk partially as a spectacle of family togetherness and
orthodox heterosexuality from which she is excluded. She then, apparently unaware of the contradictions, claims she does not "belong" in
the company of "politically active people" and their efforts to address
the underrepresentation of young people, women, and ethnic minorities. The murky problematics of autobiographical representation thus
carry over into the politics of collective self-representation: despite her
"perfect agreement" with the aims of the Walk's organizers, and her can-
didacy as a "perfect" representative for all three target groups within the
march, Lau insists on a supervening difference that renders her on the
outside.

Possibly an encrypted protest against the impassive homogeneity of
crowds, even politically active ones, the irony of Lau's self-imposed exile continues as she leaves the "throngs of marchers" and moves due
east: "The dazzle of the daylight is sickening. There's no business here. I
even move to the downtown eastside, looking for a cheap trick, but the
streets are spilling with Chinatown shoppers, and among the shuffle of
cars and passersby I am lost" (204). Besides this image of the individual's suffocation by the crowd, the insignificance of the one relative to
the many, the reader may be struck by Lau's failure to comment on the
specificity of the venue in which she currently finds/"loses" herself. The

reader may wonder how a young Chinese woman, in Chinatown on a weekend afternoon, could be disappointed not to have been "picked up," even as just one item in a sprawling marketplace. Throughout *Runaway,* Lau identifies herself as Chinese only when her ethnicity signifies a measure of difference, and not sameness or "belonging." We might remember that she sees herself, in another context, as not having a "normal" body — "one that could be sucked in as easily as any other human being's." "Lost" in the commodity spectacle that is Chinatown, from the vantage of the itinerant visitor or shopper, Lau's body may well be subsumed into a crowd of Asian bodies and reified as part of the general, exotic scenery. Thus, I would suggest, Lau takes her place in a racial text that she neither writes nor interprets.

To invoke Vancouver as a text, and one that facilitates a more macrological consideration of these kinds of local ironies, is not necessarily to give into the reveries of relativism and abstraction against which some critics have warned. The runaway subject can be seen as an accelerated version of Michel de Certeau's "walkers" — "ordinary practitioners of the city..., *Wandersmanner,* whose bodies follow the thicks and thins of an urban 'text' they write without being able to read it" (1984, 93) — rendered both ordinary and extraordinary by her relations to the crowds. Lau's movements within and outside the city number among innumerable "pedestrian speech acts" performed by all "down below" who make everyday use of the streets, the possibilities and interdictions, organized by cartographers, urban planners, and city officials (de Certeau, 1984). That such "discrete" rewritings of the spatial order are the tactics of the weak is emphasized whenever Lau moves uncertainly, at times the better or worse for methadone or hash, along Vancouver's thoroughfares. That these local "enunciations" have both a "utopian" and a "polemological" content is borne out whenever Lau abruptly flees one location or person (often both simultaneously: the psychiatrist to whom she dedicates the book is given the architectural pseudonym "Dr. Hightower") in search of a better or "proper" place.

"To walk is to lack a place. It is the indefinite process of being absent and in search of a proper. The moving about that the city multiplies and concentrates makes the city itself an immense social experience of lacking a place" (de Certeau, 1984, 103). To walk — perhaps especially to run — dis-places the city by re-creating it as a shifting constellation of participations and alienations, of performative relations to "the sign of what ought to be, ultimately, the place but is only a name" (103). Yet the city-sign interpellates its subjects/practitioners differently, according to localized constructions of their vulnerabilities and strengths; and thus do "multiple, fluid structures of domination . . . intersect to locate women differently at particular historical conjunctures" (Mohanty, 1991, 13).

For all her running, Lau may demonstrate this best when she comes to an impasse, when the street-corner signs by which she stands signify congealed social relations, advertising her body as an item for sale. Once she is accosted by a would-be rapist in an off-Broadway alley in broad daylight (33). On another occasion, Lau finds herself stuck, literally, between a rock and a hard place, between "an angry man and a cliff" (214–16). In yet another instance, she stops to clarify her situation:

> I took the bus up to Broadway, then stopped. I'd decided to turn a trick, because I couldn't even afford a pack of cigarettes, and what could a kid do except steal, deal or trick? Out on Broadway, in the rain, thumb out. A sadness in the downpour, in the night. Two guys picked me up and we went to their place in Kitsilano. (195–96)

The Vancouver most familiar to Lau may be a city in which "there's no one in sight" (33) to take notice or stock of these events as they occur. On the streets, she is visible primarily to men for whom her gender, ethnicity, and age have fetishistic appeal. She is only partially visible to the police who patrol "her" corner of Broadway and Commercial (314), and to the occasional stranger with good intentions and ulterior motives. Lau's readers may qualify as ordinary "passersby" in de Certeau's sense: pedestrians and commuters caught up in their own searches for their own places, and who may thereby contribute to the obscurity of the teenage runaway, the prostitute, or the homeless person — except when they reach for spare change, or pause to stare.

> Two boys hopping onto the bus grab the seats behind me, and to my horror I hear one of them saying, "No, she's not," and the other laughing knowingly, "Yes, she's a hooker," and afterwards when I turn around they are staring at me. (205)

By encountering the reifying gaze as simultaneously horrifying and appropriate, Lau offers herself as an analogue for the spaces in which she operates. Hooking, as an "urban image problem," has a particular resonance for Vancouver. A mid-1980s installment of the U.S. tabloid news program *Hard Copy* focused on Davie Street's sex-trade workers and strip clubs, and reappointed Vancouver, on the basis of less than a mile, "Sin City." One has reason to eye this sort of representation — its appeal to morality and its peep-show promotion of sex tourism — with skepticism; most pornographic material in Canada is imported from the United States (Bell, 1987, 15). Moreover, we can begin to consider points of affinity and difference between Vancouver and other "bad girl" seaport cities of the world, so devised and received. Bangkok and Manila, for example, are cities within nations "feminized" by the multinational powers to which they are economically, culturally, and/or militarily subordinated;[13] a similarly gendered power dynamic, mediated by similar interests, may contribute to the image of Vancouver as "Sin City," projected by an at once prurient and morally superior American gaze.

Geographic and personal identity is a relational matter, and not always or ideally a quantity that can be known. "There were so many men, they all thought I was a hooker, and most unbelievably of all I *was* a hooker" (Lau, 1989, 206). While she at times capitulates to the gazes that freeze her into delimiting categories, Lau never quite assimilates herself into the identities prefabricated for her. "I think it might have been healthier for me to run," she writes, "and emphasize my differences" (144). For Lau, writing is indeed the difference that makes the difference: "I hope to live long enough to make a name for myself from my writing; I'm even thinking as far ahead as moving to Toronto when I'm older" (231).

Deferring her arrival as a writer and as an adult to the time when she might make it to Canada's cultural capital — "that cold city people tell [her she] will hate" (246) — Lau serves yet again to interrogate her own location on overlapping maps of life and text. Lau may not physically get to Toronto in the course of her journal, but that text, in so many ways her surrogate in the "real world," is finally published and recirculated from there. And where does Lau go from there, or here?[14] What do borders look like from the perspectives of those who "don't fit in anywhere"? Another British Columbia writer, Sky Lee, has reinterpreted home as a guerrilla base in an extended war: "The circumstances are often such as to make it necessary to run away. The ability to run away is precisely one of the characteristics of the guerrilla; running away is the chief means of getting out of passivity and regaining the initiative" (Mao Tse-tung, quoted in Lee, 1990, 108). Writing is one kind of homing device, one way of regaining the initiative, available to the runaway subject and her potential allies — the migrant, the nomad, and the guerrilla.

Notes

A different version of this chapter appeared as "Where the 'Street Kid' Meets the City: Feminism, Postmodernism and Runaway Subjectivity," in Delany (1994, 97–120).

1. A Canadian Broadcast Corporation film adaptation of *Runaway* aired on Canadian television in 1994.

2. The red-light district currently located along Vancouver's East Broadway, for example, is a displacement of the even more notorious Davie Street after the gentrification campaigns of the early to mid-1980s.

3. In many respects, Lau resembles Deleuze and Guattari "nomad": the "deterritorialized par excellence" whose variable and polyvocal directions in space are localized, nonglobal, and "close vision-haptic" (1987). By referring to Lau as a "runaway" and not a "nomadic" subject, however, I mean to locate her movements within the urban-industrial West, and her strategies as partially participating in what Deleuze and Guattari call "relative global" space, as distinct from "nomad space." Another, possibly more compelling, corollary to what I am calling the runaway subject is the figure of the migrant or émigré, on whom much postcolonial scholarly and creative literature has focused. Lau's "migratory" flight from her parents, both of them Chinese immigrants, could for instance be seen as at once reproducing and departing from recognizable patterns of Asian diaspora, resettlement and assimilation in the Americas. I regret my inability to pursue these connections here, but recommend as relevant reading Takaki, especially his historical and ethnographic analysis of second-generation Chinese Americans (1989, 257–69), and Li (1990).

4. See Adrienne Rich, "Notes toward a Politics of Location" (1986), for a detailed critique of ethnocentrism within feminism.

5. In the context of interrogating the modernism/postmodernism opposition that continues to dominate academic debate, Andreas Huyssen has argued that "the term '*post*modernism' itself should guard us against such an approach as it positions the phenomenon as relational" (1986, 3).

6. Such ambiguity of generic boundaries might be considered a feature of contemporary women's autobiographical practices in general. In their introduction to *De/Colonizing the Subject: The Politics of Gender in Women's Autobiography,* Smith and Watson suggest that "the more [autobiographical writing] surrounds us, the more it defies generic stabilization, the more its laws are broken, the more it drifts toward practices, the more formerly 'out-law' practices drift into its domain" (1992, xviii).

7. Many of these moments correspond to a level of sexual sophistication, as "adult" knowledge, apparently imported into the diaristic narrative after the fact. For example, shortly after the incident in Joe's cabin and well before her first consensual sexual encounter, Lau reflects on a proposition made by a group of drunken high school students on their graduation night (e.g., her age seniors): "Maybe I should have clambered over that fence and fucked that rather beautiful blond boy, but the street lamps are lonely moons hanging over the alley" (1989, 46). A "poetic" register contributes to the density of narration in this and many other examples.

8. This would seem to apply to reader-detractors as well. In her review of *Runaway* for the *Women's Review of Books,* Jennifer Kornreich offers the pronouncement that "Lau isn't truly a street kid" and faults the memoir for what it does not deliver—among other things, "a savvy expose of street culture" and "the anthropology of sex work" (1996, 17). Given the expectations of the reviewer, and her aversion to what she defines as Lau's "simply whiny...adolescent pout about the cruelty of established authority" (18), it is perhaps not surprising that Kornreich's reading of *Runaway* should differ considerably from my own. At issue is precisely the question that interests me here: how one draws boundaries around the subject, distinguishing between the "raw" and the "cooked," the collectivist and the individualistic, testimonial and autobiographical aspects or modes of self-representation. Whereas, in other words, Kornreich sees Lau failing on both "anthropological" and "literary" counts, I am trying to trace negotiations and contradictions between the two, not at all autonomous, sets of critical assumptions—a process undertaken both by Lau and her readers. In such a context, the "failures" and omissions of *Runaway* may be just as compelling as, if not more compelling than, the extent to which Lau can be said to "succeed."

9. I have tried to engage examples of these writings in an interior critique of feminist identity politics (Chang, 1994).

10. The attribution of a prepolitical "innocence" to dispossessed individuals and groups may be considered not only that which underwrites dominant constructions of "the self," but also that which permits Western idealizations of "the other." Aijaz Ahmad has argued that Fredric Jameson's postulation of "third-world literature" as a coherent theoretical and pedagogical category relies on the "empirically ungrounded" removal of the Third World from global economic systems and the history of capitalist development (1987, 6–7). Whereas the First and Second Worlds, by Jameson's account, are defined by their modes of production (1986, 65, 88), the Third World is distinguished "purely in terms of an 'experience' of externally inserted phenomena" (Ahmad, 1987, 6–7). In taking issue with "homogenizing and reactive critical descriptions of Third World literatures," Gayatri Chakravorty Spivak (1988, 253) has similarly called attention to an "ontological/epistemological confusion that pits subaltern being against elite knowing" (268). Ahmad and Spivak suggest how contests over the status of self-knowledge always take place within a wider terrain of debate. If the ability to know and to analyze one's own conditions is considered a series of operations separate from "experience" and "being," then certain agents and forms of knowledge are necessarily, and artificially, excluded—regardless of the values assigned to the categories (e.g., knowledge/ignorance) in question.

11. Lau's efforts to differentiate herself from "other" drug addicts, prostitutes, and teenage runaways serve as a reminder that, given unequal access to literacy and publication, writing is always a mark of social privilege. Yet *Runaway*'s most compelling proof of the writer's elite cultural location and its power to determine individual and collective identity is the ongoing battle between Lau's ambitions and her self-doubts. For all her performative and wishful assertions that she is foremost a writer, Lau chronically questions her qualifications for the job. "I could become one of the top writers in Canada, or I could be a drug addict, or I could die. Those are the choices" (1989, 230). "Who's going to be fascinated by the writing of a kid who has ability but chooses time and again to run away, take drugs or prostitute herself?" (247). Lau reads James Joyce, Dylan Thomas, and E. L. Doctorow, but identifies with the deceased writer of *Go Ask Alice,* "a big sensationalist hit" published by "someone else" (299). She does not mention authors like William S. Burroughs or Jack Kerouac — that is, male writers for whom drugs, "illicit" sex, and running away or amok have not been antithetical to their pursuit of the literary vocation.

12. "Lately I've been getting on a lot of buses and riding them around and around. It increases my sense of irresponsibility, of being in limbo, of . . . 'freedom' " (Lau, 1989, 94).

13. For an excellent analysis of the cultural economy of sex tourism in Southeast Asia, see Truong, who demonstrates how "the ideology of hospitality, servitude and self-sacrifice inherent in the traditional female role" (1990, 128) is mobilized for the purposes of attracting foreign capital, manipulated as a means by which to socialize and recruit women into the tourist industries, and generalized by potential consumers as a national or regional trait.

14. Since *Runaway*'s publication, Lau has written and received less than laudatory reviews for *Fresh Girls and Other Stories* (1993) and her first novel, *Other Women* (1995). Vancouver remains her home.

Works Cited

Ahmad, Aijaz. 1987. "Jameson's Rhetoric of Otherness and the 'National Allegory.' " *Social Text* 17: 3–25.

Bell, Laurie. 1987. "Introduction." In *Good Girls/Bad Girls: Feminists and Sex Trade Workers Face to Face,* ed. Laurie Bell. Toronto: Seal.

Bell, Susan Groag, and Marilyn Yalom, eds. 1990. *Revealing Lives: Autobiography, Biography, and Gender.* Albany: State University of New York Press.

Chang, Elaine K. 1994. "A Not-So-New Spelling of My Name: Notes toward (and against) a Politics of Equivocation." In *Displacements: Cultural Identities in Question,* ed. Angelika Bammer, 251–66. Bloomington: Indiana University Press.

de Certeau, Michel. 1984. *The Practice of Everyday Life,* trans. Steven Rendall. Berkeley: University of California Press.

Delany, Paul, ed. 1994. *Vancouver: Representing the Postmodern City.* Vancouver: Arsenal Pulp Press.

Deleuze, Gilles, and Félix Guattari. 1987. *A Thousand Plateaus: Capitalism and Schiz-ophrenia*, trans. Brian Massumi. Minneapolis: University of Minnesota Press.

Gagnier, Regenia. 1991. *Subjectivities: A History of Self-Representation in Britain, 1832–1920.* New York: Oxford University Press.

Haraway, Donna. 1991. *Simians, Cyborgs, and Women: The Reinvention of Nature.* New York: Routledge.

Hawkesworth, Mary E. 1989. "Knowers, Knowing, Known: Feminist Theory and Claims of Truth." *Signs: Journal of Women in Culture and Society* 14.3: 533–57.

Huyssen, Andreas. 1986. *After the Great Divide: Modernism, Mass Culture, Postmodernism.* Bloomington: Indiana University Press.

Jameson, Fredric. 1984. "Postmodernism; or, The Cultural Logic of Late Capitalism." *New Left Review* 146: 53–92.

———. 1986. "Third World Literature in the Era of Multinational Capitalism." *Social Text* 15: 65–88.

Jelinek, Estelle C., ed. 1980. *Women's Autobiography: Essays in Criticism.* Bloomington: Indiana University Press.

Kornreich, Jennifer. 1996. "Selling Her Body, Selling Her Soul." *Women's Review of Books* 13.6: 17–18.

Lau, Evelyn. 1989. *Runaway: Diary of a Street Kid.* Toronto: HarperCollins.

———. 1993. *Fresh Girls and Other Stories.* Toronto: HarperCollins.

———. 1995. *Other Women.* Toronto: Random House.

Lazreg, Marnia. 1988. "Feminism and Difference: The Perils of Writing as Woman on Women in Algeria." *Feminist Studies* 14.1: 81–107.

Lee, Sky. 1990. "Women in Touch Coming Home." In *Telling It: Women and Language across Cultures,* ed. Telling It Book Collective, 105–9. Vancouver: Press Gang.

Li, Peter S., ed. 1990. *Race and Ethnic Relations in Canada.* Toronto: Oxford University Press.

Martin, Biddy, and Chandra Talpade Mohanty. 1986. "Feminist Politics: What's Home Got to Do with It?" In *Feminist Studies/Critical Studies,* ed. Teresa de Lauretis, 191–212. Bloomington: Indiana University Press.

Mohanty, Chandra Talpade. 1991. "Cartographies of Struggle: Third World Women and the Politics of Feminism." In *Third World Women and the Politics of Feminism,* ed. Chandra Talpade Mohanty et al., 1–47. Bloomington: Indiana University Press.

Nicholson, Linda J. 1990. "Introduction." In *Feminism/Postmodernism,* ed. Linda J. Nicholson. New York: Routledge.

Personal Narratives Group, ed. 1989. *Interpreting Women's Lives: Feminist Theory and Personal Narratives.* Bloomington: Indiana University Press.

Pratt, Minnie Bruce. 1984. "Identity: Skin Blood Heart." In *Yours in Struggle: Three Feminist Perspectives on Anti-Semitism and Racism,* 11–63. New York: Long Haul.

Rich, Adrienne. 1986. "Notes toward a Politics of Location." In *Blood, Bread, and Poetry: Selected Prose, 1979–85,* 210–31. New York: Norton.

Smith, Sidonie, and Julia Watson, eds. 1992. *De/Colonizing the Subject: The Politics of Gender in Women's Autobiography.* Minneapolis: University of Minnesota Press.

Spivak, Gayatri Chakravorty. 1988. *In Other Words: Essays in Cultural Politics.* New York: Routledge.

Takaki, Ronald. 1989. *Strangers from a Different Shore: A History of Asian Americans.* New York: Penguin.

Trinh T. Minh-ha. 1989. *Woman, Native, Other: Writing Postcoloniality and Feminism.* Bloomington: Indiana University Press.

Truong, Tranh-dam. 1990. *Sex, Money and Morality: Prostitution and Tourism in Southeast Asia.* London: Zed.

SIX

Compromised Narratives along the Border: The Mason-Dixon Line, Resistance, and Hegemony

Russ Castronovo

> There is, perhaps, no line, real or imaginary, on the surface of the earth—not excepting even the equator and the equinoctial— whose name has been oftener in men's mouths during the last fifty years.
>
> JOHN LATROBE, *The History of Mason and Dixon's Line*, 1855

Although literary critics, writers, and intellectuals have emphasized the diversity and newness emerging along the "border" zones of literal geopolitical boundaries as well the more figurative limits of subjectivity, accounts of the people and texts who inhabit these liminal spaces tend to coalesce into a single, undifferentiated narrative line. Commentators who treat the distinct experiences of nationality, alternative permutations of sexuality, racial marginalization, and varying degrees of political oppression that appear in such works as Gloria Anzaldúa's *Borderlands/La Frontera* or Américo Paredes's *With His Pistol in His Hand* nonetheless tell similar stories when they describe how such texts perform within the tricky ambiguities that mark borders. The stories latent in this criticism, for the most part, contribute to a narrative, teleologically successful and consistent, that reads like a story of classic heroism: a text overcomes the impediments of being marginal to two or more cultures, and indeed subversively benefits from these limitations and prejudices to undermine the oppressive structures that in the first place differentiated and hierarchized Texas and Mexico, heterosexuality and homosexuality, Spanish and English—whatever the particular geography of the border in question may be. This critical account usually concludes optimistically as the text that challenges division and separation provides a glimpse of a region infused with new understandings of nationality (or nonnationality), gender, and identity in which subjects are not forced to choose between sexualities, languages, or political geographies in order to live in the world.

Critical accounts often narrativize the conflicts emerging along and between cultural boundaries by representing border writing as a discursive strategy capable of deconstructing ossified structures like patriarchy or the nation. I want to explore, however, a different strain in this narrative, one that examines the interstices between border and nation to suggest that the border involves more than tactics that undermine the inviolate sovereignty of the nation, for negotiations along the border also have the unintended counterpurpose of solidifying and extending racial and national boundaries. "No once-for-all victories are obtained," reminds Stuart Hall in his comments on resistance within popular culture, because culture is a shifting terrain—a "battlefield," as he puts it— where the attainment of autonomy is too often only a temporary phenomenon (1981, 233). Not only does the border push up against and disturb the nation, but in a strategic turnabout, the nation also employs the border to imagine the limits beyond which it might expand, to scout horizons for future settlement, to prepare the first line of attack. As a site of contested cultural production, the border offers a shifting ground ripe for articulations of oppositional consciousness; however, this uncertain terrain is laden with "traps," according to Abdul JanMohamed, that suture homogeneity and confirm hierarchical structures (103). Border crossers are not the only ones who find advantage in the liminality at the margins of culture. The nation regulates this space as well, except that in this case such boundaries figure as occasions to imagine, often aggressively, fixed and unrelenting standards of citizenship and belonging.

The epigraph that heads this essay resounds with these unpredictable moments of national consolidation that appear within narratives of border crossing. Latrobe offers *The History of Mason and Dixon's Line* to remind his audience that this implied boundary line did not always imply national disintegration. He invokes the border to posit a history of homogenity; he expounds upon the border to recall a nation not of divided loyalties, but of singular purpose. Even as Latrobe acknowledges the severe ideological and institutional differences emanating from this imaginary line running between Maryland and Pennsylvania, his prose also figures the Mason-Dixon line as an exemplar of American exceptionalism that surpasses all other history being lived and experienced anywhere else "on the surface of the earth" (5). The unsettling of the United States occurring between North and South prompts a retreat into an imperial language that allows the 233-mile Mason-Dixon line to outsignify the 25,000-mile equator. At the very least, antebellum Americans can share the common pride that their border strife is the most important in the world. The border—as a site of internal discord—is forgotten through indulgence in a sense of international competition that judges this moment of U.S. history as superior to any incidents of contemporary global politics. In similar fashion, James Veech, another nineteenth-century historian of the border, argued in 1857 that the ideological battles—what he euphemistically called the "interest"—waged across the Mason-Dixon line pointed to the future and durability of the United States: "Empires have risen and fallen; dynasties have sunk into nothingness. Yet this line still stands; and its story increases in interest as time grows older. Nor is its history yet ended. God grant that it may never have to be written of it that it severed this glorious Union!" (47). Nationalism—a force that consolidates, demarcates, and hierarchizes—is here the response to the permeability and fluidity of border culture. As the site of difference, the border becomes strategic in promoting the desire for sameness.

In this volume devoted primarily to theorizing the many borderlands of the Southwest, a discursive examination of the Mason-Dixon line no doubt seems out of place.[1] An inquiry into the cultural history of the Mason-Dixon line, however, can be useful for reframing the critical narratives that describe the outcome of contact in the border zones. The attempt to translate "border theory" from the Tex-Mex region to the Mason-Dixon fails to produce an easy fit, not simply because of the chronological, cultural, and specific historical discrepancies involved, but because the narrative inherent to a good deal of theorizing about *la frontera* does not adequately tell the story of other historically significant borders. Indeed, this mistranslation suggests that critical narratives about the border may leave untheorized some of the more difficult movements — most notably counterinsurgency and national consolidation — that appear along cultural and political boundaries, including the ones that divide and connect Mexico and the United States. "Border theory," and the narratives of resistance and subversion that it supplies, does not travel well; it too readily formulates a perspective that overlooks the force and appeal of the nation-state. Although not quite the topic of conversation it was in Latrobe's day, the Mason-Dixon line, I would argue, nonetheless provides a site for examining the pitfalls of racial ideology and the cul-de-sacs of inescapable nationalism predatorily inherent to borders.

Why Hegemony Likes Borders

Before examining the autobiographies, speeches, and polemics that crisscrossed a boundary line first surveyed prior to the founding of the United States, I want to identify the latent narrative shared by many accounts of the border. Hayden White's argument that historians emplot history in certain definable narrative modes, each of which implies an ideological position, may be productively applied to writing about the border (1973, 1–21; 1987, 1–24). As the account offered by critics such as Gloria Anzaldúa, José David Saldívar, and Paula Gunn Allen goes, border writing is an oppositional discourse, battling tremendous odds, including multinational corporations, cultural imperialism, racial prejudice, and traditional patterns of gender identification. But by not settling down on either side of these divisions imposed by culture, border texts disturb rigid constellations of power. Voices and identities situated in the in-between of a hybrid land — what Anzaldúa calls a "third country" — carve out spaces laden with possibilities of liberation, as, for instance, the speaker of *Borderlands/La Frontera* does by refusing to accept either the patriarchal codes of Mexican culture or the narrow confines of mainstream U.S. feminism (5). José David Saldívar thus identifies Chicano border narrative as an "oppositional voice" that offers "a literary form of resistance to the encroachment of Anglo-Americans" (170, 172). Such positioning, according to Maggie Humm's *Border Traffic*, though often the seat of limitation and disempowerment, now works ironically and proves advantageous to "contemporary women writers [who] build something out of marginality" (4). Using a similar plot, Sonia Saldívar-Hull points to this subversive quality in Anzaldúa's *Borderlands/La Frontera,* arguing that "border feminism...deconstructs geopolitical boundaries," and in the process reconfigures the dominant cultural geography of gender and sexuality (210–11). Her conclusions echo the successful outcome of the gendered border struggle examined by Humm, where "women's writing destabilises literary hierarchies" (4). Though pronouncements such as Humm's (not to mention those of other Anglo/American feminists) often do not include or address women of color, Chicana feminists, according to Saldívar-Hull, also redirect their marginality in such innovative ways that the strictures that seek to circumscribe Chicanas' speech, actions, and consciousness are radically destabilized. Saldívar-Hull thus witnesses in Anzaldúa the formulation of "a feminism that exists in a borderland not limited to geographic space, a feminism that resides in a space not acknowledged by hegemonic culture.... Anzaldúa explodes the power that the dominant culture holds over what is 'normal' or acceptable" (211). "Border theory" narrativizes a history in which culturally transgressive texts, actions, and bodies circumvent traditional structures of power, but this emplotment of resistance can mute another narrative in which power can and does reassert itself.

To imagine a space divested of "hegemonic culture," however, is to mistake the nature of hegemony and confuse it with domination. Although it is unclear whether Saldívar-Hull intends *hegemonic culture* and *dominant culture* as synonyms, this slippage enables her to sketch a new cultural landscape, a terrain analogous to Anzaldúa's "third country." Whereas it may be possible to "explod[e]...dominant culture," hegemony is not built on the sheer force of domination, but instead regulates the discourses of legitimacy, institutions, and nation in which resistance and challenges appear. Hegemony improves upon domination by creating a "complex 'system'...conducted on several different fronts at once" instead of a monolithic display that relies on out-and-out force (Hall 1986, 19). The border is more than a site of domination: it is also a "differentiated terrain" grooved with "different discursive currents"; it is an ambiguous ground whose penetrable boundaries prove advantageous not only for border crossers, but for ideological formations that structure social realities (Hall 1986, 22). Foremost among these ideological structures is the nation, which often eagerly looks to the border zone for the conquest and annexation of new territory. The misrecognition of domination for hegemony allows for a narrative that begins with the rebellion of an unruly underdog against "hegemonic culture" and concludes with a glimpse of a landscape whose geographic and psychic dimensions outstrip traditional categories. Border crossers, as one critic writes, create "new myths . . . [that] provide radical alternatives to the existing social structures" (Keating 73). But this narrative of newness is not without its debts to cultural forces coincident with nationalism. The search for fresh possibilities and innovative communities is actually a version of a much older story of America: optimism about the "New World," and later the "new" lands west of the Mississippi, was fueled by the notion of the *translatio,* which held that the drama of human history unfolds in five great acts, each located progressively westward, chasing the horizon from Eden to Jerusalem to Rome to England to America.[2] As the promised and final installment of the *translatio,* America rises up as the pinnacle of civilization because its exceptional newness surpasses the worn-out cultures of the "Old World." Imagined as a break from what had come before, America represents a new beginning not destined to repeat the excesses of Rome. Clearly the *translatio* authorizes a colonial and rapacious vision that "border theory" does not repeat and indeed forcefully critiques, but the imperial frontier and the border do correspond in their indebtedness to a romanticized novelty about regions beyond traditionally mapped boundaries. This overlap suggests that resistant narratives borrow — perhaps are compelled to borrow — from narratives made available by hegemonic culture.

Encompassing more than geography, the border as a theoretical space provides commentators with a frontier of alternative identities fortuitously disconnected from antecedents of predation and exploitation. *Borderlands/La Frontera,* for instance, is constructed so that the chapters progress from "The Homeland, Aztlán" to "*La conciencia de la mestiza*: Toward a New Consciousness," which celebrates a hybrid identity — neither male nor female, neither American nor Mexican, neither English nor Spanish — that inhabits the crossroads, discovering "new meanings" spoken in a "new language" (Anzaldúa 81). Renato Rosaldo charts a similar movement in the work of Sandra Cisneros, citing her experimentation with narrative as means of producing "a fresh vision of self and society" (81). Like Anzaldúa's, Rosaldo's discussion is indebted to geographic metaphors that lead to a narrative of new, optimistic encounters: he discovers "an alternative cultural space, a heterogeneous world," bountiful in creative possibilities, rich in the "potential of borders in opening new forms of human understanding" (165, 213). Certainly the consequences of discovering yet another world are different for border writers and the seventeenth-century colonists authorized by the *translatio,* one envisioning avenues for political enfranchisement and cultural autonomy, and the other implementing a history of conquest and genocide. Moreover, the capacity of border writing to lead the way past an "invidious, white supremacist rhetoric" and toward "the possibility of a revitalized Chicano present and future," as José David Saldívar puts it, is not a questionable goal simply because the narrativization of that goal, in part, corresponds to other narratives whose effects have been catastrophic (178).

Though border writing has the capacity to "counter the hegemonic national narratives" and thereby envision "other, perhaps more enlightening heliotropes," I want to invoke the Mason-Dixon line as border in order to question how alternative, how unencumbered this new territory is that emerges in the shifting zones of cultural interaction and overlap (R. Saldívar 42). Although abolitionists such as Wendell Phillips proclaimed "the soil of the Pilgrims as an asylum for the oppressed" and touted the North as a land of freedom, too often and too soon fugitive slaves who crossed the Mason-Dixon line encountered national policies and racial prejudices that compromised the sanctity of the supposed refuge (Douglass 1968[1845], xviii). Even before the passage of the Fugitive Slave Law in 1850, runaways had been subject to recapture, and this legislation only laid bare the complicity between the new land of freedom and the old land of bondage. When John Latrobe, a white citizen from Maryland, came North in 1854 to lecture to Pennsylvanians about this rift in the national fabric, he denied that destabilization occurs along the border; instead, he predicted a time of ideological consolidation when "the Mason and Dixon's line of politics will gradually change its position until, as cloud-shadows pass, leaving earth in sunlight, we shall be seen, of all, to be a united and homogeneous people" (51). Borders need not be sites of division; rather, as the sutures of national cohesion, they can offer an imaginative topos for the articulation of "transcendent" ideals of racial supremacy and political unity. As black activists charged, the Compromise of 1850 and its provisions for remanding fugitives only confirmed that inextricable connections between North and South were so strong that Northerners consented to hunt slaves for a social system they often derided as tyrannical and unjust. Added to these institutional trappings, race prejudice permeated the Mason-Dixon line to such an extent that discrimination and exploitation followed the ex-slave in his or her efforts to gain access to education, religion, housing, and employment. These overlaps between North and South show that Latrobe's comments are right on the mark: instead of fragmenting regions and identities, boundaries may encourage consolidation and consensus. Poised against such forces, new territories of political possibility may slide back into repressive regimes. The surest signs that crossings along this antebellum border do not end in freedom are found in slave narratives such as Harriet Jacobs's *Incidents in the Life of a Slave Girl* and Frederick Douglass's *My Bondage and My Freedom,* whose plots continue to unfold long after their protagonists reach the North.[3]

The textual traffic in the antebellum United States that runs back and forth across the Mason-Dixon line illustrates that although crossing borders is a powerfully subversive act, its impact may be limited, capable of dismantling a construct like the nation only temporarily before the deconstructive potential of border discourse is reconstructed *back* within the very system being challenged. Of course, the human traffic that escaped bondage and fled to the North was, especially after passage of the Fugitive Slave Law, subject to recapture: yet not only were bodies in continual jeopardy, but the fugitive textual expressions that challenged and undercut the peculiar institution were assailed by slaveholders and returned to discursive frameworks riddled with the workings of oppression. Almost as soon as fugitive slaves stood up at reformist pulpits and abolitionist lecterns in Boston and New York, proslavery editors and writers reappropriated the slave's story, rechaining it to an ideology it had sought to escape.

Although I don't disagree with the optimism expressed in critical stories about border writing, I nonetheless contend that this narrativization obscures other ways of thinking about the border that must be recognized if negotiations involving nations, hybrid identities, and cultural liberation are to acknowledge not simply the celebratory potential of the contact zone, but also the ineradicable trappings of power that patrol the boundaries of any area of culture. This thinking, strongly indebted to Gramsci's work on hegemony, suggests the need to create cautionary tales about the border.[4] To tell a story that casts border writing with a "subversive nature" disruptive of national culture ignores how discursive acts that undermine the nation are also susceptible to recontainment and suppression (Hicks xxvii). Speaking of class antagonisms, Stuart Hall rejects "heroic" accounts of a working-class culture that thoroughly evades encapsulation by commercial modes (1981, 232). Instead, he offers a more difficult rendering of a dialectical "battlefield" in which sides, positions, and victories occupy a fluctuating terrain where boundaries are redrawn from struggle to struggle. The "heroic alternative" of resistance deployed by the narrative of border theory I am critiquing here implies a position that does not see a more ambivalent and compromised story of continuing struggle, where the forms of liberation and escape prepared by deconstructing boundaries remain intricately linked with power (Hall 1981, 232).[5] "What is wrong" with a story in which marginal expression undercuts domination, states Hall, is that it "neglects the absolutely essential relations of cultural power — of domination and subordination — which is an intrinsic feature of cultural relations" (232).

The "cultural relations" mapped by critical theorists of the border at first seem attuned to this continually shifting interplay between suppression and resistance. Yet the emphasis falls too predominantly upon resistance as the final and sustained outcome; the result is that "cultural relations" get read as a unidirectional narrative line that begins with oppression and ends with a dissident stance impervious to compromise or setback. Ramón Saldívar, for example, employs Foucault's famous dictum that "where there is power, there is resistance" as part of his argument that border texts can thwart national teleologies, but in Foucault's text it is not the word "resistance" that is emphasized (R. Saldívar 36;

Foucault 1978, 95). Rather, the sentence continues, hinging on words not quoted by Saldívar: "and yet this resistance is never in a position of exteriority in relation to power," writes Foucault (95). The "and yet" does not so much discount the viable existence of cultural critique as it underscores the constant complicity between power and resistance that allows for some points of resistance to act as the "adversary" of power and others to act as the "support" of power (Foucault 1978, 95). Ramón Saldívar's partial quotation of Foucault aptly typifies the desire to narrate a story of the border that ends with resistance. Too often, however, the story continues and resistance is neither a new conclusion nor a promised land, but a temporary victory susceptible to national retrenchment. What ensues from this misplaced stress on resistance is a "cultural dualism" that, according to Eric Lott, makes for static models of interpretation that posit cultural artifacts as either "wholly authentic or wholly hegemonic" but not as a more entangled mixture, not as part of a more complex topography in which oppressive forces can and do reassert themselves (35).

Conceptualizations of borders in the twenty-first century need to consult the seemingly out-of-date cultural maps offered by fugitive slaves. African American slaves who crossed the Mason-Dixon line offer uncannily accurate descriptions of the forces amassed along the sites of national suture. Their tales of a tenuous freedom argue for a reexamination of the stories we tell ourselves of discursive defiance and textual emancipation. Although freedom seems the obvious conclusion of the slave narrative, the material circumstances surrounding instances of antebellum black discourse ambiguate any teleology of freedom.

The Escape and Capture of Fugitive Discourse

As a border crosser subject to recapture, trenchant racism, and open hostility, Frederick Douglass perceived the necessity of *not* fashioning a narrative that ends with resistance; instead, he extended his story beyond his own rebellion to the slave regime, because he saw all too clearly that hegemony could reframe and manage rebellion so that its power could become not antagonistic toward but supportive of the U.S. system of slavery. His 1845 *Narrative* boldly details his defiance to the "peculiar institution," *and yet* Douglass is careful not to overemphasize the emancipatory qualities of resistance. His very plot of freedom is threatened by readers who would use the slave's story as a means to gain knowledge of and thus counteract strategies of escape and subversion. Douglass abruptly announces, "I deem it proper to make known my intention not to state all the facts" of his flight; he understands that any merchandise, bodies, or articulations that cross the border can take on an oppositional status without fully invalidating the force of a slaveholding logic coincident with the nation itself (1968[1845], 105).

In his speeches and writings, Douglass displays an incisive understanding of the extent to which slavery's influence spread far beyond the actual sanctioned geography of human bondage. "The evils resulting from this huge system of iniquity," he wrote in 1850, "are not confined to the states south of Mason and Dixon's line. Its noxious influence can easily be traced throughout our Northern borders" (1950, 2:145). His awareness of how capitalism, love for the Union, and a nationally sanctioned ideology of racism all overcame sectional differences led Douglass to seek a position impervious to Southern manipulation. Placing himself on terrain that could not be crisscrossed by national loyalties, Douglass wrote from Ireland, "I have no end to serve, no creed to uphold, no government to defend; and as to nation, I belong to none" (1950, 1:126). Little over a year later, however, Douglass's articulations would be forced to take sides; the sentiment behind these words, which offer no obeisance to a country that denies him citizenship, is repositioned back within the very borders he tried to evade. One of the first speeches made by Douglass to be published as a pamphlet appeared not in some Northern furnace of abolitionism, but in Baltimore, under the title *Abolition Fanaticism in New York. Speech of a Runaway Slave from Baltimore, at an Abolition Meeting in New York* (1847) (see Figure 6.1). Though slave catchers could not recapture a chattel once called Fred Bailey and now prominently lauded by the name Frederick Douglass, proslavery forces had little difficulty in pirating his speech and returning it to the very city from which he had run away.

The circumstances of publication undercut the freedom of the fugitive's voice. The title records the fact of his escape "from Baltimore," but the materiality of the pamphlet, produced in the South, counteracts that flight and insists on senses of geographic specificity and belonging

Figure 6.1. The cover of the pamphlet *Abolition Fanaticism* uses visual stereotypes and commercial markings in an attempt to defuse the potential subversiveness of Frederick Douglass's antislavery activities.

that Douglass had resisted. Offered to the public — "price six cents" is plainly printed on the cover — the pamphlet reinitiates the conditions of slave labor as once again the work of the slave (in this case, a speech) is expropriated and surrendered to the financial and ideological profit of slaveholding society. In this context, one cannot forget Eric Lott's reminder that such interest in black performance on the part of white Americans "was indeed a matter of ownership" (43). Could these signs of recontainment effectively silence the critical facts ironically memorialized by this publication, namely, that a runaway had spoken out against the peculiar institution and that white persons had gathered to hear him do so? No — but then again acknowledgment of marginal speech is never pure and simple; instead, it always involves expropriation or, to recall the words of Hall, "the absolutely essential relations of cultural power — of domination and subordination." Thus, in the case of *Abolition Fanaticism* recognition does not entail respect, for slavery's supporters admit that Douglass can speak only to undermine his words and shackle their import to another agenda.[6] It is at this point that racist caricature, made popular by the minstrel show, literally enters the picture of Douglass's speech. Accenting the way in which the word "Speech" stands out on the title page, a racialized portrait of Douglass in the act of delivering his oration to a white audience forms the most prominent aspect of the pamphlet's face. But any echo the graphic image provides of this "speech" is a sinister one: the illustration does not underscore that a runaway can discourse intelligently so much as it presents Douglass as the "dandy," puffed up to ironic heights, which mocks any pretensions to seriousness contained in the "speech" advertised. Lott's remark that "print caricature was probably a necessary but not a sufficent condition for racial burlesque, for it lacked the crucial presence of the body" is instructive, for it reveals how the juxtaposition of Douglass's "speech" and Douglass's "body" muffles his denunciation, reminding readers of the corporeal forms they can by law and custom silence (41). The image supersedes the textual message, thereby burying Douglass's words under stereotyped visual references to comic animality. Whereas the very idea of an oration delivered in the free states by a fugitive slave marks the abrogation and transgression of borders between North and South, man and chattel, and resistance and docility, the material circumstances and encompassing frame appended to his speech prove the need for a critical narrative, which questions the permanence and profundity of the deconstructive forces that arise with border crossing.

Ironic reversals severely afflict the oppositional impetus of Douglass's address. Much of his discourse obviates national boundaries, challenging the petty allegiances that curtail honest and forthright reflection. By declaring, "I have no country. What country have I?" Douglass locates himself outside the entanglements of the American political geography, beyond any expectations that he conform to or abide by the customs of a particular territory or the rules of its institutions (1847, 3). Self-identified in this manner, he asserts his right, against the protests of several American representatives, to address the London World's Temperance Convention in 1846 by stressing that "it was the *World's* Convention . . . not the convention of any particular Nation — not a man's nor a woman's Convention, not a black man's nor a white man's Convention, but the *World's* Convention, the convention of ALL, *black* as well as *white, bond* as well as *free*" (1847, 7). Independent of national borders and the divisions they maintain, Douglass has the freedom to speak. By confronting these boundaries, a writer, according to Paula Gunn Allen, "can erect a criticism that speaks to . . . spiritual independence," which "must lead to freedom from domination" (314). For Douglass and *Abolition Fanaticism,* however, discursive freedom is fleeting, a temporary space in an ideological world subject to retrenchment and counterattack. The opening paragraph of *Abolition Fanaticism,* the only supplement to a speech that is otherwise reprinted verbatim from the *New York Tribune,* reestablishes a geography of fixed borders and, in the process, confronts the text's desires to place itself on a self-reliant ground unsullied by national barriers:

> The following Report will show to Marylanders, how a runaway slave talks, when he touches the Abolition regions of this country. This presumptive negro was even present at the World's Temperance Convention, last year; and in spite of all the efforts of the American Delegates to prevent it, he palmed off his Abolition bombast upon an audience of 7000 persons! Of this high-handed measure he now makes his boast in New-York, one of the hot-beds of Abolitionism. The Report is given exactly as published in the New York Tribune. The reader will make his own comments. (2)

These few sentences, combined with a title and image that are not Douglass's own, recodify the aberrant, contestory expression, ushering it into what Foucault calls a "discursive regime" that overlaps all too perfectly with a racial regime (1980, 113). Independence does not lie with the author, who has passed on to other "regions of this country"; instead, the editorial frame establishes the Southern reader as autonomous. In contrast to Paula Gunn Allen, who forecasts border crossers traversing routes of "freedom from domination," this brief preface declares that freedom is found *through* domination, through the interpretive control of the reader who will judge the text and its author at his leisure. Douglass, as critic of the slave regime, forfeits his active discursive opposition, which is enacted through public speaking, and now passively awaits the perusal of the pamphlet's purchaser. Annexed and recolonized, the unbounded border text is converted into a sectional articulation addressed not to the citizens of the world Douglass faced at a temperance meeting, but to the "Marylanders" who claim his body as property.

The peculiar circumstances encircling this one oration by Douglass certainly do not nullify his emancipatory activism, which revolutionized the abolition movement, resulted in the establishment of a distinct and sustained African American editorial presence in the United States, and successfully combated various forms of segregation. But *Abolition Fanaticism* is not an isolated instance of Southern retrenchment; it is merely one trace of a pervasive struggle waged not on both sides of the Mason-Dixon line, but *across* the Mason-Dixon line, in which fugitive texts and insurgent voices were preempted and deflated by literary and ideological productions designed expressly to quell opposition. As Gramsci notes, when subaltern groups pose a crisis that threatens hegemony, the ruling class acts "swiftly" and "reabsorbs the control that was slipping from its grasp" (210). Culture is never a site of absolute resistance or absolute domination, but is an uncertain arena of uncertain struggles, shifting back and forth between Douglass's recontainment and his meaningful and radical dissent. So although it is clear to anyone familiar with Douglass's corpus that the vast bulk of his editorials, correspondence, and speeches were too powerful and ideologically irresolvable for assimilation, the fate of this one speech underscores the dangers in celebrating a discursive freedom that Douglass himself, long after his early fight for literacy, still understood as precarious and always endangered.

Harriet Jacobs's *Incidents in the Life of a Slave Girl* documents this complex interplay of textual dissent and recolonization. Although confined and hidden in her grandmother's garret, Linda Brent devises a strategy so that her letters can evade the patrols and slave hunters who define and give meaning to the Mason-Dixon line. From her "loophole of retreat" in North Carolina, she writes a series of letters that she entrusts to a sailor friend headed North, who will mail them from New York to deceive her master into thinking that she is beyond his grasp, and not just a few houses away from his own home. Her master, Dr. Flint, intercepts Linda's letter home, and substitutes his text as though it were Linda's, palming it off on her family as though it were an authentic communication. Manipulating the literal frame that the slave's envelope provides, Flint inscribes his own interest over the slave's voice. "The old villain!" writes Jacobs. "He had suppressed the letter I wrote to grandmother, and prepared a substitute of his own" (130). Transposed within the discourse of the slaveholder, Linda's understanding of freedom, her resistance to slavery, and her commitment to her children are perverted and minimized. Gramsci's statement that hegemony works by "bringing about . . . intellectual and moral unity, *posing all the questions* around which the struggle rages" (181–82; emphasis added) illuminates how within this "competition in cunning," as Jacobs calls it (128), power resides with the person best able to set the terms of the discourse and draw a compass around the debate.[7] The envelope, at times controlled by Flint and at times by Brent, but ultimately controlled by Jacobs in the narrative "written by herself," is the literal incarnation of a framed discourse, the embodiment of a prescribed range of available positions in the "struggle," that sets and regulates the exchange between master and slave. Even though she emerges victorious and gets the last laugh by encircling Flint's adulterations in her autobiographical *Incidents,* Jacobs recognizes that subversion always runs the risk of being reframed within less threatening articulations: insurgent traffic along the border flows in several directions, never reaching a final point of liberation or domination.

So honed did the strategies of reappropriation become that Southerners published their own slave narratives. The slave narrative—a genre whose very existence undermines the South's claims about the benevolence or naturalness of human bondage—in some singular instances appeared not as a fugitive or subversive expression, but as an artifact firmly ensconced in the practices and doctrines circulating below the Mason-Dixon line. That is, a cultural form having oppositional value precisely because it has traversed a series of barriers—from slave to free, South to North, chattel to human—is now produced as an affirmation of the social institutional system it had been originally devised to question and challenge. Just as "Marylanders" facilitated the publication and pirating of Douglass's oration, they enabled the printing of *A Narrative of the Life of Rev. Noah Davis, a Colored Man, Written by Himself, at the Age of Fifty-Four* in 1859.[8] On the one hand, this text evades its geographic specificity to indict the system that holds its author and his family as property. Davis's *Narrative* records a tireless desire for freedom in the exertions of a father and husband who raises the funds necessary to buy first himself and then his wife and children. When Davis learns that "it was now considered that the children had increased in value one hundred dollars and that I was told that I could buy them by paying in cash six hundred dollars, and giving a bond, with good security, for three hundred more, payable in twelve months" (38), the ineradicable and enduring financial complications record the ambiguities of a situation that, like the seesaw critique in this passage, evidences both resistance and containment, for enveloping this subtle denunciation of a slaveholder's intractable rapacity is the more obvious and sanctioned testimony to a slaveholder's benevolence that allows Davis to purchase his family in the first place.

On the other hand, Davis's *Narrative* defuses social antagonisms, remanding disruptive criticisms to a more secure ideological arena. As a cultural artifact, then, this text exists in a state of flux, affirming certain assumptions and practices of the "peculiar institution" even as it rejects and overturns others. "There are points of resistance; there are also moments of suppression," writes Stuart Hall (1981, 233). Although laws existed prohibiting free blacks from passing back and forth between

Northern and slave states, once he had bought himself, Davis crossed and recrossed the Mason-Dixon line in an effort to gather subscriptions to free his family. He visited Baptist churches in Philadelphia, and then continued on to Boston, the center of abolitionism, before returning to Baltimore. At first, this text can hardly encompass the subversive meaning and promise Boston offers: "I know, I shall fail to present a true picture of this heavenly place; for such it was to me, and many others" (62). Through indirection and intimation, Davis offers a critical, even inflammatory, allusion to fugitive slaves who have also found Boston to be "heavenly." This mention of "others" who have found refuge in the North encourages stirrings of resistance that defy the Southern materiality of this slave narrative; the radical import of Boston remains excessive to the text, uncircumscribed by the Marylanders who publish Davis's autobiography. Yet Davis's text next undercuts such implied escapes as an effective means of resistance: "I reflected, suppose I had stayed away, when I was in Boston, twelve years ago, begging money to buy myself—how would it be with me and my family to-day?" (65).

Suppression follows close on the heels of defiance, muting the disruptive mention of fugitive slaves in a text written by a black man and published below the Mason-Dixon line. In short, Davis lets go of Douglass's self-reliance to work within the confines of a dependency translated as Southern humanitarianism. Not exactly or thoroughly dominated, Davis's mission develops within a framework "posing all the questions," setting limits on the range of his discourse instead of the range of his movements. Within these boundaries, his story can only affirm Southern kindness and indulgence, abandoning the flirtation with Boston radicalism as a shortsighted and selfish endeavor. As Dick Hebdige notes, within a hegemonic situation, "subordinate groups are, if not controlled, then at least contained within an ideological space which does not seem at all 'ideological'" (366). Like its author, who traversed the sectional borders between free and slave states, *A Narrative of the Life of Rev. Noah Davis* operates in constrained circumstances, both upsetting and acceding to a discourse regulated by an economic and racial system.

When Saldívar-Hull writes that "Chicana feminism challenges boundaries defined by the hegemony," she certainly records the oppositional work performed by a text such as *Borderlands/La Frontera*, yet this statement also risks underestimating the ability of hegemony to annex and even to win the consent of its social adversaries (220). The distinctive success of hegemony, according to Gramsci, comes about "in securing the development of the group which they represent with the consent and assistance of the allied groups—if not out and out with that of groups which are definitely hostile" (148). In other words, by its very nature, hegemony entails that any moment or expression of culture is constantly enmeshed in a network of competing social forces, so entangled and so compromised that ultimately a "new" territory, a promised land of thoroughly successful opposition, can never be reached. Gramsci's statement that culture is "a relation of forces in continuous motion and shift of equilibrium" leads to a remapping of borders—in this case those transecting antebellum America—because it projects the unceasing pitfalls strewn across a discursive landscape defined by the Mason-Dixon line (172). It is no suprise, then, that the South became increasingly adept at capturing fugitive expressions and reinstalling them with the borders of hegemonic discourse. So positioned, "hostile" voices can be acted upon, influenced, and even fabricated so that they affirm forces they had previously defied.

A Georgia slave master named S. W. Price temporarily rendered inert the social protest of slave writing when he agreed to the publication in Atlanta of *Slavery and Abolitionism, as Viewed by a Georgia Slave* in 1861. Attacking Northern editors as fanatical, abolitionists as unpatriotic, and Republicans as diabolical, this text's purported author, Harrison Berry, reproduces the dominant strains of proslavery arguments. And although historical evidence casts severe doubts about the authenticity of this tract,[9] the white editor who prepares the public for Berry's volume, a probable masquerade, describes a scenario ripe for securing what Gramsci calls the "active consent" of the opposition (244):

> I will not merely say that I *think* he wrote it, for I can safely say I know him to be the author—the sentiments are his, for I have heard him express them time and again, long before I ever dreamed of his writing a book.... Harrison fully understands the position of a *Slave*, and has uniformly kept himself in his proper place. He is neither insolent or impudent, but humble and polite. He is honest and trustworthy, and has ever enjoyed the confidence of those who know him. (Berry vii)

He is the model slave and his is the model discourse, agreeably disposed toward its own subjection. Assertions of Berry's authorship verify that the text's defense of the South comes willingly; however, the strong probability that Berry serves only as a mouthpiece reveals a once supposedly consensual arena to be a conflicted zone of manipulated speech and enforced politics, much like the situation in *Incidents* when Linda Brent's master encrypts his own message in the envelope she freely sent to her mother. The words "before I ever dreamed of his writing a book" signal more than this editor's amazement at a literate slave; they also unveil an admission that the project itself has been generated and organized — in short, "dreamed" up — by the slaveholding class. "Active consent" is not so much given voluntarily as it is framed, produced, and won.

The title page, which continues to disclose that *Slavery and Abolitionism* is written by "Harrison Berry, the Property of S. W. Price, Covington, Georgia," demonstrates the brilliance of hegemony as a relation of consent and suppression. At one moment this statement admits traces of compulsion by labeling its author "property," but at the next it documents the achievement of a man who reportedly spent his free time and Sundays laboring to produce a text that justified his own enslavement. The announcement "Copy-Right secured by Wood, Hanleiter, Rice & Co., for the use of Harrison Berry, A Slave," creates an enduring irony that textual property is being held in trust for an article of human property, further underscoring an awareness that culture permits no final outcomes (Berry ii). Just as Davis's intimations of "heavenly" Boston are soon overseen by the slaveholder's frame, here the external constraints upon Berry, whether or not he is the author of this polemic, do not maintain any ultimate invisibility, because they are exposed and undercut by the unavoidable confession that force pervades the material circumstances surrounding the text and its production. Certainly this slave author argues against abolition, but does the enveloping discourse allow other possibilities? If hegemony is "posing all the questions," assuredly only a delimited set of questions will be asked — a regulation clearly seconded in the prefatory letter of S. W. Price, which declares, "HARRISON. . . . By this letter I give you full permission to print and publish your MS" (Berry vi). Within the story of liberty, the possibilities of compulsion cannot be ignored, and neither can the traces of force and suppression be effaced from the "active consent" that leads to the consolidation of hegemony.

In *Slavery and Abolitionism,* the "slave" writes about freedom only to refuse it. He chafes against the discursive boundaries that decree that slaves should not read and write, speak of abolitionists, or circulate material about freedom, merely to reconfirm other, more encompassing, confines. Arguing that whatever liberties allowed by masters have been curtailed by the "infernal agitations" of the North, Berry insists on censorship and sectional autonomy (16). He takes it upon himself to patrol the borders and stem the invasive cant of freedom: "The agitation of Slavery put a manacle on the hands of every Slave South of Mason and Dixon's Line" (12). Even though Berry rebukes liberal Northerners who tresspass onto the ideological domain of the South, *Slavery and Abolitionism* takes care not to disrupt the sanctity of the United States. It is border discourse in service of the nation. In a passage filled with political sentiments seemingly capable of splintering the national fabric, Berry writes:

> It is not that I am opposed to freedom, that actuates me to address them [abolitionists] in the manner which I do, for I believe it to be one of the greatest blessings earthly, when not contaminated with fanatical dispositions. But rather would I die, were I a citizen of the United States, than to disturb the peace, or act in any way that would be detrimental to the onward progress and prosperity of my country. (14)

Laden with half-revealed desires for freedom and an indirect reproach that he is not a citizen, Berry's criticisms remain posed in the conditional, subordinated to the overall "progress and prosperity" of a nation that disenfranchises him. Though the irony of a noncitizen offering political advice is not dispelled, the slave's discourse ultimately reconfirms the sovereign boundaries of the United States. Questions about the denial of citizenship get subsumed by larger, more patriotic concerns for the integrity of the entire nation. The slave body disappears before the body politic. The ideological discord contained in the figure of the slave succumbs to a plea for homogeneity. Slavery is not tearing apart the nation; instead, as Berry repeatedly charges, divisive interference that crosses Southern borders poses the real threat to national unity. Once framed by a context of Unionism that transcends abolitionist meddling, Berry's partisan narrative passes itself off as a nonsectional performance that overcomes deep political conflicts to argue for the sanctity of nation. So often a radical figure who defied institutional limitations and geographic restrictions, what is here only the framed figure of the literate slave upholds a sublime national ideology devoted to dissipating social and political contradiction.

The Border as National Sublime

Of course, such sentimental appeals to the nation proved ineffective as a means of quieting secessionist fervor. And though by 1861 the Mason-Dixon line demarcated the boundary between two warring armies, this militarized division only confirmed that the border had always been a site of battle and contestation. The Civil War, on one level, merely signified that this continual conflict was now being enacted in more traditional and recognizable terms. Military campaigns into Southern territory, counterattacks to push the aggressors back, new fronts in the West and along the Mississippi, raids upon enemies' stores all provided graphic echoes of the textual skirmishes of the preceding decades, exemplifying Foucault's mutation of Clausewitz's aphorism into the statement that politics is war by other means (1980, 90). As this discursive history of the Mason-Dixon line suggests, the border thus never images a final geography; instead, it is perhaps merely the most heavily traveled route, a path beaten by the incessant "double movement of containment and resistance" (Hall 1981, 228). Telling this story demands an ambivalent narrative, one that refuses a clear teleological narrative line in favor of a series of competing tales that compromise and undercut one another. Single stories cannot be told because stories do not exist in some sort of fixed isolation, but are instead always bordered by some other story. In their several overlaps, they describe a culture crisscrossed by defeats that are ultimately as temporary as the victories to such an extent that perhaps the only certain thing that can be said about national-border culture is that it is experienced across spaces of continuing struggle.

More often than not, this continuing struggle is one front in an entire hegemonic campaign that includes moments of opposition as well as moments of stability; this continuing struggle all too frequently has the effect of (re)configuring such border skirmishes as episodes in a story of national consolidation. This murky map helps to pinpoint little, but it does adequately sketch the larger unsettling lesson that those attempting to read the cultural map best pay particular attention to the borders, for it is in these uncertain regions where the landscape of politics is most susceptible to sudden change and reversal. Indeed, it is within this landscape that the nation can reappear with sublime force.

Notes

I would like to thank Tom Goodman for his help and suggestions in developing an earlier draft of this essay.

1. Clearly, the most significant contributions to understanding border writing have emerged from studies of the hybrid culture of the Tex-Mex region, although approaches that look at other contact zones, such as those between race and gender, or between women's writing and patriarchal canons, raise the contention that culture itself can be mapped only by changing margins of identity and fluctuating fringes of power. D. Emily Hicks, for instance, in her study *Border Writing: The Multidimensional Text,* looks at Latin American writers such as Gabriel García Márquez and Julio Cortázar, who are not usually associated with the peripheries and overlaps between cultures. Likewise, Paula Gunn Allen points to the ubiquity of borders for writers of "whatever color, class, gender or sexual orientation" who "have been bound by ideological barriers a mile thick and two miles high" (305). Or see Maggie Humm, who uses the idea of the border to investigate the encounters of woman writers with conventional literary forms. To cite these examples, however, is not to say that studies of the U.S.-Mexico boundary are wholly rooted in the literalness of geography; rather, it is to echo Héctor Calderón, who calls borders "those spaces geographical as well as conceptual where the contradictions of displacement, resistance and rebellion are most plainly visible" (23).

2. For a discussion of the *translatio* in its American incarnations, see Kermode (83–90).

3. Again, I want to emphasize that my understandings of the border as a region laden with the pitfalls of recontainment do not necessarily obviate the enactment of oppositional strategies. Slaves who ran away disproved many proslavery notions, among them fictions that blacks were content with bondage and that they were unconcerned with freedom. Moreover, narratives that relate successful instances of passing, such as William Craft's *Running a Thousand Miles for Freedom* and William Wells Brown's *Clotel; or, The President's Daughter,* illustrate how the crossing of racial and gender boundaries can become a viable and threatening source of resistance.

4. Mae G. Henderson has recently sounded a similar note of caution: "Naive, facile valorization of border crossings must be deemed risky and unwarranted" (26).

5. There are, of course, readings that do not fit this overarching critical narrative. See, for instance, Genaro Padilla, whose investigations of the U.S.-Mexico border reveal "a consciousness that participates in its own submission, transformation, and erasure" (43), and Carl Gutiérrez-Jones, who discusses "the routinization of the potentially transformative aspects inherent in the culture of the borderlands [that comes about] by selectively incorporating elements" (48). After sighting "new forms of polyglot cultural creativity," Renato Rosaldo takes incisive note of similar dangers: "All of us inhabit an interdependent late-twentieth-century world marked by borrowing and lending across porous national and cultural boundaries that are saturated with inequality, power, and domination" (217).

6. Nineteenth-century "black" performance, both authentic and inauthentic, is plagued by such predations; see especially Lott, who understands the minstrel show as "a truly American combination of acknowledgment and expropriation" (49).

7. Authors from the Birmingham Center for Contemporary Cultural Studies have put the matter of "framing" this way: "A hegemonic order prescribes, not the specific content of ideas, but the *limits* within which ideas and conflicts move and are resolved" (Clarke, Hall, Jefferson, and Roberts 39).

8. What is remarkable about this title is that it culminates in a clause that would suggest Davis's biggest adversity is his age, natural and unstoppable, as opposed to the highly elaborated artifices and institutions of racism.

9. Maxwell Whiteman calls *Slavery and Abolitionism* "a highly suspect" document: "If the words were the words of Berry, the ideas were the ideas of his master. Later in life, as a freedman, Berry issued another pamphlet which showed him as a semi-literate man not even equal to the logic of apologetics of his first literary venture, giving credence to the likelihood that the work was not his own."

Works Cited

Allen, Paula Gunn. 1992. " 'Border' Studies: The Intersection of Gender and Color." *Introduction to Scholarship in Modern Languages and Literatures,* 2d ed. Ed. Joseph Gibaldi. New York: Modern Language Association of America.

Anzaldúa, Gloria. 1987. *Borderlands/La Frontera: The New Mestiza.* San Francisco: Aunt Lute.

Berry, Harrison. 1969[1861]. *Slavery and Abolitionism, as Viewed by a Georgia Slave.* Philadelphia: Rhistoric.

Brown, William Wells. 1989[1853]. *Clotel; or, The President's Daughter.* New York: Carol.

Calderón, Héctor. 1991. "Texas Border Literature: Cultural Transformation and Historical Reflection in the Works of Américo Paredes, Rolando Hinojosa and Gloria Anzaldúa." *Disposito* 16: 13–27.

Clarke, John, Stuart Hall, Tony Jefferson, and Brian Roberts. 1976. "Subcultures, Cultures and Class: A Theoretical Overview." *Resistance through Rituals: Youth Subcultures in Post-War Britain.* Ed. Stuart Hall and Tony Jefferson. London: Hutchinson. 9–66.

Craft, William. 1991[1860]. *Running a Thousand Miles for Freedom; or, The Escape of William and Ellen Craft from Slavery.* New York: Ayer.

Davis, Noah. 1969[1859]. *A Narrative of the Life of Rev. Noah Davis, a Colored Man, Written by Himself, at the Age of Fifty-Four.* Philadelphia: Rhistoric.

Douglass, Frederick. 1847. *Abolition Fanaticism in New York. Speech of a Runaway Slave from Baltimore, at an Abolition Meeting in New York.* Baltimore: n.p.

———. 1950. *The Life and Writings of Frederick Douglass,* 5 vols. Ed. Philip S. Foner. New York: International.

———. 1968[1845]. *The Narrative of the Life of Frederick Douglass, an American Slave, Written by Himself.* New York: Signet.

———. 1969[1855]. *My Bondage and My Freedom.* New York: Dover.

Foucault, Michel. 1978. *The History of Sexuality,* vol. 1, *An Introduction.* Trans. Robert Hurley. New York: Vintage.

———. 1980. *Power/Knowledge: Selected Interviews and Other Writings, 1972–77.* Ed. Colin Gordon; trans. Colin Gordon, Leo Marshall, John Mepham, and Kate Soper. New York: Pantheon.

Gramsci, Antonio. 1971. *Selections from the Prison Notebooks of Antonio Gramsci.* Ed. and trans. Quintin Hoare and Geoffrey Nowell Smith. New York: International.

Gutiérrez-Jones, Carl. 1991. "Rethinking the Borderlands: Between Literary and Legal Discourse." *Disposito* 16: 45–60.

Hall, Stuart. 1981. "Notes on Deconstructing the Popular." *People's History and Socialist Theory.* London: Routledge & Kegan Paul. 227–40.

———. 1986. "Gramsci's Relevance for the Study of Race and Ethnicity." *Communication Inquiry* 10.2: 5–27.

Hebdige, Dick. 1993. "From Culture to Hegemony." *The Cultural Studies Reader.* Ed. Simon During. New York: Routledge. 357–67.

Henderson, Mae G. 1995. "Introduction." *Borders, Boundaries, and Frames: Essays in Cultural Criticism and Cultural Studies.* Ed. Mae G. Henderson. New York: Routledge. 1–26.

Hicks, D. Emily. 1991. *Border Writing: The Multidimensional Text.* Minneapolis: University of Minnesota Press.

Humm, Maggie. 1991. *Border Traffic: Strategies of Contemporary Women Writers.* Manchester: Manchester University Press.

Jacobs, Harriet A. 1987[1860]. *Incidents in the Life of a Slave Girl, Written by Herself.* Ed. Jean Fagan Yellin. Cambridge: Harvard University Press.

JanMohamed, Abdul R. 1992. "Worldliness-without-World, Homelessness-as-Home: Toward a Definition of the Specular Border Intellectual." *Edward Said: A Critical Reader.* Ed. Michael Sprinkler. Cambridge, Mass.: Blackwell. 96–120.

Keating, AnnLouise. 1993. "Myth Smashers, Myth Makers: (Re)Visionary Techniques in the Works of Paula Gunn Allen, Gloria Anzaldúa, and Audre Lorde." *Critical Essays: Gay and Lesbian Writers of Color* 26: 73–95.

Kermode, Frank. 1975. *The Classic: Literary Images of Permanence and Change.* New York: Viking.

Latrobe, John. 1855. *The History of Mason and Dixon's Line, an Address.* Philadelphia: Press of the Historical Society of Pennsylvania.

Lott, Eric. 1993. *Love and Theft: Blackface Minstrelsy and the American Working Class.* New York: Oxford University Press.

Padilla, Genaro. 1991. "Imprisoned Narrative? Or Lies, Secrets, and Silence in New Mexico Women's Autobiography." *Criticism in the Borderlands: Studies in Chicano Literature, Culture, and Ideology.* Ed. Héctor Calderón and José David Saldívar. Durham, N.C.: Duke University Press, 43–60.

Paredes, Américo. 1958. *With His Pistol in His Hand: A Border Ballad and Its Hero.* Austin: University of Texas Press.

Rosaldo, Renato. 1989. *Culture and Truth: The Remaking of Social Analysis.* Boston: Beacon.

Saldívar, José David. 1991. "Chicano Border Narrative as Cultural Critique." *Criticism in the Borderlands: Studies in Chicano Literature, Culture, and Ideology.* Ed. Héctor Calderón and José David Saldívar. Durham, N.C.: Duke University Press. 167–80.

Saldívar, Ramón. 1993. "Lyrical Borders: Modernity, the Nation and Narratives of Chicano Subject Formation." *Narrative* 1.1: 36–44.

Saldívar-Hull, Sonia. 1991. "Feminism on the Border: From Gender Politics to Geopolitics." *Criticism in the Borderlands: Studies in Chicano Literature, Culture, and Ideology.* Ed. Héctor Calderón and José David Saldívar. Durham, N.C.: Duke University Press. 201–20.

Veech, James. 1857. *Mason and Dixon's Line: A History. Including an Outline of the Boundary Controversy between Pennsylvania and Virginia.* Pittsburgh: W. S. Haven.

White, Hayden. 1973. *Metahistory: The Historical Imagination in Nineteenth-Century Europe.* Baltimore: Johns Hopkins University Press.

———. 1987. *The Content of the Form: Narrative Discourse and Historical Representation.* Baltimore: Johns Hopkins University Press.

Whiteman, Maxwell. 1969. "A Bibiliographic Note." Harrison Berry, *Slavery and Abolitionism, as Viewed by a Georgia Slave.* Philadelphia: Rhistoric.

SEVEN

Resketching Anglo-Amerindian Identity Politics
Scott Michaelsen

> But what has been fancied as life in the forest, has had no little
> resemblance to those Utopian schemes of government and
> happiness which rather denote the human mind run mad.
> HENRY ROWE SCHOOLCRAFT, *The Myth of Hiawatha*, 1856

I

Daniel K. Richter's magisterial history of early Iroquois politics and identity, *The Ordeal of the Longhouse* (1992), moves from the deep past (approximately 1000 A.D.) forward: "The story perhaps best begins in the
beginning," reads the first line of the text (8). Richter is able to accomplish this feat through the process that historians call " 'upstreaming,'
that is, the interpretation of historical sources in light of ethnological
and folkloric materials collected in later periods; one moves 'up' the
historical stream from a better to a less well documented era" (Richter
1992, 5).

There are good reasons to be suspicious of narratives about identity
and, therefore, "identity politics" produced through upstreaming.[1] Such
narratives—produced through the rose-tinted memories and memo-
rizations of informants, living and dead, and filtered again through the
similarly colored preconceptions of the historian-anthropologist—tend
to produce the most astonishingly stereotypical and, recently, romantic-
utopic-inflected versions of Amerindia. In Richter's case, he produces
Amerindians of "sublimely" "spiritual unity" — "busy," "calm," "warm,"
"peaceful" (7, 18). This is an Amerindia of "nuclear families" linked by

an "ethic of sharing and reciprocity," an "upside-down capitalism" in which leaders competed to "give the most away" (19, 22). To give this its proper name, Richter's Iroquois are liberal communitarian, a kind of cross between Andrew Carnegie and his "Gospel of Wealth" and Christopher Lasch's sense of American lower-middle-class values in *The True and Only Heaven* (1991). This is, above all, an Amerindia of "consensus" — a "noncompetitive" and "noncoercive society" that, in Richter's most remarkable claim, engaged in a series of terrible wars against neighbors only because their neighbors failed to live up to Iroquois values of reciprocity or gift giving (22, 45, 40, 49). Algonquian peoples, then, from an Iroquois perspective, simply were not giving enough to justify their continued existence. Strangely, all of this comes after Richter has signaled that he does not want to essentialize the Iroquois, that he hopes to present the Iroquois "simply as peoples … caught up by forces … over which they had little control," and that "most of the mental world of the men and women who populate these pages is irrevocably lost" (2, 4). But it is upstreaming that has saved the day, permitting Richter to say that there is a "rock of traditional rituals," a "spiritual … unity," that transcends history, even hundreds of years of encounter history. Iroquois identity is "flexible," he concedes, but "perdurable" (3). He says that "core traditional values" "survived" the whole of colonization — that year 1000 Iroquois are the *same* people who entered the middle 1700s (4).

The problems with this approach are rather obvious. On the basis of literally nothing, it assumes one thousand years of identity without epistemological breaks or even bends in the road — folklore collected "today" can tell the truth about Amerindian identity in the deep past. In Richter's case, what Amerindians "remember" about themselves need not be subjected to the obvious questions: Does the collected folklore reflect what Amerindians *want* to be remembered as (is it fantasy)? Does it reflect *present* consciousness rather than past (is folklore in general always about the here and now)? Is the informant simply telling the folklorist what she or he wants to hear ("Tell me about your wonderful past")? Are various informants ideologically positioned *within* Amerindian thought (for example, male or elite, or senior, or Indianist)? Furthermore, Richter assumes one thousand years during which the "spiritual" values and Amerindian identity are one and the same, and during which period Iroquois identity manages to exclude everything else as secondary or even utterly marginal to itself, such as the colonial, the diplomatic, the economic, the political, the juridical, the sexual.[2] Nothing, it appears, can alter a monolithic Iroquois identity, save a dissolution of its conception of the spirit world.[3]

Rather than begin at this sort of "beginning," one alternatively might choose to start with the very end of Anglo-Amerindian identity politics — with two quite radically defamiliarizing historical texts: Oren Lyons and John Mohawk's collection *Exiled in the Land of the Free* (1992) and Sam D. Gill's *Mother Earth* (1987). Both texts rely more subtly upon upstreaming; in both cases, the scholars primarily attempt to read an existing documentary record of red-white relations. Yet the problem of upstreaming remains impossible to avoid, given the ambition of the arguments.

It is the contention of Lyons and Mohawk, both of whom claim Iroquois identity as well as identity as American studies scholars at the State University of New York-Buffalo, that the framers of the Articles of Confederation and the U.S. Constitution sought "to take the applicable principles of the visible Indian democracy" in constructing the polity of the United States (Lyons 1992, 33). In order to make this contention stick, Mohawk argues that *no* intellectual traditions of the European Enlightenment harbored ideas of equality: "No important political thinker of the seventeenth century proposed a government representative of the population to be governed" (1992b, 68). And all ideas of equality, of radical democracy, emanated then from "the Indian camp fire" (69). As one example, "the origin" of the natural rights ideas in the Declaration of Independence, says Mohawk, "is clearly rooted in exchanges with the Indians" (71). And whereas Mohawk concludes that Amerindian politics is merely "one of the streams" of the Constitution and the Bill of Rights, this argument is of a piece with that of Lyons, who concludes that everything in the Constitution that is *not* Iroquois amounts to a compromising of League of the Iroquois principles, mortgaging them to "private property interest" (Lyons 1992, 33).

The language used by Lyons in order to suggest a League of the Iroquois origin for all major U.S. political ideals is indeed striking: Iroquois polity is organized around "freedom from coercion," "free speech" and the "individual . . . right to voice an opinion," freedom of dissent ("free to disagree"), "participatory democracy," concepts of "peace" and the "just," states' rights, and, in general, a deep "tradition of democratic thought." Iroquois democracy was a "revolution" similar to the American Revolution, designed to promote such bourgeois ideas as "healthy minds and bodies," and rational "clear thinking" as opposed to "confuse[d]" emotionality (32–34, 38–40). At the limit of this sort of rhetoric, Lyons argues that the Iroquois Peacemaker conceptualized a version of multiculturalism—"the Haudenosaunee principle of respect for the laws and customs of different cultures," which amounts to a politics of "the right of peoples and their societies to be different" (42). The implication of Lyons and Mohawk's volume in terms of a politics of identity is clear: Amerindia literally invented the humanistic, bourgeois, democratic individual. Everything most crucial for modern U.S. self-identity and self-ideality is, in fact, an Iroquois cultural construction, and U.S. personhood, then, is Iroquois through and through.

Sam Gill's *Mother Earth* files the grand counterclaim, contending that everything most central to a pan-Indian spiritual identity—that is, the very idea of the earth as a mother, and therefore the whole of the modern Amerindian sense of religion, of nature worship, of the stewardship of the environment, and of a kind of deep ecologism—is, in fact, part of the cultural baggage of Europe. Gill reads John Smith's story of Pocahontas, for example, as the story of the first Amerindian "earth mother." Once Smith publishes his tale, "the seeds are thus sown. The conception of Mother Earth in North America has taken place" (1987, 39). And although Gill goes on to argue that Amerindians have altered the Mother Earth concept in creative, "reasoned," and even "sophisticated" ways (64), the bulk of his story concerns the constant imposition of the idea upon Amerindians, as late as the end of the nineteenth century, by anthropologists such as James Mooney and A. S. Gatschet. After three hundred years of prodding and cajoling, then, Amerindians finally "appropriated" the spiritual/ecological idea of Mother Earth (Gill 1987, 66).

In both cases, the claims made rely primarily upon a benevolently inflected, white colonial record that depicts Amerindians, for Lyons and Mohawk, as democrats and, for Gill, as ecologists. The difference between the claims is that Lyons and Mohawk read documents about Amerindians as speaking the truth about Amerindian identity, whereas Gill reads the same record as a history of white stereotyping that eventually appealed to Amerindians and became part of Amerindian identity claims. In both cases, the authors upstream by implication: before contact, Amerindians really were progressive political philosophers and, before contact, Amerindians really were not progressive nature philosophers. Not surprisingly, both of these dramatic positions have come under methodological attack from significant sources: by Elisabeth Tooker (1988), for example, with respect to the contours of Lyons and Mohawk's argument, and by Ward Churchill, an Amerindian cultural studies scholar, who has issued a stinging critique of the Gill volume, quoting Martin Sheen's character in *Apocalypse Now* for his final verdict on the book: "'Frankly, sir, I can't find any valid method at all'" (1992, 206).

But one might suggest, as another way of thinking, that these two narratives are in some sense inevitable. Such are the tricks and traps of the five-hundred-year-long attempt to essentialize the "differences" between Anglo and Amerindian cultures. The two narratives are locked into abyssal relation — each one ceaselessly trying to empty out the other. And if one were to accept both of these narratives, it would be Amerindians who are bourgeois subjects, protective of their individual rights and liberties and concerned with their physical and mental health,[4] and it would be Anglos who have spent the past five centuries worshipping at altars of earth. At the maximum expansion of the anthropological thinking of the "other," one may no longer know who "we" and "they" are — and identity comes to seem extremely precarious, contingent, and without a center.

This is necessarily so because it is theoretically impossible to construct a description of radical alterity, of the absolutely other. If Amerindians and Anglos *were* each other's radical "others," the differences would be, in principle, incomprehensible. It is not surprising, then, that the most "radical" accounts of Amerindian otherness (for example, Indians as singularly anticapitalists or protocapitalists, and/or the definitive individualists or anti-individualists)[5] are, ironically, those that most clearly expose the web that holds together Anglo and Amerindian identities. The anthropology of the other is and always has been entirely "self"-motivated — moralizing for and to its Anglo audience, and in mostly banal ways.[6]

II

Contact changes everything. The very possibility, for example, of sites of translation and communication *between* cultures implies that the cultural situation is always already shaped in such a way that something more than cultural translation or cultural crossing takes place. And the tenacious metaphors of cultural travel and assimilation do not begin to grasp how fundamental is the ground rending and remending that takes place in such contact situations between incommensurable cultures at the level of identity or personhood. The historian Richard White has argued, for example, that a "middle ground," or "elaborate network of economic, political, cultural, and social ties," opened up between French and Amerindian peoples in the Great Lakes region in the seventeenth and eighteenth centuries (1991, 33). White focuses on "basic issues of sex, violence, and material exchange" to make his point that such and other matters needed joint juridico-economic resolution through "cultural fiction" and improvisation, thereby producing a new culture, new identities (56, 80–81). "Such changes, worked out on the middle ground, could be remarkably influential, bringing important modifications in each society and blurring the boundaries between them" (93). But to White's account one must add that cultural *difference* is a product, too, of the same encounter — produced at the very same moment as the most minimal "middle ground." A middle ground, in fact, is culture's very condition of possibility, of visibility. Culture quite literally cannot appear until such a space is opened. And today, Anglo and Amerindian identities remain wedded together within a contentious shared space, even though White's particular middle ground "withered and died" in the early nineteenth century (523).

   This can be explored further with reference to two protoanthropologies, in both cases in the form of folklores, written just after White's "middle ground" period, during the Jacksonian era — David Cusick's *Sketches of the Ancient History of the Six Nations* (1827) and Henry Rowe Schoolcraft's *Algic Researches, Comprising Inquiries Respecting the Men-*

tal Characteristics of the North American Indians (1839), which he was drafting and prepublishing with the assistance of his wife, Jane Johnston Schoolcraft, and other members of her family, as early as 1826. These are, then, precisely contemporaneous texts, in quite similar formats, and yet there are differences — and no end of them.

Cusick is not very well known today, whereas Henry Schoolcraft may be *the* crucial protoanthropologist, bent on establishing a *method* (however vague, in the final analysis) for collection, digestion, and historical reflection upon Amerindian oral knowledge and stories. During the middle third of the nineteenth century, his work on the Amerindian mind was nearly impossible to avoid: avid readers of Schoolcraft include prominent midcentury litterateurs (most dramatically, Henry Wadsworth Longfellow), historians (Francis Parkman), and anthropologists (Lewis H. Morgan), as well as Amerindian autoanthropologists (Ely S. Parker, George Copway).

The difference in subject position of the authors of *Algic Researches* and the *Sketches* is both dramatic and not. Cusick represents himself as Iroquois (specifically, Tuscarora), and explains that he is researching his own culture's beliefs and stories, whereas Schoolcraft clearly represents himself as Anglo, intent on studying the ancient Amerindian "other." And yet Jane Johnston, whose contribution to the final text is difficult to overestimate, was the child of an Irish fur trader, John Johnston, and a Chippewa mother, Neengay (later Susan Johnston), and "Jane and the other children were educated in Ojibwa lore by their mother" (Parins 1990b, 1216).

Cusick, in turn, was the son of Nicholas Cusick, who, far from living the life of imaginary Amerindians, had served as Lafayette's bodyguard during the Revolutionary War (Parins 1990a, 1225). Nicholas Cusick's time on the Tuscarora reservation, then, followed life lived primarily within the so-called Anglo world, and David Cusick lived across the divide as well. He had a "fair education," according to William Beauchamp, and he "was thought of as a good doctor by both whites and Indians" (1892, 41). So, even if one accepts, on some level, narratives about the cultural difference of Amerindians and Anglos (and if one could be quite particular about the status of that difference — understanding it as radical, relational, or utterly trivial, to give just three possible choices), what can be said with any conviction about culture and text in these particular cases?[7]

Henry Schoolcraft, for his part, is rarely unsure about the unique status of Amerindian culture, even though, at first, there are indications in *Algic Researches* that he accepts the idea of a universal human subject—that the "Indians" or "aborigines," as Schoolcraft says, share a "desire" "implanted in the minds of all men, to convey to their contemporaries and transmit to posterity the prominent facts of their history and attainments" (1991[1839], 5).[8] So Amerindians desire to speak history, just as Anglos do, although Schoolcraft's remark is more a reflection of nineteenth-century historical consciousness than of some timeless drive or desire.[9]

But once past a certain minimal humanistic intelligibility, everything else about the Amerindian is differently constructed—distinctly non-European. Just as in Columbus's writings, or the contemporaneous novels of James Fenimore Cooper and Catharine Maria Sedgwick, Schoolcraft divides the Amerindian in two, presenting a "fierce and dominating" Ostic, or Iroquois, and a nearly idyllic Algic, or Algonquin—"mild and conciliating," full of the dreams of "independence" at the level of "personal or tribal freedom" (1991[1839], 7). (Here, one might note, Lyons and Mohawk's Iroquois are turned upside down, with the Algonquin made the Northeast's liberal individuals.) Schoolcraft argues: "One is descended from . . . shepherds or pastoral nomads, and the other from a line of adventurers and warlike plunderers" (1991[1839], 7). Reading Schoolcraft, it seems, at times, as if anthropology has traveled no distance at all from Columbus's imagined Taino and Caribs.[10] Henry Schoolcraft is at no remove from this hoary "split image" of Amerindia, which, as John McWilliams has argued, "allows the white reader to mourn for the loss of the heroic red man without having to protest against it" (1990, 360).

Schoolcraft's occasional discussion of the Amerindian according to the opposition of savage/civilized is of no more recent vintage,[11] but what makes his text a bit more "modern" is, first, his quite inchoate notion of "race," which, as Winthrop Jordan has shown, is a concept that was not explicitly and fully thematized until the late 1700s—and the

1770s in terms of its application to Amerindia.[12] The shepherds and the plunderers are "races," says Schoolcraft, and he argues that Amerindians can be divided into four different ones — the Algic, Ostic, Abanic, and Muskogee (1991[1839], 5). These races, however, it seems, share certain features, as part of a larger Amerindian race. They have "distinctive opinions" as a result of a unique "mental constitution" (1991[1839], 4).[13]

Also more "modern," but perhaps contradicting the race narrative, is Schoolcraft's occasional, evolutionary model of man. One of the key purposes of collecting Amerindian stories, according to Schoolcraft, is "rescuing . . . an important link in the chain" of humanity (1991[1839], 11). Although Schoolcraft is vague on this point (the details are hardly worked out at all), *Algic Researches* seems partly intended to explain the origin and transformation of human beings. Tracing this out, Amerindians can be shown to be in various "states"; the Algic, upon encounter, were in "the hunter state," for example, and lagging behind those quasi-capitalist Iroquois/Ostic.[14] The Algic race did not yet know "the value of time," and "could not endure the tension, mental and physical, of long-continued exertions" (1991[1839], 8). In short, the Algic race had not yet learned the work ethic, a seemingly central evolution for production of a higher order of "man."[15]

None of this is particularly novel, but what is interesting is that Schoolcraft's views of Amerindia encapsulate all of the several hundred years' worth of paradigm shifts within protoanthropologies described in Bernard McGrane's work.[16] As close as Schoolcraft gets to doubting such metanarratives of identity, and then the aboriginal tales that bolster or support the metanarratives, is a diary entry of 26 January 1838, where he wonders about the future reception of *Algic Researches*: "There are so many Indian tales, fancied, by writers, that it will hardly be admitted that there exist any *real* legends" (1991[1839], 310). But Schoolcraft seems to have accepted the ancient veracity of everything that *he* managed to collect, believing, like Richter, that a singular, still-existing "mythology" "furnishes the best clue to their hopes and fears, and lies at the foundation of the Indian character" (1991[1839], 10).[17]

This is a perception not necessarily shared by Jane Johnston. The closest one can come to finding her voice in its singularity is in Schoolcraft's earliest published anthropological research — a self-produced magazine that he called *The Literary Voyager* (1826–27). *The Literary Voyager* was an idiosyncratic grab bag of random Amerindian lore (stories and customs), family poetry, personal information (issue 14 is devoted to the death of Schoolcraft and Johnston's child, Henry), and humor (acrostics and conundrums), with various family members providing material under numerous pseudonyms. One of Jane Johnston's several *Literary Voyager* pseudonyms is "Leelinau," and it is under this name (and in the magazine's first number) that she published her only attempt to speak to the problems of cultural anthropology and, more particularly, of historical upstreaming.[18] In "Character of Aboriginal Historical Tradition," Johnston writes:

> Now the stories I have heard related by old persons in my nation, cannot be so true, because they sometimes forget certain parts, and then thinking themselves obliged to fill up the vacancy by their own sensible remarks and experience, but it seems to me, much oftener by their fertile flights of imagination and if one person retains the truth, they have deviated, and so the history of my country has become almost wholly fabulous. (in Schoolcraft 1962, 6)

Johnston's, or Leelinau's, argument is that, with the possible exception of "one person," the recording of Amerindian tradition is an impossible task. There is forgetting, of course, and the quite unremarkable fact that each storyteller retells the tale according to new lived experience. The tales that Henry Schoolcraft, Jane Johnston, her relatives, and others collected for *Algic Researches* were, at least to begin with, told by these same "old persons" (perhaps fifty such elders, perhaps more) among whom new versions and new meanings so endlessly proliferate that only the "almost wholly fabulous" exists. *Algic Researches,* from this perspective, is just another collection of whoppers.

But who is the "one person" of truth to whom Leelinau refers in her sketch? It is, quite strangely, her "father," "descended from one of the most ancient and respected leaders of the Ojibway bands" (Schoolcraft 1962, 6).[19] Now, Johnston's actual father, as noted earlier, claimed no Amerindian identity, and this other father, then, is sheer make-believe— a phantom conjured by Jane Johnston in order to assert the bare fact that, yes, some truth, somewhere, exists.[20] But not here, perhaps, because Leelinau also explains that her father is dead. Will Leelinau, with her memories of her father, be able to pass on to Schoolcraft the "ancient traditions and customs," the old stories (Schoolcraft 1962, 7)? "I should strive to," she says, provided she could write her own letters (which she cannot because she is Amerindian, raised within Amerindian culture). At the end of the sketch, therefore, the "truth" of Amerindian life remains unknown.

It is possible to read Jane Johnston's text as part of a microbattle for authority within the Schoolcrafts' joint protoanthropological project. For example, when Leelinau returns to the pages of *The Literary Voyager*, in January 1827, Henry Schoolcraft frames her tale of "The Origins of the Robin" in a way that does violence to her original narrative. She now, according to the editorial frame, is able to write English, and Henry Schoolcraft says that she is descended partly from "European parentage" (1962, 38). So "The Origins of the Robin" is *not* pure Amerindian legend, says Schoolcraft. Rather, Leelinau's story "derives additional interest" because of "the position she [Leelinau] occupies between the European and aboriginal races" (Schoolcraft 1962, 38–39). Leelinau is here interesting as a hybrid storyteller, and Schoolcraft's frame at least hints, in a reversal of Johnston's argument in the first Leelinau piece, that it is *she* who is not quite Amerindian enough to speak the pure truth of the Amerindian mind.[21]

Again, perhaps, this is an abyss. Or, more precisely, the rhetorical figure that describes this conversation is *aporia*; two roads diverge, and both are blocked. On the one side, according to Jane Johnston, Schoolcraft cannot know the truth of Amerindia because all of the figures he has interviewed are radically cut off from the "traditional" past. On the other side, according to Henry Schoolcraft, Leelinau (and Johnston too, of course) cannot speak with a singular cultural tongue about Amerindia because of her partial European birth and background. In this case, if one accepts both narratives, both arguments, as true, no one can speak anything for certain about the Amerindian past. There is literally no entry point — no access to it.

One more turn — a kind of coda — on the Schoolcraft-Johnston relationship: a number of *The Literary Voyager* texts, including Jane Johnston's folklore contributions, were reprinted in *Algic Researches,* and Henry Schoolcraft added yet more matter, including a tale titled "Leelinau, or The Lost Daughter." It is hard to resist reading this text, and its later transformation in Schoolcraft's revision of *Algic Researches* (published in 1856 as *The Myth of Hiawatha* in order to cash in on Longfellow's acknowledged debt to Schoolcraft), as Schoolcraft's attempt to have the final word on Jane Johnston's authority, her autoanthropology. In "The Lost Daughter," Leelinau is described as a young girl, both "pensive and timid" and "dissatisfied with the realities of life" (Schoolcraft 1991[1839], 155, 156). Leelinau is, in short, prone to "fancy" of the most odious sort (157)—communion with the fairies of the woods—and, on the evening before she is set to be married and enter the world of adult responsibilities, she retires to her favorite "fairy haunted grove" and disappears forever, presumably turned into a spirit or sprite by the chieftain of the wood fairies (158). Schoolcraft, as per his usual habit, turns this into a moral tale about parental supervision: Leelinau was "a daughter whose manners and habits they had not sufficiently guarded, and whose inclinations they had, in the end, too violently thwarted" (158).

Two things, perhaps, should be noted about this portrayal of Leelinau. First, one might consider it an act of representational violence against Jane Johnston that Schoolcraft literally makes her pseudonymic incarnation vanish—disappear from the world. This is precisely the action of *Algic Researches,* which, unlike *The Literary Voyager,* does not acknowledge Jane Johnston's hand in the collection and production of its texts; for example, *The Literary Voyager* attributes "Mishosha, or the Magician and His Daughters," to "Bame-wa-wa-ge-zhik-a-quay," another of Jane Johnston's Amerindian pseudonyms, whereas in *Algic Researches* it, and, indeed, every story in the book, appears as the product of Henry Schoolcraft's own researches.[22] In the "Leelinau" story, as in the Schoolcraft-Johnston folklore corpus, Jane Johnston's presence is erased. The necessarily joint Anglo-Amerindian production of anthropological discourse is effaced.

Second, the moral frame makes clear that Leelinau, and therefore Johnston, lives in a world of make-believe; this is precisely the charge that Schoolcraft leveled again and again at David Cusick's book, as will be shown below. This infantilization is Schoolcraft's preferred method for contextualizing, and thereby neutralizing, the large fact, and therefore the truth claims, of autoanthropology. Although Schoolcraft acknowledged the Amerindian presence in his work — he was, after all, a folklorist and cultural anthropologist *in the field,* and depended primarily upon Amerindian informants — he at the same time denied that Amerindian minds might be able to fathom the depth of or ferret out the truth of their own identities. It is up to the Anglo anthropologist, finally, to make historical, cultural, and racial sense out of the welter of confused data that, admittedly, only Amerindians can provide.

Finally, Schoolcraft's greatly shortened poetic rendering of the Leelinau tale in *The Myth of Hiawatha* (as the book's final story, "Leelinau: A Chippewa Tale") further etherealizes Leelinau by poeticizing language and form. This version of the story ends:

> Night came but Leelinau was never more seen, except by a fisherman on the lake shore, who conceived that he had seen her go off with one of the tall fairies known as the fairy of Green Pines, with green plumes nodding o'er his brows; and it is supposed that she is still roving with him over the elysian fields. (1984[1856], 236)

In this rendering, Jane Johnston is frozen in sentimental pastoral, a magical but insubstantial girl wandering distant landscapes (235–36). She is, in short, turned into an Indianism — romantically banished and vanished. At one and the same time, she is less likely than ever to contribute to knowledge of the Amerindian, and she becomes a dehistoricized, mythic subject fit for Schoolcraftian analysis.

III

David Cusick's text points toward a way that permits one to think through the aporia produced by Schoolcraft's and Johnson's critiques of one another. Henry Schoolcraft knew of Cusick's short book. In fact, one might go so far as to suggest that he brooded upon it. Between 1847 and 1855, Schoolcraft's works took up the problem of the very existence of the Cusick text at least six times. Here was a book, an Amerindian book, written in English, that covered all of Schoolcraft's topics of concern: Amerindian folklore, culture, history. Matters of expertise and authority mark every turn in Schoolcraft's recurring reference to *Sketches of the Ancient History of the Six Nations.*

In republishing several pages of the Cusick text in 1847, in his *Notes on the Iroquois,* Schoolcraft prefaced it by suggesting that Cusick's "full blooded Indian" nature and his book's "style, or grammar" were "evidence of the authenticity of the traditions recorded" (1975[1847], 475). Yes, this was an "Indian book." Considered as such, Schoolcraft said, Cusick's *Sketches* was "remarkable," but he also summarized his feelings about the work by calling it a "curious publication," as if something about the book remained cause for wonder. But what might that be? After all, Schoolcraft is quizzical about a text written almost entirely within the terms of his own emerging discipline. Other than the fact that *Sketches* is written by an Amerindian, what is so strange or odd about a text that, in so many ways, resembles Schoolcraft's own works on Amerindian legend and lore?

Schoolcraft had an answer to this question, but it did not come to him right away. A reading of Cusick emerged over the course of the next decade, as Schoolcraft began production and publication of his monumental six-volume (seven-hundred oversized pages each) *Historical and Statistical Information Respecting the History, Condition and Prospects of the Indian Tribes of the United States* (1851–57). Although the volumes include a number of contributions from contemporaneous scholars, Schoolcraft wrote the bulk of the work, digesting, abstracting, and rendering judgment upon hundreds of works about Amerindians in general and their various races, nations, tribes, and language families.

Schoolcraft virtually ignores autoanthropology in these volumes. There is no mention of Jane Johnston (perhaps not surprisingly), but, strangely, no reference to William Apess's or George Copway's then-available anthropological works, nor to Ely S. Parker, even though Parker was one of his correspondent-informants during the writing of *Notes on the Iroquois*. (Schoolcraft's major section on Amerindian writers, in volume 4 of *Historical and Statistical Information* [1854], is devoted exclusively to translations of scripture, school primers, and hymns into Amerindian languages—safe enough to acknowledge.)[23] But Cusick's name comes up five times over the several thousand pages, and with increasing attention. This process culminates in volume 5 (1855), where Schoolcraft reprints the whole of Cusick's book, with an extended comment (Schoolcraft 1851–57, 5:632–46). Cusick's text, then, represents the problem of autoanthropology for Schoolcraft, and a careful look at this set of remarks is quite revealing.[24] Finally, Schoolcraft's critique (for that is what it is) centers upon the matter of writing *history*. In volume 1 (1851), Schoolcraft writes that Cusick's "mind" was "replete with traditions" — a point in Cusick's favor — but

> his ignorance of general chronology, and of the very slow manner in which the dialects and languages of the human race must have been formed, was profound; and his attempts to assimilate the periods of the several Atotarhoes or leading magistrates of that famous league of aboriginal tribes, are utterly childish and worthless. Not so with his traditions of events. When he comes to speak of the Indian mythology, and beliefs in spiritual agencies, the monster period, and the wars and wanderings of his people, he is at home, — and history may be said to be indebted to him for telling his own story of these things in his own way. So much for Cusic [*sic*]. (1851–57, 1:125)

"History" is indebted to David Cusick, but only so long as he stays "at home," telling the stories that he knows without historical context, without method, "in his own way" — an Amerindian way of knowing the world. For Schoolcraft, the "genuineness" of Cusick's text depends upon Cusick's presentation of belief without an overarching understanding: "a mass of incongruous details" that remains unassembled in terms of chronology or race theory (Schoolcraft 1975[1847], 63).

In volume 4, Schoolcraft again refers to Cusick as the author of "that curious publication" by a "native archaeologist." The issue of history is again foregrounded: "The chronology and dynastic terms of his pamphlet are believed to be conjectural, or faulty" (4:137). Finally, in volume 5, as a preface to his reprinting of Cusick "*verbatim et literatim*," Schoolcraft begins by noting that "this extraordinary piece of Indian penmanship," Cusick's "entire tract is, specially, left in the literary garb in which it came from his hands." Yet, at the same time,

> like many writers of far higher pretensions, he falls into the error of trying to generalize and systematize matter which would be better if left in its accrete state. The greatest merit of such traditions consists in their being told in a simple manner, without any attempt at chronology or embellishment. By putting the time-frame of a suppositional chronology to the traditions, he entered on quicksands where stouter feet have sunk. This part of the narrative may be regarded as a mere excursion of a North

American Indian into the fields of imagination. The assertion that there had been "*thirteen*" Atatarhos, or presiding rulers, at Onondaga, the seat of the confederacy, may be regarded as the tradition; although, if we regarded each Atatarho as ruling thirty years, it would carry the antiquity of the confederacy a century farther back than is generally conceded. (5:631)

Schoolcraft, in short, accuses Cusick of upstreaming without a paddle: "putting the time-frame of a suppositional chronology" onto a collection of folklore in order to produce a history of undocumented eras. Curiously, the "fields of imagination" within which Cusick tarries are, according to Schoolcraft, only one hundred years removed from the "generally conceded" truth of Anglo historical reconstruction. (At the end of this passage, Schoolcraft inserts a footnote instructing the reader to refer to his own work, *Notes on the Iroquois*—meaning that Schoolcraft himself is the "generally conceded" expert on such matters.) One hundred years: Schoolcraft's rhetorical tone—"childish," "worthless," "faulty"—borders on the hysterical, given the minimal magnitude of the mistake (if it is one) he discovers.

But consider matters from another angle. The two longest remarks on Cusick in *Historical and Statistical Information,* both partially cited above, focus on Cusick's reconstruction of the chain of thirteen Iroquois Atatarhos, or rulers, and the events that occurred under each successive reign. One might well agree with Schoolcraft that it is this very feature of Cusick's text that most clearly distinguishes Cusick from mid-nineteenth-century anthropology. It is at these moments in *Sketches of the Ancient History of the Six Nations* that ethnic or racial history is reworked in a most dramatic way. It is at these moments that one can locate and identify a previously unthought methodological difference between Schoolcraft and Cusick: whereas Schoolcraft understands Amerindian and Anglo identities as separate and distinct, Cusick figures them as necessarily relational.

A passage from *Algic Researches*'s "Preliminary Observations" makes explicit Schoolcraft's view that Amerindia and Europe have shared nothing, exchanged nothing—that no borders have ever been crossed, much less crossed out. Schoolcraft says that the history of "contest" for North America has been anything but favorable to the production of right feeling and a reciprocal knowledge of real character on both sides. The Indians could never be made to appreciate the offers of education and Christianity by one portion of the community, while others were arrayed against them in arms. Their idea of government was, after all, the Eastern notion of a unity or despotism, in which everything emanates from the governing power, and is responsible to it. Nor has their flitting and feverish position on the frontiers been auspicious to the acquisition of a true knowledge of their character, particularly in those things which have relation to the Indian mind, their opinions on abstract subjects, their mythology, and other kindred topics. Owing to illiterate interpreters and dishonest men, the parties have never more than half understood each other. (1991[1839], 17)[25]

This quite complex narrative makes it clear that a long string of contingencies has prevented anything but a "half" knowledge of the other. With Amerindians "flitting" on the "frontiers" and Anglos either "illiterate" or wildly divided in their presentation, it seems, more than 230 years after Champlain, as if the colonial encounter has not yet taken place.

Of course, there is little truth to this narrative, and within a few pages, *Algic Researches* produces a quite contradictory argument—one that chastises the Amerindian because "he does not seem to open his eyes on the prospect of civilization and mental exaltation held up before him" (1991[1839], 22). Schoolcraft now argues that "these scenes have been *pictured before him* by teachers and philanthropists *for more than two centuries*; but there has been nothing in them to arouse and inspire him to press onward in the career of prospective civilization and advancement" (22). Instead of taking this good advice, says Schoolcraft, the Amerindian "pines away as one that is fallen, and despairs to rise," while meditating upon "a sort of golden age, when all things were better with them than they are now" (22).

This is hardly the Amerindian who does not know the European, nor is this the Amerindian untouched by colonialism, "flitting" beyond the space of contact. This is, instead, a portrait of a mind transformed by massive redefinitions of physical/psychic space, albeit in the tragic mode. This is, absent the tragedy, Cusick's Amerindian. Cusick begins his narrative, however, with a "cross-cultural" trope that essentializes cultural difference. "I have taken much pains," he says, not only "procuring the materials" for the book, but crossing the cultural divide and "translating it into English language":

> I have been long waiting in hopes that some of my people, who have received an English education, would have undertaken the work as to give a sketch of the Ancient History of the Six Nations; but found no one seemed to concur in the matter, after some hesitation I determined to commence the work; but found the history involved with fables; and besides, examining myself, finding so small educated that it was impossible for me to compose the work without much difficulty. (in Beauchamp 1892, 1)

Cusick's reference in his first line to the Tuscaroras as "my people" makes it clear how he comprehends his own identity and how he understands his audience as other, Anglo. It is his very identity, it seems, that makes for "difficulty" in the writing of a book for "the public." Crossing over a cultural divide with an entire people's history on his back hurts — it comes with great "pains."

The first indication, however, of a counternarrative at work in the *Sketches* is in this same paragraph, when Cusick starts to undermine his attempt to write "history." It is all "involved with fables," he says, which suggests the same problem for historical upstreaming that Leelinau raised. And although it is true that *Sketches* claims to reproduce the mental world of the "ancients," just as Schoolcraft did (Beauchamp 1892, 1), at the same time, Cusick's various sketches are deployed less as historical truths than as political fictions that make recurrent, specific reference to the politics of Amerindian removal.

Cusick makes it quite clear, in the "tale of the foundation of the great island (now North America)," that the earth is a "possession" of the Amerindians, the "real people":

> When he [the "good mind," Enigorio] had made the universe he was in doubt respecting some being to possess the great Island; and he formed two images of the dust of the ground in his own likeness, male and female, and by his breathing into their nostrils he gave them the living souls, and named them Ea-gwe-howe, i.e., a real people; and he gave the Great Island, all the animals of game for their maintenance. (in Beauchamp 1892, 3)

One might note that Cusick seems primarily to be recounting the Christian creation myth — and Cusick may or may not be aware of this — but more interesting is the way that this story, read as a tale of original Amerindian possession, resonates throughout the short book.[26] Relatively late in the text, Cusick tells of an ancient Tuscarora prophecy by this good mind (who has taken the form of an old man) in which he says that Europeans "would in some future day take possession of the Big Island, and it was impossible to prevent it" (in Beauchamp 1892, 31). But Cusick finishes this tale by recounting how "the aged man died among them, and they buried him; but soon after some person went to the grave and found he had risen, and never heard of him since" (31). In this passage, again marked by Christianity (and, some might argue, the "culture hero" myth), it is clear that even though the "Big Island" will be lost, the creator of the "real people" has symbolically promised a resurrection for them. And right at the end of the *Sketches*, in the next-to-last paragraph, "Holder of the Heavens" appears in a dream to an Iroquois prophet and advises the tribe "not to comply with the wishes of the whites, lest they should ruin themselves and displease their Maker" (in Beauchamp 1892, 37). To invoke Schoolcraft, these are "remarkable," potentially dangerous, words — *"not to comply with the wishes of the whites"* — written, as they were, in the middle of removal debate.[27]

But, so far, all that has been suggested is that Cusick, who foregrounds the fablelike or "fabulous" ground of ancient Amerindian history and identity, much like Jane Johnston, uses this to his advantage and explicitly constructs a history in the shape of a politics — thereby intervening in the ongoing, asymmetrical conversation about removal.[28] More "curious," however, is the way in which Cusick's versions of Iroquois and hemispheric history converge. Iroquois history points toward the successful military and political conquest of all area tribes following the founding of the Iroquois confederacy, "after which the kingdom enjoyed without disturbance for many years" (in Beauchamp 1892, 38). Cusick explains that at the very same moment of peace, however, Columbus arrives on the continent, and shatters the Iroquois dream. "Columbus" and the successful "confederacy" happen at the same moment, and this is not a coincidence in Cusick's narrative. This is, instead, the determination of a History with a capital *H,* a History with a vector, and a *telos.* Twelve times throughout the *Sketches,* Cusick connects Columbus to events in his Iroquois history:

> This fate happened probably between two thousand five hundred winters before Columbus discovered the America. (in Beauchamp 1892, 9)

> Perhaps about two thousand two hundred years before the Columbus discovered the America.... (10)

> Perhaps about 1250 years before Columbus discovered the America.... (15)

> Perhaps 1,000 years before Columbus discovered the America.... (16)

> Perhaps about 800 years before the Columbus discovered the America.... (20)

> In the days of King Ototarho VI, perhaps 650 years before the Columbus discovered the America.... (23)

> In the reign of King Atotarho VIII, perhaps 400 years before the Columbus discovered America.... (27)

> In the reign of King Atotarho IX, perhaps 350 years before the Columbus discovered the America.... (31)

> In the reign of Atotarho X, perhaps 250 years before Columbus discovered America.... (36)

> Atotarho XI, perhaps about 150 years before Columbus discovered America.... (36)

> In the reign of Atotarho XII, perhaps about 50 years before Columbus discovered America.... (37)

> In the reign [of] Atotarho XIII, in the year 1492, Columbus discovered the America. (38)

Undoubtedly, several things are happening in these repeated intonations. For one, the use of the term *discovery* should be understood ironically, given that each time, it appears in a sentence that documents either complex tribal history or kingly consolidation and rule. More important for my purposes, however, this constant locking together of Columbus and the Six Nations makes it impossible to think one without the other. In the *Sketches,* the very ability to "sketch," the very ability to narrate "ancient history," is entirely dependent upon the presence of

Columbus. Put another way, it is "the Columbus" that enables the discourse of folklore anthropology, that makes it possible in the first place. "The Columbus," in this sense, literally produces the past in the Cusick text, in that the "ancients" can be narrated only with reference to him.

"The Columbus" and whatever he stands for literally appear at the same moment as Cusick's Amerindians and their project of peace. They are born together. They must mean everything to each other. Which is why, in the first place, Gill's and Lyons and Mohawk's texts stand in such strange relation to each other. The very possibility that these figures can make their claims with *any* degree of credibility supports a massive revision of their understanding of identity. It is not a question of Mother Earth or democracy belonging to one or another, but rather that each is produced within sight of the other, with reference to a site for the other.[29]

Interesting, too, is the type of precontact Iroquois identity Cusick constructs. His narrative, as noted, is primarily one of conquest and consolidation: the Iroquois were centralizing, empire builders, intent on bringing an entire world under one stable rule through battles with cannibal giants, stonish giants, flying heads, giant mosquitoes, and tribe upon tribe of indigenous peoples. A god, in fact, has taught the Iroquois to agglomerate territory: "The Holder of Heavens visited the Five Families and instructed them in the arts of war, and favors them to gain the country beyond their limits" (in Beauchamp 1892, 16). In a manner that might best be described as Cortésian, they raid and conquer beyond their territories and "make incursion upon the enemy that may be found within the boundaries of the kingdom" (23). And the Iroquois, according to Cusick, also go out on "expeditions" to "explore" the world, and discover, like Columbus, strange, unevolved "others" who seem to be more animal than man. Cusick writes that when the Iroquois met the "Dog Tail Nation," "they were astonished that the people had short tails like apes; a hole was made through their seats where they put their tails" (24). This is similar to an incident reported by Columbus in a letter concerning his fourth voyage: "A crossbowman wounded a creature that was like an ape, only much larger and with a human face. He had pierced him with an arrow from the breast to the tail but had to cut off the fore and hind paw because he was so fierce. . . . The hunting of this animal was so strange and splendid that I have had to describe it" (1969, 298).

In these ways, Cusick's Iroquois are a kind of mirror for Columbus and/or Cortés, and Cusick provides no rhetorical resources with which one could sketch significant identity differences between Anglo and Amerindian. The importance of the *Sketches* for identity politics is that, unlike *Algic Researches,* Cusick's book constructs an Amerindian identity entirely circumscribed by colonial relations, and in which the Iroquois are colonizers every bit the equal of the Europeans. Amerindian identity is, in Cusick's text, both relational and decentered, and, at the same time, curiously identical to Anglo identity.

IV

Of course, it would be tempting to reintroduce Cusick's nearly unknown text to wider readership as part of what Edmund Wilson aptly refers to as *Apologies to the Iroquois* (1959), and to Amerindia in general. But this would be repeating a very old colonial gesture—one produced as early as 1827, when Dr. D. B. Coates introduced Hendrick's Aupaumut's "A Narrative of an Embassy to the Western Indians" (c. 1794) to his Historical Society of Pennsylvania audience as an authentic product of the "sons of the forest," and one that would compensate for the fact that "no apologists have arisen to celebrate and exalt their [the Indians'] great actions" (63). Here apology for conquest and the "discovery" of autoethnic narrative are conjoined in a way that should remind one of the entire history of European "othering"—from Cortés's pity for the conquered, even as he produces Moctezuma's voice, to Cooper's attempt, in *The Last of the Mohicans* (1826), to salvage the vibrant masculinity of Amerindian semiotics while reciting a funeral oration for "real" Amerindians. It is undoubtedly so, as David E. Johnson points out, that anthropology of the other is always in the form of an apology of one sort or another—and that the "primal scene" of the production of otherness involves tears.[30] The word *a(nthro)pology* itself is framed by an "apology."

So rather than recover Cusick's text within, for example, a multicultural framework, which might comprehend it as an anthropological counternarrative or autoethnic account of identity (making him either nineteenth-century anthropology's inventor or its interlocutor),[31] Cusick can be configured as an identity dissenter — arguing from entirely different grounds. Simply put, he shows the border effects that Schoolcraft hides, and this destabilizes the very possibility of *Algic Researches*.

Cusick's most general writing strategies and his identity politics, far from finding a ready home within anthropological discourse, even in this century, are *still* on the margins of anthropology.[32] Even a good deal of postmodern ethnographic practice and postmodern critique of ethnography does little more than foreground the subjectivity of the anthropologist at the expense of the "other," forcing her or him into the position of maximum alterity, of the occult — when, in fact, it is possible to argue that the great scandal of our lives is that "our" so-called differences hold no meaning.[33] Identity difference, then, may be, at maximum, relational, and often closer to the realm of the trivial — blank custom and habit masquerading as significance. One need only think of Schoolcraft's random accumulation of cultural oddities in his "grab bag" texts (*The Literary Voyager, The Indian in His Wigwam*) to understand this anthropological model: lists of Amerindian foods, clothes, implements, places, ritual, words — a strategy that multiplies the principle of othering, but adds up to nothing in particular; anthropology as an "accrete state." But furthermore, if the Iroquois are, fundamentally, protocapitalists *and* anticapitalists, *and* democrats, *and* ecologists — then what's the difference?[34]

One thing more with reference to this problematic: I noted earlier that Cusick's notion of Amerindian identity rings and rhymes with accounts of Anglo identity. Yet it is not precisely *Anglo* identity that is at stake, but rather *Spanish* identity, given that Cusick's text refers to conquest and colonization only through "the Columbus." This seeming anomaly in Cusick is, on closer inspection, a more general Iroquois conceit. Iroquois materials from before and after Cusick sometimes evidence the same interest in Spaniards and Columbus. Richter notes that on 2 September 1723, an Anglo transcriber of a treaty negotiation reported what an Iroquois orator told his white and red audience:

Formerly We lived alone and were Masters of this Land. Afterwards one came over the seas from afarr who had a skin like one of us and Entred our land and was Master of our Rivers Who We had discursed with and was welcome to us, he was a Spaniard. (quoted in Richter 1992, 278)

The second text is from 1992, and it appears as the epilogue to a volume of essays titled *The State of Native America*. The book as a whole presents a summary of various sorts of modern Amerindian struggles over law, land, water, religion, gender, education, and military service. The piece is written by a figure encountered earlier in this essay, John Mohawk, and is titled, "Looking for Columbus: Thoughts on the Past, Present, and Future of Humanity." "Looking for Columbus"—the very title tells us something. Mohawk, a member of one of the Iroquois confederacy tribes, whose home grounds are in Upstate New York and Canada, is searching for "Columbus" in order to comprehend his own "state." And whereas this brief text criticizes a European tendency to imagine all of the peoples of preencounter America as just one—"Indians"—he himself collapses all of his arguments about "Europeans" and "Eurocentrism" onto only Spanish source materials: texts by Columbus and Sepúlveda (Mohawk 1992c, 440). For Mohawk, these two figures produce the two possible models for all European colonialism, and they are Spanish. Therefore, the Spanish alone set the tone and terms for conquest; they make the largest arguments to and on behalf of this thing called "Europe." To understand American colonialism in general and to combat it, one must "find the real meaning of Columbus" and "bury it" (443).

What can one make of Cusick's "the Columbus"? And of the anonymous Iroquois speaker's "Spaniard"? Why is "he" "here," in Massachusetts, tens of hundreds of miles from New Spain? And what can one conclude about Mohawk's ongoing fixation upon Columbian discourses—a gesture he has repeated in other work?[35] What does it mean that, in this Senecan account of colonization and its consequences, names such as Samuel de Champlain do not appear, much less Dutch and English names—nor reference to Northern European colonial records, or evidence of Northern European home country debates over the fate of the Amerindians?[36] The trope of the "Spaniard" in Iroquois discourse—or, more broadly, the production of the identity of the "Spanish Iroquois"—is a curious problem for the project of comparing, contrasting, and, finally, distinguishing the colonialisms in the Americas. At stake are complex questions of colonial identities — strategies of Amerindian self-definition that, at one and the same time, strategize self-identity in ways that cut against the historical-anthropological work of Anglo investigators and produce, in certain specific ways, more revealing accounts of the very process and possibilities of identity self-fashioning.

The hundreds of years of Spanish Iroquois, finally, are not strange identity anomalies, but are as "real" as anything else in this world; they are a necessary possibility and a reminder of the intellectual limitations that come with the project of determining *particular* identities, or even *local fields* of identities — the sheer poverty of demarcating and explicating identities based on a reading of particular material practices or conditions. A historian might describe it as a Pan-Indianism that predates most historical accounts of such, explain it as an early and enduring dissemination of the stories of Spain and the "Black Legend," and/ or argue that it is a manifestation of modernity's world economy, with signs and texts in constant, turbulent interaction.

All of this may be "true," as far as causal explanations go, but the significance, in any case, is that there are not, nor have there ever been, any Amerindians (or Anglos, for that matter) *as such.* Push the colonial record back to its beginning, and, in the beginning, Amerindians comprehend themselves as Amerindians only through the mechanism of — the text that is — Europe. Which is to say, Amerindia has always been Spanish, and Anglo, and whatever else was conceptualized and embodied at time of contact. This is not a detour, not a colonized subjectivity or mentality: this figure or trope marks the limit of self-representation.

And if the rhetorical strategies of Cusick's *Sketches* have anything to tell us today, it is that, far from living in a world of singular cultures and their borders and contact zones, "we" are stitched together and shot through with all of "our" others. "Our" condition is critical, borderline. And the hope for any "other" world is tied not to rediscovering precontact Amerindia, to upstreamed longings and imaginations, but rather to the limit recognition that "our" so-called differences are part of a more-encompassing, yet, in principle, never-closed sketch — circles without a center, drafted in pencil; remains on a yellowing sheet of paper.

Notes

Portions of this essay, in earlier versions, were presented at the Fourth International Native American Studies Conference (1993), the 1993 meeting of the American Studies Association, and the 1995 meeting of the American Historical Association.

1. By *identity politics,* I simply mean any normative or prescriptive politics whose entry points are, for example, ethnic, racial, class, gender, or sexual identities. Multiculturalism is an identity politics, as are its reverse — "melting pot" accounts of American identity.

2. Some of this is quite explicit in Richter's text. "International relations," for example, are part of a "mundane" world, and of relatively little consequence for Iroquois identity (1992, 41).

3. See Asad, who attempts to "problematize the idea of an anthropological definition of religion by assigning that endeavor to a particular history of knowledge and power (including a particular understanding of our legitimate past and future)" (1993, 54).

4. On the connection between the bourgeoisie and health, see Foucault (1980, 122–27).

5. Anthony F. C. Wallace's (1972) well-known work on the Iroquois, first published in 1969, imagines Iroquois men as maximal competitive individualists in need of psychic healing — the very opposite of Richter's account. Wallace produced, for the 1960s, the Iroquois as New Left straw men; Richter produced the Iroquois as 1990s paragons of new age spirituality. The very fact that Richter and Wallace both moralize about community and acquisitiveness, with the Iroquois positioned in polar ways, should make one suspicious of the production of cultural history.

6. See, for example, Marcus and Fischer (1986, 157–64), who are enamored, however, of the possibility of a "stronger" version of the tactic I am describing, which they call "cross-cultural juxtaposition." And I am making a larger claim than do Marcus and Fischer, who appear to believe that it is only one specific genre of anthropology that makes such "self"-motivated comparisons or juxtapositions.

7. Here I would explicitly like to separate my argument from that of Mary Louise Pratt. In her introduction, she talks usefully about "contact zones" — "social spaces where disparate cultures meet, clash, and grapple with each other, often in highly asymmetrical relations of domination and subordination" (1992, 4). For her, however, the contact zone is a place where cultures meet and even mix but are not fundamentally problematized. This makes her identity politics somewhat more conservatively essentialist than Richard White's. For example, Pratt argues that "transculturation" occurs in contact zones: "Subordinated or marginal groups select and invent from materials transmitted to them by a dominant or metropolitan culture" (6). Sometimes such transculturation takes the form of "autoethnography," in which colonized subjects act in "partial collaboration with and appropriation of the idioms of the conqueror" (7). All of her metaphors suggest that cultures can be crossed — that people can live biculturally — but that fundamental cultural positions remain unchanged. Her descriptions, then, of the "autoethnographies" of both Felipe Gua-

man Poma de Ayala and Garcilaso de la Vega are at some distance from the manner in which I attempt to contextualize David Cusick's *Sketches* in this essay.

8. It should be noted that although Schoolcraft grants Indians a "history" (a gesture Eric R. Wolf [1982] found necessary to repeat 140 years later), it is not one in which very much *happens*. Indian history in Schoolcraft's terms is perhaps best understood as a mostly static difference from everything European.

9. See White (1973) and, more particularly, McGrane (1989, 93–100), who discusses historicism in relation to nineteenth-century anthropology.

10. Another remnant of Columbian discourse is Schoolcraft's figuring of Amerindians as Oriental (1991[1839], 22). Also, see Said (1979) for his famous reading of the politics of such "Orientalism"; this key topic within "postcolonial theory" has generated a massive secondary literature — too large to do anything but acknowledge here.

11. See Schoolcraft (1991[1839], 10) for an example. McGrane understands the savage/civilized polarity as part of the heritage of the "Enlightenment" (1989, ix). The classic study of the concepts *savage/civilized* in American writing is that by Pearce, whose discussion of Schoolcraft's work locates it as "the culmination of a tradition, the culminating episode in the history of a mode of belief" (1988[1953], 120–28).

12. See Jordan, who says that the first narratives to suggest that Amerindians constituted a separate race are dated 1775 and 1778, respectively (1969, 240 n. 49). See, more recently, the essays collected by Gates (1986).

13. Bieder's chapter on Schoolcraft makes clear that Henry Schoolcraft considered himself an opponent of "polygenism," or separate racial creations (1986, 179–82). In *Notes on the Iroquois,* Schoolcraft succinctly declares that Indians "are a branch of the original Adamic stock" (1975[1847], 58). And it is this belief, perhaps, that permits Schoolcraft to forecast Amerindians' reclaiming their Christian heritage. But the term "branch" means that, somewhere in early biblical history, the Indians branched off — became a subspecies of "man" that calcified within a relatively low position on the scale of human development. "The early migrations must have been necessarily confined to portions of the old world peopled by the *red race* — by a race, not only of red skins, black hair and eyes, and high cheek bones, who would reproduce these fixed characteristics, *ad infinitum,* but whose whole mental as well as physiological developement [*sic*] assimilates it, as a distinct unity of species" (1975[1847], 60). In a passage like this one, the difference between polygenism and monogenism is nearly meaningless, as Schoolcraft suggests that the inferiority of Amerindians is physiologically based.

14. Later, a more pessimistic and monological Schoolcraft would argue that even the Iroquois were in the "absolute barbaric state" at time of contact — that all Indians were in the "hunter state": "We are in want of all evidence to show that there ever was in America, a pastoral state" (1975[1847], 11, 16).

15. "Evidence" of human evolution is also furnished by Schoolcraft's evolutionary model of language — from simple to complex words — which is explained in some detail in Schoolcraft (1991[1839], 18–21).

16. See McGrane (1989, ix–x) for a summary statement.

17. Permitting Schoolcraft his complications, he notes that "superstition has en-grafted upon the original stock" of Indian lore, meaning that even his stories are partly contaminated by spiritual ideas of more recent date. Finally, Schoolcraft also readily acknowledges that a "moral point" has been added to some of his texts, al-though the "original" texts always "justify it" (1991[1839], 19).

18. Philip P. Mason believes that this text was orally transmitted by Jane's mother to Jane, which may or may not be true, and which, if true, would not alter the dy-namics I am noting (see Schoolcraft 1962, 171 n. 39). Henry Schoolcraft, as evi-denced below, treated the character "Leelinau" as a stand-in for his wife.

19. The Ojibwa are a "tribe" constructed at a relatively late date out of refugees from the Iroquois wars. See White (1991, 19) and Wolf (1982, 171). See also Fried (1966) on the very idea of "tribe."

20. The story of Jane's father, John, is told in brief by Tomaszewski (n.d.).

21. Thomas McKenney, a friend of the Schoolcrafts, and respected and admired in his own right as a scholar on Amerindian matters (for example, by George Cop-way), describes Johnston as more European than Chippewa: "She dresses with great taste, and in all respects in the costume of our fashionables, but wears leggins of black silk, drawn and ruffled around the ankles, resembling those worn by our little girls. I think them ornamental. You would never judge, either from her complex-ion, or language, or from any other circumstance, that her mother was a Chippe-way, except that her moderately high cheek bones, her dark and fine eye, and breadth of the jaw, slightly indicate it — and you would never believe it, except on her own confession, or upon some equally responsible testimony, were you to hear her converse, or see her beautiful, and some of them highly finished compositions, in both prose and poetry.... Mrs. S. is indebted, mainly, to her father, who is doat-ingly [sic] fond of her, for her handsome and polished acquirements" (quoted in Tomaszewski n.d., 19–20).

22. Compare Schoolcraft (1962, 71) to Schoolcraft (1991[1839], 168).

23. The only place in Schoolcraft's published writings where he discusses his wife's work directly locates her within this corpus: "The writer, who from early years was a member of the church, had made a translation of the Lords prayer, and, occasionally, as delicate and declining health permitted, some other select pieces from the sacred writings, and hymns" (Schoolcraft 1978[1848], 409). Schoolcraft makes no mention of her ethnographic work.

24. In the first place, one might wonder what is happening when Schoolcraft drops a letter from Cusick's name between the time of his reference to him in *Notes on the Iroquois* in 1847 and the *Historical and Statistical Information* volumes. In the former text, Schoolcraft writes about "Cusick," whereas in the latter it is always "Cusic." This may be a small enough matter, a simple proofreading oversight, but it is interesting in light of Schoolcraft's temporary transformation of his own name during the 1840s from "Schoolcraft" to "Colcraft" — dropping the letters *s, h,* and an *o* from his surname. Were one so inclined, one could tease out cabalistic signifi-cances from these shortenings. On another level, Bieder reports that at least one scholar believes the shift to "Colcraft" was a "symbolic act of suicide" during a des-perate time of "debt and ravenous insecurity" (1986, 173). And even less dramati-

cally, one could suggest that *both* name changes are diminutions—subtractions from the authority of the signature. The more Schoolcraft reflected upon "Cusick," the smaller the worth of the "Cusic" project.

25. Curiously, Schoolcraft appears to be making Amerindia entirely Ostic in the first part of this passage—as if he has forgotten his previous distinction between Algic and Ostic sociopolitics.

26. Schoolcraft at one point, perhaps, understood the text in this manner. In a paragraph from *Notes on the Iroquois* that includes discussion of Cusick's book, he notes that Iroquois folklore is produced with "the intent, perhaps, that they might put forth an undisputed title to the country they occupied" (1975[1847], 48).

27. See Rogin (1976) for a useful intellectual history of the removal debates.

28. Cusick's text was in a highly marginalized position within the Anglo cultural marketplace. Although three editions of Cusick's book were published by 1848, all were by western New York local/regional presses (Beauchamp 1892, 41). Even the Beauchamp reprint, which is the most readily available edition today, was self-published at the turn of the century. The first edition of *The Heath Anthology of American Literature* (1990) republished a portion of Cusick's text, but it was deleted from the second edition. Cusick's cultural force has been small indeed compared with that of a Cooper or even a Schoolcraft.

29. Michael Taussig's *Mimesis and Alterity* is entirely about this sort of strange relation to the seemingly "other" within a postcolonial world—where the "reaction" to the other "tears at identity and proliferates associations of a self bound magically to an Other, too close to that Other to be but dimly recognizable, too much the self to allow for satisfying alterity" (1993, 253).

30. Johnson cites Jacques Derrida's *Of Grammatology*: it is "remorse that produces anthropology" (1993, 12 n. 8).

31. See Judkins (1987), for example, who celebrates Cusick's classically anthropological achievement.

32. I am explicitly thinking of Cusick's relationship to anthropology as *unlike* what Prakash (1990) sees as a dialectical relationship between colonizer and colonized historiography in India.

33. Stephen A. Tyler, for example, says of postmodern ethnography: "It does not describe, for there is nothing it could describe.... It begins and ends in concepts" (1986, 137).

34. An interesting counteraccount from a humanist perspective is given by Todorov, even though he is equally critical of recent work on "othering" that ends up erasing the other—"refusing these Others any specificity at all" (1986, 374).

35. See Mohawk (1992a). Also, in Mohawk's "Indians and Democracy," which focuses on the transmission of democratic values from the Iroquois to the British, the narrative of colonialism is, again, almost entirely "Spanish" in content (1992b, 47–51).

36. The reverse gesture is not deployed in the earliest or even latest indigenous accounts of conquest from Mexican or Central or South American perspectives—and here one might specifically cite the texts produced by the Florentine Codex informants, Guaman Poma de Ayala and Garcilaso de la Vega.

Works Cited

Asad, Talal. 1993. "The Construction of Religion as an Anthropological Category." In *Genealogies of Religion: Discipline and Reasons of Power in Christianity and Islam,* 27–54. Baltimore: Johns Hopkins University Press.

Beauchamp, W. M. 1892. *The Iroquois Trail, or Footprints of the Six Nations, in Customs, Traditions, and History, by W. M. Beauchamp, S.T.D., in which are included David Cusick's Sketches of Ancient History of the Six Nations.* Fayetteville, N.Y.: Beauchamp.

Bieder, Robert E. 1986. *Science Encounters the Indian, 1820–1880: The Early Years of American Ethnology.* Norman: University of Oklahoma Press.

Columbus, Christopher. 1969. *The Four Voyages,* ed. and trans. J. M. Cohen. New York: Penguin.

Churchill, Ward. 1992. *Fantasies of the Master Race: Literature, Cinema and the Colonization of American Indians.* Monroe, Maine: Common Courage.

Coates, D. B. 1827. "A Narrative, &c." *Memoirs of the Historical Society of Pennsylvania* 2: 63–74.

Foucault, Michel. 1980. *The History of Sexuality,* vol. 1, *An Introduction,* trans. Robert Hurley. New York: Vintage.

Fried, Morton H. 1966. "On the Concepts of 'Tribe' and 'Tribal Society.'" *Transactions of the New York Academy of Sciences* (ser. 2) 28: 527–40.

Gates, Henry Louis, Jr., ed. 1986. *"Race," Writing, and Difference.* Chicago: University of Chicago Press.

Gill, Sam D. 1987. *Mother Earth.* Chicago: University of Chicago Press.

Johnson, David E. 1993. "*Contando Cuentas:* The Economies of Conquest." Paper presented at Narrative: An International Conference. Albany, N.Y., 1 April.

Jordan, Winthrop. 1969. *White over Black: American Attitudes toward the Negro, 1550–1812.* Baltimore: Penguin.

Judkins, Russell A. 1987. "David Cusick's *Ancient History of the Six Nations:* A Neglected Classic." In *Iroquois Studies: A Guide to Documentary and Ethnographic Resources from Western New York and the Genesee Valley,* ed. Russell A. Judkins, 26–40. Geneseo: State University of New York, Department of Anthropology.

Lasch, Christopher. 1991. *The True and Only Heaven: Progress and Its Critics.* New York: Norton.

Lyons, Oren R. 1992. "The American Indian in the Past." In *Exiled in the Land of the Free: Democracy, Indian Nations, and the U.S. Constitution,* ed. Oren Lyons and John Mohawk, 13–42, 338–39. Santa Fe, N.M.: Clear Light.

Lyons, Oren, and John Mohawk, eds. 1992. *Exiled in the Land of the Free: Democracy, Indian Nations, and the U.S. Constitution.* Santa Fe, N.M.: Clear Light.

Marcus, George E., and Michael M. J. Fischer. 1986. *Anthropology as Cultural Critique: An Experimental Moment in the Human Sciences.* Chicago: University of Chicago Press.

McGrane, Bernard. 1989. *Beyond Anthropology: Society and the Other.* New York: Columbia University Press.

McWilliams, John. 1990. "The Historical Contexts of *The Last of the Mohicans*." In James Fenimore Cooper, *The Last of the Mohicans*, 355–63. New York: Oxford University Press.

Mohawk, John. 1992a. "Discovering Columbus: The Way Here." In *Confronting Columbus: An Anthology*, ed. John Yewell, Chris Dodge, Jan DeSirey, 15–29. Jefferson, N.C.: McFarland.

————. 1992b. "Indians and Democracy: No One Ever Told Us." In *Exiled in the Land of the Free: Democracy, Indian Nations, and the U.S. Constitution*, ed. Oren Lyons and John Mohawk, 43–71, 339–43. Santa Fe, N.M.: Clear Light.

————. 1992c. "Looking for Columbus: Thoughts on the Past, Present, and Future of Humanity." In *The State of Native America: Genocide, Colonization, and Resistance*, ed. M. Annette Jaimes, 439–44. Boston: South End.

Parins, James W. 1990a. "David Cusick (Tuscarora) ?-1840." In *The Heath Anthology of American Literature*, vol. 1, ed. Paul Lauter et al., 1225–26. Lexington, Mass.: Heath.

————. 1990b. "Jane Johnston Schoolcraft (Ojibwa) 1800–1841." In *The Heath Anthology of American Literature*, vol. 1, ed. Paul Lauter et al., 1216–17. Lexington, Mass.: Heath.

Pearce, Roy Harvey. 1988[1953]. *Savagism and Civilization: A Study of the Indian and the American Mind*. Berkeley: University of California Press.

Prakash, Gyan. 1990. "Writing Post-Orientalist Histories of the Third World: Perspectives from Indian Historiography." *Comparative Studies in Society and History* 32.2: 383–408.

Pratt, Mary Louise. 1992. *Imperial Eyes: Travel Writing and Transculturation*. New York: Routledge.

Richter, Daniel K. 1992. *The Ordeal of the Longhouse: The Peoples of the Iroquois League in the Era of European Colonization*. Chapel Hill: Institute of Early American History and Culture/University of North Carolina Press.

Rogin, Michael Paul. 1976. *Fathers and Children: Andrew Jackson and the Subjugation of the American Indian*. New York: Vintage.

Said, Edward. 1979. *Orientalism*. New York: Vintage.

Schoolcraft, Henry Rowe, ed. 1851–57. *Historical and Statistical Information Respecting the History, Condition and Prospects of the Indian Tribes of the United States*, 6 vols. Philadelphia: Lippincott, Grambo.

————. 1962. *The Literary Voyager or Muzzeniegun*, ed. Philip P. Mason. Lansing: Michigan State University Press.

————. 1975[1847]. *Notes on the Iroquois; or, Contributions to American History, Antiquities, and General Ethnology*. New York: AMS.

————. 1978[1848]. *The Indian in His Wigwam, or Characteristics of the Red Race of America. From Original Notes and Manuscripts*. New York: AMS.

————. 1984. *The Hiawatha Legends: North American Indian Lore*, ed. Larry B. Massie. AuTrain, Mich.: Avery Color Studios. (Originally published as *The Myth of Hiawatha and Other Oral Legends, Mythologic and Allegoric, of the North American Indians*, 1856.)

————. 1991. *Schoolcraft's Indian Legends*, ed. Mentor L. Williams. East Lansing: Michigan State University Press. (Originally published as *Algic Researches, Comprising Inquiries Respecting the Mental Characteristics of the North American Indians*, 1839.)

Taussig, Michael. 1993. *Mimesis and Alterity: A Particular History of the Senses*. New York: Routledge.

Todorov, Tzvetan. 1986. " 'Race,' Writing, and Culture." In *"Race," Writing, and Difference*, ed. Henry Louis Gates Jr., 370–80. Chicago: University of Chicago Press.

Tomaszewski, Deidre Stevens. n.d. *The Johnstons of Sault Ste. Marie: An Informal History of the Northwest, as Portrayed through the Experience of One Pioneer Family*. Sault Sainte Marie, Mich.: Tomaszewski.

Tooker, Elisabeth. 1988. "The United States Constitution and the Iroquois League." *Ethnohistory* 35.4: 305–36.

Tyler, Stephen A. 1986. "Post-Modern Ethnography: From Document of the Occult to Occult Document." In *Writing Culture: The Poetics and Politics of Ethnography*, ed. James Clifford and George E. Marcus, 122–40. Berkeley: University of California Press.

Wallace, Anthony F. C. 1972. *The Death and Rebirth of the Seneca*. New York: Random House.

White, Hayden. 1973. *Metahistory: The Historical Imagination in Nineteenth-Century Europe*. Baltimore: Johns Hopkins University Press.

White, Richard. 1991. *The Middle Ground: Indians, Empires, and Republics in the Great Lakes Region, 1650–1815*. New York: Cambridge University Press.

Wilson, Edmund. 1959. *Apologies to the Iroquois*. New York: Farrar, Straus and Cudahy.

Wolf, Eric R. 1982. *Europe and the People without History*. Berkeley: University of California Press.

Afterword: Further Perspectives on Culture, Limits, and Borders

Patricia Seed

Culture

As a teenager I thought that *culture* was principally a verb, "to culture." It meant growing an unidentified substance often in a gelatinous medium inside a petri dish. Culturing was a means of distinguishing something not visibly identifiable and, in all likelihood, very unpleasant. Both implications of culture have stayed with me; culturing means rendering something indistinguishable into something identifiable, and its content is often quite nasty.

In many of these essays, as well, culture is not so easily identifiable. A Northerner in the United States would probably call the war that took place between 1860 and 1865 the Civil War — implying a domestic dispute, soon overcome — whereas a Southerner may well call it the War between the States, stressing the independent political ambitions of the southern states. There are no visible clues — dress, hairstyle, skin color, or even accent — that can consistently distinguish those who call the conflict the Civil War from those who term it the War between the States. Yet using one or the other name for the same military contest implies a critique of the other's point of view. The tone may be polite, but the message often is not.

Likewise in Ben Sáenz's and his students' accounts of growing up on the Texas-Mexico border, it is often difficult to tell nationality by visible signs. Mexican citizens may have light complexions, and U.S. citizens may have dark ones. Blue jeans and T-shirts with identical messages are ubiquitous on both sides of the border. Accents and vocabulary can sometimes distinguish regional origins, but not national ones along the border. As Scott Michaelsen observes, " 'We' are shot through with all our 'others.' " But that does not mean we are equally generous with all of our "others." Some of our others are those whose influences we deny, regret, or try to forget.

Limits

A second perspective comes from the same teenager who thought *culture* was usually a verb in English — a fascination with the mathematical idea of limits, for a limit is an approximation.

Used throughout mathematics, limits estimate exact quantities, such as finding the area inside a curve, using the limit of approximations by rectangles. They are also the means for fixing the rate of change of a function or the derivative. Because the rate of change of a function can be expressed geometrically as the slope of the tangent line at a point, the limiting ratio represents the actual slope at a particular point.

All of these essays describe processes of approximation. Scott Michaelsen criticizes a well-known historian's technique for approximating seventeenth-century Iroquois culture. Ben Sáenz estimates the Chicano and Anglo regions of West Texas. Russ Castronovo uses slave narratives and literature to approximate the Mason-Dixon line in the mid-nineteenth century. Louis Kaplan explores how "Chaplin's signature in *The Pilgrim* [operates] as a wavering border that moves between convict and chaplain," as a kind of "staged straddling of the border" rather than a lived experience (an anthropological perspective). And he suggests that rather than assuming a border, we should understand the limits of any possible relation to an other.

Limits in mathematics show a function approaching something based upon what surrounds it. Limits are used to assign values to functions at points where no (numerical) value is defined. Sometimes the limit is reached because no value can be defined, because, for example, it requires division by zero, which is not a valid mathematical operation. Limits define such values in a way that makes them consistent with nearby values. Limits in mathematics are processes that depend upon the closeness between numbers, points, or functions.

David Johnson's reading of Borges's "La biblioteca de Babel" seems indeed to be trying to approximate limits using words rather than a mathematical equation, for there is no physical boundary to this library, only a mathematical limit — an approximation to something on the basis of what surrounds it.

Borders

Whereas a border is more often considered a decorative object, there is a parallel in the field of mathematics called a boundary. A boundary is a line, point, or plane that indicates or fixes a limit or extent. The solution to boundary questions comes from mathematical physics, an arena that did not interest me until I was in my twenties, but has sustained my interest longer. Boundary values are mathematical solutions in the form of differential equations that must satisfy two distinct requirements. First, the equation must describe how a quantity behaves in a region, but it is the second condition that defines its complexity. The boundary value must also either describe the future behavior of a function or characterize the influence from outside the region. This latter condition on a mathematical boundary value — describing the inside while simultaneously characterizing the influences from outside — comes closest to summarizing the majority of the diverse approaches to "border" in this volume.

Elaine K. Chang objects to interpretations in which one category is posited as mobile and operative while the other is presumed immutable, if portable, and subordinate. Chang prefers a more relational approach — one that resembles a boundary value. For Chang, Evelyn Lau's *Runaway* characterizes both the runaway and the constant efforts from outside to define her.

Chang criticizes the idea that autobiographies must contain "transparent or transcendent self-knowledge," for, as she points out, without the luxuries of time, money, and distance, self-knowledge exists in fragments and packets. To me the runaway's packets of self-knowledge resemble the physical world's discrete natural units of energy or momentum, the packets of light called photons, flashing their illumination and then being absorbed elsewhere.

In a number of the essays here there are accounts of the Texas-Mexico border. As in mathematical physics, there is an actual physical phenomenon called "the border" that divides Texas from Mexico. Once an imaginary line, "the border" is today often visibly marked by barbed wire and concrete. But it is the relation between the sides of the border that interests Ben Sáenz and David Johnson, for like their counterparts in mathematics, these contributors are concerned with describing both the region and the influence from the other side of the boundary/border.

Another essay in this volume deals with a largely intellectual boundary. Alejandro Lugo's reading of the interactions between the contemporary literary movement — "cultural studies" — and the tradition of cultural anthropology focuses on a different kind of boundary, one that often underlies a kind of academic politics not yet marked by barbed wire.

The language of limits and approximation and boundary values seems to me to be far closer to what the contributors to this volume are trying to do than are other, more conventional, approaches that start with the phenomenal world. Beginning with the phenomenal world seems to have led discussions of borders and limits to a morass of philosophical essentialisms directed more toward characterizing objects than toward describing border and limits.

Contributors

Russ Castronovo is associate professor at the University of Miami, where he teaches English and American studies. He is the author of *Fathering the Nation: American Genealogies of Slavery and Freedom*.

Elaine K. Chang is assistant professor of English at Rutgers University. Her essays have appeared in the collections *Vancouver: Representing the Postmodern City; Displacements: Cultural Identities in Question;* and *Revisioning Italy: National Identity and Global Culture* (Minnesota, 1977); and in the journal *Emergences*.

David E. Johnson teaches Spanish and English at the State University of New York at Buffalo. He has published essays in *American Literary History, Arizona Quarterly, Americas Review,* and *Amerindian Images and the Legacy of Columbus*.

Louis Kaplan is visiting assistant professor of modern art at Tufts University. He is the author of *László Moholy-Nagy: Biographical Writings*. He is currently concerned with exploring the borders of twentieth-century art history, pop culture, and media studies.

Alejandro Lugo received his Ph.D. in 1995 from Stanford University in cultural anthropology. He is assistant professor of anthropology at the University of Illinois at Urbana-Champaign, and is currently completing two book projects: an ethnography of factory workers at the U.S.-

Mexican border and an edited volume in honor and memory of feminist anthropologist Michelle Z. Rosaldo.

Scott Michaelsen is an assistant professor of English at Michigan State University. He has taught at the University of Texas at El Paso, and was a Fellow in 1995–96 of the American Council of Learned Societies. He is completing a book on the nineteenth-century, multicultural foundations of American anthropological literatures.

Benjamin Alire Sáenz is assistant professor of English at the University of Texas at El Paso. His first book of poetry, *Calendar of Dust,* received an American Book Award in 1992. In 1993 he received a Lannan Poetry Fellowship. His other books include the short story collection *Flowers for the Broken; Dark and Perfect Angels,* a collection of poems; and the novel *Carry Me Like Water.*

Patricia Seed teaches history at Rice University in Houston, Texas. She is the author of *Ceremonies of Possession in Europe's Conquest of the New World, 1492–1640,* and the Bolton Prize-winning *To Love, Honor, and Obey in Colonial Mexico: Conflicts over Marriage Choice, 1574–1821.*

Index